C0-EEA-196

Donald Trump and the Prospect for American Democracy

Voting, Elections, and the Political Process

Series Editors: Shauna Reilly and Stacy Ulbig

Receptive to studies in the American and comparative settings, the Voting, Elections, and the Political Process series examines the broadly defined electoral process. The series seeks scholarly monographs and edited volumes that investigate the ways in which voters, candidates, elected officials, parties, interest groups, the media, and others interact in the context of electoral politics. Works with a focus on individual attitudes and behavior, institutional and contextual influences, and the legal aspects of the electoral process are welcome. This series accepts interdisciplinary work using a variety of methodological approaches.

Recent Titles

Unconventional, Partisan, and Polarizing Rhetoric: How the 2016 Election Shaped the Way Candidates Strategize, Engage, and Communicate edited by Jeanine E. Kraybill

Donald Trump and the Prospect for American Democracy: An Unprecedented President in an Age of Polarization by Arthur Paulson

The 2016 Presidential Election: The Causes and Consequences of a Political Earthquake edited by Amnon Cavari, Richard J. Powell, and Kenneth R. Mayer

The Resilient Voter: Stressful Polling Places and Voting Behavior by Shauna Reilly and Stacy Ulbig

Donald Trump and the Prospect for American Democracy

An Unprecedented President in an Age of Polarization

Arthur Paulson

LEXINGTON BOOKS
Lanham • Boulder • New York • London

Published by Lexington Books
An imprint of The Rowman & Littlefield Publishing Group, Inc.
4501 Forbes Boulevard, Suite 200, Lanham, Maryland 20706
www.rowman.com

Unit A, Whitacre Mews, 26-34 Stannary Street, London SE11 4AB

Copyright © 2018 The Rowman & Littlefield Publishing Group, Inc.

All rights reserved. No part of this book may be reproduced in any form or by any electronic or mechanical means, including information storage and retrieval systems, without written permission from the publisher, except by a reviewer who may quote passages in a review.

British Library Cataloguing in Publication Information Available

Library of Congress Cataloging-in-Publication Data

Names: Paulson, Arthur C., author.
Title: Donald Trump and the prospect for American democracy : an unprecedented president in an age of polarization / Arthur Paulson.
Description: Lanham, Maryland : Lexington Books, [2018] | Series: Voting, elections, and the political process | Includes bibliographical references and index.
Identifiers: LCCN 2018011205 (print) | LCCN 2018016017 (ebook) | ISBN 9781498561730 (electronic) | ISBN 9781498561723 (cloth : alk. paper)
Subjects: LCSH: Trump, Donald, 1946– | Presidents—United States—Election—2016. | Polarization (Social sciences)—Political aspects—United States. | United States—Politics and government—2017–
Classification: LCC E912 (ebook) | LCC E912 .P38 2018 (print) | DDC 973.933092—dc23
LC record available at https://lccn.loc.gov/2018011205

∞™ The paper used in this publication meets the minimum requirements of American National Standard for Information Sciences—Permanence of Paper for Printed Library Materials, ANSI/NISO Z39.48-1992.

Printed in the United States of America

Contents

List of Figures		vii
List of Tables		ix
Acknowledgments		xi
1	An Unprecedented President	1
2	From Umbrella Parties to Polarized Parties in American Politics	15
3	Trumping the Republicans and Berning the Democrats: Post-Reform Presidential Primaries and the Case of 2016	43
4	The Presidential Election of 2016 in Historical Perspective	75
5	The Irony of Polarization: Parliamentary Parties Without Parliamentary Government	103
6	The Trump Era and Beyond: Postindustrial Democracy in America	123
Conclusion		149
Bibliography		151
Index		161
About the Author		167

List of Figures

2.1	Democratic Convention Balloting on Civil Rights, 1924 and 1948	25
2.2	Balloting for President at Republican National Conventions, 1952 and 1964	39
4.1	Surge Realignment of States in Presidential Elections 1896–1944	82
4.2	Interactive Realignment of States in Presidential Elections 1896–1944	83
4.3	Realigning Coalitions of States in Presidential Elections 1880–2012	84
4.4	Surge Realignment of States in Presidential Elections 1968–2012	87
4.5	Interactive Realignment of States in Presidential Elections 1968–2012	88
4.6	States in Presidential Elections 2012–2016	90
5.1	States in Presidential and House Elections 1896–1962	110
5.2	States in Presidential and House Elections 1964–2016	111
5.3	Party Polarization in the House 1964–2015 (ADA Scores)	114
5.4	Party Polarization in the Senate 1964–2015 (ADA Scores)	115
5.5	Party Unity in the House of Representatives 1964–2014	116
5.6	Party Unity in the Senate 1964–2014	116

List of Tables

3.1	Front-Runners for Presidential Nominations: Polls, Campaign Finance, and Party Endorsements after Invisible Primary	51
3.2	Typologies of Contested Presidential Nominations (Keech and Matthews Model)	53
3.3	Typologies of Campaigns in Post-Reform Presidential Primaries, 1972–2016 (Bartels Model)	54
3.4	"Agenda-Seekers" Who Extended Presidential Nomination Campaigns (Using Norrander Model)	55
3.5	Exit Polls in Republican Presidential Primaries, 1976–2016	59
3.6	Exit Polls in Democratic Presidential Primaries, 1976–2016	67
4.1	Correlations of Vote by States in Presidential Elections 1880–2016	80
4.2	"Modern" vs. "Traditional" Values in American Politics	89
4.3	Exit Polls in 2012 and 2016 Presidential Elections (By Population Characteristics)	95
4.4	Exit Polls in 2012 and 2016 Presidential Elections (By Party, Ideology, and Issues)	96
5.1	Republican Vote for House of Representatives by State, 1946–2014	106
5.2	State Level Correlation of Vote for President and House, 1880–2016	109

Acknowledgments

As always with projects such as this one, this book would not have been possible without the generous assistance and support of many people.

First, my thanks to the people at Lexington Books for their invaluable assistance in putting together this publication. My early discussions with Kate Tafelski gave shape to this project, and the advice and guidance of Emily Roderick, Courtney Morales, and Christine Fahey were vital to the final product. My thanks also to the series editors, Shauna Reilly and Stacy Ulbig. My thanks to proofreader Melaina Balbo Phipps, who saved me from myself at several points in the manuscript.

I also thank the anonymous reader whose thoughts made this work a better product.

William Crotty played an important role in the development of this work, giving my first book professional exposure, serving a series editor for another book, and as book editor for several chapters I have contributed. Without his support, I would not have been in a position to complete this work.

Several people generously contributed to my early thinking on the subject matter addressed in this book, particularly John Berg, Walter Dean Burnham, Thomas Ferguson, Edward S. Greenberg, William G. Mayer, Garrison Nelson, Gerald Pomper, and John K. White.

Contributions were also made through critiques and discussions at several conference panels, particularly by Randall Adkins, Brian Arbour, Donald Beachler, Mark Brewer, Lara Brown, Larry Butler, Bruce Caswell, Margaret Conway, Andrew Dowdle, Christopher Hull, Scott McLean, Maureen Moakley, Hans Noel, Barbara Norrander, Shayla Nunnally, Larry Reardon, Gary Rose, Dante Scala, Andrew Smith, Wayne Steger, and Stephen J. Wayne. I also want to recognize the late Howard Reiter, who seemed always to appear at the right time, whenever I needed an idea or some encouragement.

I owe a debt of gratitude to Don Kusler at Americans for Democratic Action. He shared data on Congressional voting records that proved invaluable to this project. I would like to thank Dave Leip for the use of his wonderful electionatlas website to build maps.

My thanks collectively to my colleagues at Southern Connecticut State University, for their professional, institutional, and personal support for my work. My colleagues in the Department of Political Science always made our workplace as pleasant as it was productive.

Harriet Applewhite and Robert Gelbach provided ideas and early encouragement. Paul Best, Kul Rai, and David Walsh extended the opportunity to publish with them on political economy.

Kevin Buterbaugh became department chair when I needed to shift my focus to this research, Jonathan Wharton and Jennifer Hopper provided thoughtful encouragement, and Theresa Marchant-Shapiro did a project of her own, critiquing my work on congressional elections and helping to make it better. Special thanks to Monica Mihailoff, our department secretary, who is unfailingly efficient, helpful, and a very good friend.

Another collective thank you to my students over the years, particularly to the graduate students who took my course on the Trump transition and presidency during the spring semester after his inauguration. The course drew public attention and the students worked hard but had a team spirit and sense of humor. I learned at least as much from them as they did from each other or from me.

Finally, thank you to Lynn Greer, my wife, who has lived with this book as much as I have. I am happy that she has shared a life with me.

Chapter One

An Unprecedented President

The 2016 Presidential primaries were certainly interesting, exciting and historic. Donald Trump beat sixteen opponents and the party establishment in the Republican presidential primaries. Senator Bernie Sanders presented former Secretary of State Hillary Clinton with a stiff challenge in the Democratic primaries. With her victory, Ms. Clinton became the first woman ever to win a major party nomination for president. The events of the primaries in both parties seemed to take observers (both journalistic and academic), the general public, and not least, party elites by surprise. Even as the presidential nominations were settled, there was wide speculation of deep systemic change in our parties, perhaps more so in the Republican party, but in the Democratic party, as well.

Then came the presidential election, and it turned out there were more surprises to come. While the public opinion polls were generally close throughout the campaign, most of them indicated that Hillary Clinton was leading, and she was almost universally expected to be elected president. The anticipation and excitement among Democrats was only heightened by the fact that she was on her way to becoming the first woman President of the United States. When there was increasing focus on examples of Trump's tasteless behavior and comments, Democrats briefly expected to win by a landslide. Even as the center of gravity of the polls indicated a closer finish down the stretch, Democrats were preparing with confidence for victory. But their celebrations were not only premature, they were unfounded, and cancelled by the outcome.

On November 8, 2016, Donald Trump was elected president. To be sure, Hillary Clinton won the popular vote by 48 percent to 46 percent, a margin only slightly smaller than had been forecast. But Mr. Trump won the electoral vote by 306 to 232, his narrow victories in Pennsylvania, Michigan, and Wisconsin proving decisive.

What has followed is an unprecedented presidency, at this writing entering its second year. President Trump has promoted a policy agenda which on some issues has been conventional, such as support for economic deregulation, tax cuts and tax reform, and repeal of the Affordable Care Act, all long supported by Republicans. But his turn away from support for open international trade reverses the pattern practiced by presidents of both parties since World War II, and his policies on illegal immigration have been extreme and tied down in legal controversy in the federal courts.

But the policy debates stimulated by President Trump are matters of degree, more unconventional in style than purely unprecedented. What is closer to unprecedented is his character and behavior in office, his tendency to broil controversy on a consistently personal level, and to engage in issues, on Twitter and in personal appearances, that take him away from his own agenda, perhaps to the point of incompetence in office. He has not adapted his personality to the fact that he is the President of the United States. His behavior has been embarrassing to leaders of both parties, even to some of his own supporters. It is his character and behavior, more than his partisan politics or ideology, that has many Americans worried about how President Trump might handle genuine international crises, such as the nuclear armament of North Korea.

The early Trump presidency has also been driven off its intended course by the issue of Russian efforts to influence the 2016 election, and investigations by House and Senate Committees and by a special counsel into suspected collusion between the Trump campaign and the Russians. The presence of questions concerning the Russian attempt to interfere with American democracy makes a longer-term policy analysis of the Trump administration all the more difficult.

This book looks beyond the drama surrounding the personality of Donald Trump to examine the 2016 election and his developing presidency in historical and systemic perspective. The election and the Trump presidency seem historic. Certainly, his election seems to be at least partly the product of fundamental change in the American economy. Will the 2016 election represent a real sea change, a realignment of American parties and electoral politics? Will the policies advanced during the Trump administration represent a real turning point, or will they amount to less change than meets the eye? Finally, and most important, what will be the longer-term impact of the politics of our time on the future of American democracy?

FROM UNCONVENTIONAL CANDIDATE TO UNPRECEDENTED PRESIDENT

Donald Trump was certainly an unconventional candidate and is, by definition, and unprecedented president. He is the first President ever to take office without any previous government or military experience.

Although unconventional, Trump is not entirely unique in our history. He is the second candidate to win a major party presidential nomination without government or military experience. The first was Wendell L. Willkie, the Republican nominee for president in 1940. Willkie and Trump share important similarities as candidates, just as they exhibit important differences.

Trump, like Willkie, is a New Yorker. Both were businessmen. Willkie was Indiana-born, but after moving to New York, became a fixture in the Manhattan establishment. Trump was also in the New York establishment. However, while Willkie's New York bona fides centered in the publishing intelligentsia of the east side of Manhattan, Trump's are centered in business and real estate. Trump and Willkie both made their appeals to voters with a colorful, personable "tell-it-like-it-is" approach to public speaking and direct connection with the crowds they addressed.

Willkie, like Trump, was not a very partisan Republican. Both had been registered as Democrats, Willkie for most of his political life, before turning Republican not long before running for President. Both took unconventional paths to the nomination, avoiding ingratiation with, and for the most part, support from, the party elite. While Trump clinched the nomination in the primaries, Willkie did not enter the primaries. But in a day when national conventions still did the nominating, Willkie built his campaign mostly outside the party hierarchy, with the support of Henry Luce and Russell Davenport at *Time-Life*, the Cowles family and *Look* magazine, and the Willkie Clubs, built across the country from a Wall Street base, under the leadership of Oren Root. Willkie emerged relatively suddenly as a serious candidate late in the preconvention period.

Neither Trump nor Willkie adhered to the party orthodoxy of their day, although their ideologies were very different from each other. Trump is a nationalist and something of a protectionist who sidesteps the support most in his party have for free markets. Willkie was an internationalist who, even during the 1940 campaign, did not oppose the efforts of President Franklin D. Roosevelt to support the United Kingdom even before the United States entered the war (Peters 2005).

After losing a hotly contested election to FDR, Willkie supported internationalism and preparation for war, backing Lend-Lease and delivering a decisive minority of Republican votes to its support in Congress. Thereafter, Willkie travelled the world meeting with Allied leaders on behalf of his president, and wrote *One World* advocating a postwar internationalist foreign policy and civil rights at home (Willkie 1943). Party loyalty was as unimportant to Willkie as it seems to be for Trump. In 1943, as he was preparing to seek renomination for president the following year, Willkie told a luncheon of party leaders, "I don't know whether you are going to support me or not, and I don't give a damn. You're a bunch of political liabilities who don't know what's going on (Neal 1989, 290)." While the ideological content of what he had to say may not be similar, Willkie's outspoken disregard of political diplomacy certainly reminds us of Donald Trump more than seven decades later.

Donald Trump shares another characteristic with Wendell Willkie: relationships with many women. Willkie was married to Edith Wilk, who remained loyal in public through a number of affairs he had with women after moving to New York. Although the press paid little public attention to the private lives of political figures in Willkie's day, his relationship with Irita Van Doren, who was well placed in Manhattan society, and who was the book review editor for the *New York Herald Tribune*, was relatively widely known and acknowledged. Indeed, she played a leading role in introducing Willkie to the opinion leaders of the New York establishment, who then had a greater influence on national public opinion than they do today, and in encouraging him to take himself seriously as a political leader (Barnard 1966; Peters 2005; Neal 1989).[1]

Personal Behavior and Public Life

While Willkie's relationships with Ms. Van Doren and others never caused him severe problems in public opinion, Trump's relationships with women, and the way he has talked about women certainly has caused him problems, and has been part of raising larger questions about his character.

Donald Trump's relationships with women were numerous and more public than Willkie's. Moreover, Trump's attitudes and behavior were apparently more tasteless and disrespectful of women, as revealed in the *Access Hollywood* tape released late in the general election campaign. American history is full of examples of presidential candidates whose affairs with women, real or imagined, had some political impact in their time. Grover Cleveland was revealed to have fathered a child out of wedlock during the 1884 campaign, which he won. Nelson Rockefeller in 1964 and Gary Hart two decades later both saw their front-runner status in nomination campaigns disappear over public revelations about relations with women considered scandalous:

Rockefeller's divorce and remarriage and Hart's extramarital dalliance on top of other suspected affairs. As a candidate and president, from Gennifer Flowers to Monica Lewinski, Bill Clinton's relations with women haunted his political fortunes. In 2016, Donald Trump would attempt to mitigate his problems after the *Access Hollywood* tape by comparing himself favorably to Clinton who, Trump said, had actually done things to women that Trump claimed only to have bragged about.

Trump's careless, or worse, designed tasteless speech hounded him throughout the 2016 campaign. In his announcement of candidacy, he implied, or outright stated, depending on your point of view, that Mexican immigrants were rapists, though he said he assumed some were "good people." He would build a wall to keep illegal immigrants out of the country. He had generalized disparaging remarks to make about Moslems, including the father of an American soldier killed in action, and suggested that Islamic immigration should be banned. Trump was certainly not the first candidate ever to make offensive statements about groups of people, but he was perhaps the first to double down on so many of his comments so consistently.

The Legitimacy of the Election

The personality of Donald Trump had much to do with public demonstrations against him immediately after his inauguration. But they would not have had the vigor they had without the general sense among opponents that the results of the presidential election had been illegitimate. There were, of course, suspicions that FBI Director James Comey had intervened in the campaign with his announcements in the final days about Hillary Clinton's e-mails, or that the Russians had interfered with our democratic process with the release of electronic "fake news."

Indeed, the early days of the Trump administration have been dominated by investigations not only into Russian interference in the 2016 election, but also into evidence of collusion between the Trump campaign and the Russians. These investigations are being conducted within the national government in three places: The House Intelligence Committee, the Senate Intelligence Committee, and by the Special Prosecutor. While Special Prosecutor Robert Mueller has handed down indictments on matters related to the investigation, it is much too early at this writing to conclude where this will all lead.

The real problem of the legitimacy of the election, in the eyes of many Trump opponents, was that Hillary Clinton had won the popular vote by a margin of about three million votes, even as Trump was elected with a majority of the Electoral College vote. Rep. John Lewis, Democrat of Georgia, went so far as to say that Donald Trump was not a legitimate President.

Dramatic as the protests were, doubts about the legitimacy of presidential elections are not unprecedented. The historic cases of doubt are, in fact, numerous, although they have never interrupted the peaceful transfer of power when one was called for by the outcome of an election.[2]

In 1800, the defeat of President John Adams, the incumbent Federalist, for reelection did not result in the clear election of a new President from the opposition. Under the constitutional system for the Electoral College then operating, electors were to cast two votes, without distinguishing a choice for president or vice president. The candidate who came in first, if he had the votes of a majority of electors, would be president, while the candidate coming in second would be vice president. If no candidate had the support of a majority of electors, the election would go to the House of Representatives. The constitutional design made it likely that the Electoral College would usually serve as a nominating institution, with most presidential elections being settled in the House (Mayer 2008a). In 1800, the candidates on the Democratic-Republican ticket, Thomas Jefferson and Aaron Burr, tied with 73 electoral votes, to 65 for Adams, 64 for Adams's running mate, Charles C. Pinckney, and 1 for John Jay (Stanwood 1888).[3] The election went to the House, not because no one got a vote from a majority of electors, but because two candidates could claim a vote from a majority of electors, and they tied. The House elected Jefferson after 36 ballots. The 1800 Presidential election led to the 12th Amendment to the Constitution, which required electors to cast one vote for President and one vote for Vice President.

By 1824, Congressional party caucuses were the generally accepted manner of choosing nominees for President, and most states were selecting electors by popular vote. As President James Monroe was leaving office after having been reelected effectively without opposition four years before, and the Democratic-Republican Party was functionally the only national party. Members of Congress, however, shared no consensus on continuing the caucus method of nomination. A small caucus, not enough to constitute a quorum, met and nominated Treasury Secretary William H. Crawford for president. A popular convention in Tennessee nominated General Andrew Jackson, while Secretary of State John Quincy Adams and Speaker of the House Henry Clay were each nominated by several state legislatures. In the general election, Jackson won a plurality of both the popular and electoral vote, but as he failed to gain a majority, the choice among the top three (Jackson, Adams, and Crawford) went to the House. Adams was elected by the House on the first ballot. When Adams appointed Clay as Secretary of State, speculation spiked, particularly among supporters of Jackson, that a deal had determined the Presidential election and thwarted the will of the people (Stanwood 1888). The 1824 controversy led to a rematch between Jackson and Adams in 1828, won by Jackson; and over the next decade or so, to the birth of the Democratic Party, and the emergence of national conventions to confer party Presidential nominations.

In 1876, Governor Samuel J. Tilden of New York, Democrat, won the popular vote, and apparently the electoral vote as well, over the Republican, Governor Rutherford B. Hayes of Ohio. But the electoral votes of four states, three of them southern states effectively governed by the Republicans under Reconstruction, were in dispute. Unable to resolve the issue in its counting of electoral votes, Congress created an Electoral Commission composed of five members of each house of Congress and five Supreme Court Justices, with a partisan division of eight Republicans and seven Democrats. The disputed electoral votes were awarded to the Republican Hayes, who was thus elected by a count of 185 to 184. The result effectively assigned the presidency to the Republicans, while Reconstruction ended when federal troops were withdrawn from the south the following year, returning self-government to the states of the former Confederacy (Stanwood 1888, 303–44).

The 1888 Presidential election was the only one, before 2016, in which there was a conventional result, without a constitutional controversy, featuring a winner in the Electoral College who lost the popular vote. President Grover Cleveland, the incumbent Democrat, won the popular vote but was defeated for reelection by Republican Benjamin Harrison.[4]

The 2000 election was accompanied by constitutional controversy and recounts in Florida. The Democrat, Vice President Albert Gore, won a narrow victory in the national popular vote over Governor George W. Bush of Texas. However, Florida remained unresolved. Recounts and court cases lingered for thirty-six days, until recounts were halted by the U.S. Supreme Court. Florida was certified to have been carried by Bush, and the final national electoral vote was 271 for Bush, 266 for Gore (*Bush v. Gore* 2000; Ceasar & Busch 2001).

It is interesting that between 1876 and 1892, a period marked by a closely divided electorate, the Democrats won the popular vote in four out of five presidential elections, but the Republicans won the presidency in three of those elections. Once again, since 2000, the Democrats have won the popular vote in four out of five elections, but the Republicans have won the Presidency in three of those elections.

After the 2016 election, Donald Trump assumed the presidency amid serious controversy and opposition, but the unrest represented nothing new or unprecedented in the American experience. What the dramatic transfer of power to Mr. Trump illustrates, like the transition to George W. Bush after the 2000 election, is the severity of political polarization in the current era of our politics. Donald Trump is much more a product of that political polarization than its cause.

Trump as a Product of Lingering Coalitions in American Political Culture

In 2016, Donald Trump appealed to a populist coalition which had deep roots in American history and corners of American political culture. His foundations of support were white, rural and small-town, working-class, disproportionately Southern and even more, Appalachian, and "unhyphenated" Americans (Arbour 2016). His appeal can be traced back to similar candidates with a variety of specific issue agendas, including Andrew Jackson, James B. Weaver, William Jennings Bryan, and populist Southern Democrats both for and against white supremacy, such as Huey Long, Jim Folsom, and George Wallace.

To those who argue that Trump violates American values, the answer is that he violates one corner of our culture while upholding another. The same society that was gifted with and celebrates the Statue of Liberty produced the Alien and Sedition Acts, the Know-Nothings, pro-business tariffs, and pro-labor anti-immigration campaigns long before Donald Trump, who offers the same mixture of protectionism sold as pro-business and pro-labor two centuries later. Moreover, battles between internationalists and isolationists are nothing new. President Woodrow Wilson fought to no avail for the Treaty of Versailles and the League of Nations against isolationists after World War I, just as before World War II, internationalists battled isolationists proclaiming, "America First!" Many of today's debates, involving the "birthers" who opposed Obama, and the alt-right now gaining footing in the White House, inspire political coalitions and language that we have seen before on similar issues. David Weigel (2016) in the Washington Post referred to the Trump coalition as nationalist, "racialist" voters of the "Alt-right." Trump assured these voters that he (in fact, *only* he) could fix their problems.[5] In office, President Trump has continued his appeal to this segment of his base, particularly in his remarks about demonstrations and violence in Charlottesville, Virginia, when he implied a moral equivalence between white nationalists and neo-Nazis on one side, and counterprotesters for racial equality on the other.

Not all, perhaps not even most of Trump's support is located on the ideological extremes. If it were, he could not have been elected President. He enjoys extensive support from Americans who see their way of life and work disappearing. These voters, too, are nothing particularly new to American history. At the turn of the twentieth century, they were farmers and rural voters who saw their way of life being overtaken by industrialization. Since the late twentieth century, they have been a product of the decline of the manufacturing and mining employment in America associated with the end of the industrial age and the development of postindustrial society. Kevin Phillips saw these white, working-class voters as the swing vote in the "emerging Republican majority" that elected Richard M. Nixon president twice, while Everett Carll Ladd (1978, 1980) identified their shift as the "inversion of the New Deal order."

David Apter (1964) contributed to an understanding of these emerging voters with his identification of a new, technologically based class system in postindustrial society. Apter identified the technologically competent and the technologically superfluous (nothing new about either of these), and the technologically obsolete, whose work and way of life were disappearing with postindustrial modernization. Walter Dean Burnham (1978) saw the "technologically obsolete" as the potential core of a working-class conservatism in postindustrial politics. Voters of this description seem to be the heart of the Trump coalition in 2016, particularly in the Appalachians and the Great Lakes states that made such a decisive difference in the election.

Donald Trump and the Presidential Character

Trump's appeal is to populist voters who are nothing new and more than a fringe in American political culture. They are not all the "deplorables" that Hillary Clinton referred to. But it is fair to say that at least a fair number of them confirm the Pulitzer Prize–winning work of Richard Hofstadter (1963), *Anti-Intellectualism in American Life*. It is anecdotal evidence, but clearly true that a number of Trump voters actually acknowledge that Trump is ignorant of the issues he has to deal with as president, but that his ignorance is preferable to knowledge within the governing establishment.

Trump appeals to attitudes long found in American culture, sometimes dormant, sometimes active, but always there. For Republicans, he represents a dangerous opportunity to win over disaffected voters (Tanenhaus, 2016), but he often declines to cooperate with party leaders or to adhere to widely shared norms of conduct for a public leader. Republican leaders themselves hardly know how to handle their president. House Speaker Paul Ryan attempts to keep his focus on issues, seeking to maintain his own libertarianism while uniting House Republicans on a conservative agenda. Senate Majority Leader Mitch McConnell attempts to push a legislative agenda while seeking to protect incumbent Republican Senators who are critical of Trump. Senators Bob Corker of Tennessee and Jeff Flake of Arizona have announced they will not run for reelection in 2018, declining to participate in Trump-era politics. Meanwhile, Senator John McCain of Arizona, the Republican nominee for president in 2008, who is near the end of his political career in the face of life-threatening cancer, has become one of the sharpest critics of Trump.

Throughout a campaign in which the speech and behavior of Donald Trump was a constant issue, there was wide speculation about when, if ever,

Mr. Trump would begin to appear more tasteful, dignified, or presidential. Republicans hoped he would "pivot" once he officially became the Republican nominee for President, or failing that, once he was elected if he were to be so fortunate. After the election, Republicans and Democrats alike, and the American people apparently hoped he would pivot and start acting like a president once he was inaugurated. At this writing in the early days of his presidency, these hopes for a pivot remain unfulfilled, even violated.

There is little reason to be surprised with President Trump, either in the policies he has pursued in the early days, or in his personal conduct. His appointments to his administration, his first appointment to the Supreme Court, his policies on border security, immigration, deregulation, national security and foreign affairs, and energy, all are consistent with what he said he would do as president if elected. His conduct remains what it almost always has been in public, and what it has been since he first declared his candidacy after descending his escalator at Trump Tower. Even his firing of both acting Attorney General Sally Yates and FBI Director James Comey should not have come as a surprise. As president, he continues to launch personal attacks on top officials in the executive branch. There is no reason to expect President Trump to change suddenly.

How unprecedented is the Trump phenomenon? As a whole character (and perhaps as a caricature?) he seems unprecedented. Probably never has a candidate said so much that was not only politically incorrect in his own time, but socially tasteless and immature. But we have seen all the parts of Donald Trump before, just not all in the same person.

An assessment of the personal character of Donald Trump, and how it might predict his behavior in office is perhaps best performed by applying the construct developed by James David Barber in his classic work, *The Presidential Character* (1972).[6] Barber categorized the Presidential character along two dimensions: The active-passive, which indicated the degree of initiative and activity in office by a president, and the positive-negative, an indicator of attitudes toward the self and other people, that is, whether or not he liked and trusted people, and whether the president positively enjoyed the useful exercise of power, or he saw power as a tool to advance him- (or her-) self against perceived opponents. The two dimensions leave four categories of presidential character, according to Barber.

The *Active-Positive* President likes and trusts him or herself and other people, enjoys the work of the presidency and the exercise of power, takes initiative, and has a task-oriented focus on achieving policy goals. Theodore Roosevelt, Franklin D. Roosevelt, and John F. Kennedy are perhaps the best examples of presidents so classified by Barber.

The *Passive-Positive* President also likes and trusts people. But unlike the active-positive, building and maintaining good and even friendly relationships is of great importance as an end in itself to the passive-positive. For a passive-positive president, the rule seems to be, "If it ain't broke, don't fix it." Perhaps the leading example of a passive-positive for Barber is Ronald Reagan.

The *Passive-Negative* President has an attitude toward the self and other people that is highly conditioned on public service and good behavior. The passive-negative serves as president out of a sense of obligation and duty, and does not particularly enjoy the activity involved for its own sake. George Washington, Calvin Coolidge, and Dwight D. Eisenhower are passive-negatives according to Barber. I might add George H. W. Bush, who seemed to run for reelection in 1992 without warming to the task.

Finally, there is the *Active-Negative* President, who wants power for the purpose of defeating opponents and protecting oneself. The active-negative cannot tolerate criticism, is closed-minded and unlikely to revisit decisions. For the active-negative president, the rule seems to be, "Do unto others before they do unto you." The active-negative will often get wrapped up in an issue, and, unable to disentangle himself, see his presidency fail. Lyndon B. Johnson saw an otherwise productive presidency on domestic policy fail with the Vietnam War, while Richard M. Nixon, so successful in foreign affairs, lost his presidency over Watergate.[7]

Donald Trump reminds us of Richard Nixon not only for the electoral coalition he attracts, but also for his style of personal conduct in office. Nixon certainly had a stronger understanding the of dignity of the office of President of the United States. But the investigations into Russian interference in the 2016 election, and possible collusion between the Trump campaign and Russia, have brought back memories of Watergate. The firing of Comey particularly generated comparisons with Nixon's firing of Attorney General Elliot Richardson in the "Saturday Night Massacre" of 1973. Finally, investigations of collusion with Russia by the Trump campaign are a reminder of suspected efforts by the Nixon campaign in 1968 to sabotage efforts by President Johnson to advance the Paris peace talks on the Vietnam War (Baker 2017).

Throughout the campaign, and in the early days of his presidency, all the evidence indicates that Donald Trump is an active-negative personality. Whether challenged on issues, or his statements, or personal behavior, Mr. Trump doubles down on with an attack on whomever poses the question at hand. His conduct consistently indicates that his default position is to do unto others either before they do unto him, or to do unto others more than they have done unto him. Anyone who hopes or expects Donald Trump to "pivot" away from this pattern has no basis for that expectation. As president, Trump will be Trump.

PLAN FOR THE BOOK

This book examines the election of Donald Trump and the prospects for his presidency in historical and systemic perspective. Going beyond Trump personally, this book becomes an inquiry into the longer-term impact of this moment in our history on the health of American democracy, assessing directions of change in our economy, public policy, and our political institutions. The analysis that follows considers Donald Trump to present a severe problem for the American body politic. But Trump is not the source of the polarized condition of American politics today. While he aggravates that condition, he is more the product of it than the cause.

Chapter 2 traces ideological change within the two major parties in American politics, with emphasis on the national parties and presidential nominations. It presents the historic character of the American two-party system, starting with the umbrella parties born in the nineteenth century which thrived as diverse factional systems well into the twentieth century, then traces the decline of umbrella parties and emergence of ideologically homogenized and polarized parties in the latter half of the twentieth century.

Chapter 3 discusses Presidential nominations since the ideological realignment of American political parties and party reforms of the 1960s. It discusses patterns of factional conflict and consensus in postreform presidential nominations, and seeks evidence of stability and change in the presidential nominations of 2016.

Chapter 4 examines the election of 2016 in historical perspective, offering an analysis of the relationship between ideological realignment and electoral realignment over the past half century. Going beyond the questions of how Donald Trump was elected and how Hillary Clinton lost in 2016, this chapter considers the short-term and longer-term impact of the 2016 election. How did the 2016 election represent stability in our electoral politics, and how did it present change? What electoral coalitions from 2016 are likely to persist, and what electoral behavior is a passing phase? What will be the foreseeable impact on the American party system?

Chapter 5 discusses the separation of powers in the American constitutional system, and its relationship to the two-party system. The focus will be on the decline of umbrella parties and the spread of ideological polarization to Congress. The crisis of the party system is presented: While the separation of powers provided the setting for the development of the old umbrella party system, our polarized parties that developed over the last half century are more appropriate to party government in a parliamentary system. That is, we have developed parliamentary parties without developing parliamentary government. which has led to dysfunction in policy making, commonly called "gridlock." While parliamentary systems, particularly in the United Kingdom, are often called "responsible party government," Americans today are sensing that we are burdened with what could be called "irresponsible party government."

Chapter 6 addresses postindustrial democracy in America. Alexis de Tocqueville visited an America developing during the industrial revolution, and made observations of a culture which describes the "American dream." Americans of his day and ours have believed in an "equality of condition" in which individuals enjoy the opportunity for upward mobility toward the "good life." What is the impact of political and economic change on that culture almost two centuries later? What realities can be attached to policy proposals by the new president and his political opponents today? How relevant to our future will their debate prove to be? What are the longer-term challenges we face? What is the outlook for American political institutions designed for an industrial age to come and persisting in an industrial age now over? What are the prospects for American democracy in the twenty-first century?

The answers to these questions will not be clear for some time to come. Donald Trump says he will pursue different policies, and that he will do things differently. Trump's claims to the contrary notwithstanding, our future will not be shaped by Donald Trump alone. But by their conduct over the next four to eight years, President Trump, his supporters, and his opposition will impact the responsiveness of the American system, and the range of choices Americans, elites and citizens alike, will have left to them in the years thereafter. This book is offered in the hope that it will help explain how we came to this moment in time while contributing to our thinking about the alternative futures we face.

NOTES

1. The movie, *State of the Union*, was modeled on Willkie's story. Spencer Tracy played a businessman running for a presidential nomination, with Katherine Hepburn as his wife who tolerated his affairs to support him. Angela Lansbury played the socialite who encouraged the Tracy character to run for president. (See Neal 1989, 143).

2. With the reasonable qualification that one might consider the War Between the States as an "interruption" of the peaceful transfer of power. Abraham Lincoln took office following constitutional form, but eleven states seceded from the union, and war followed.

3. The Federalists did what the Democratic-Republicans failed to do: They coordinated their electoral votes to ensure that their candidate for president finished ahead of their candidate for vice president. Unfortunately for them, they lost the election.

4. It should be noted that Grover Cleveland, who was elected again in 1892, was the only president other than Franklin D. Roosevelt to win the popular vote in more than two presidential elections.

5. Indeed, in his acceptance speech at the convention Trump proclaimed that "only I" can fix it.

6. Barber gained public notice with his first edition by predicting that President Nixon, then headed for reelection, would get caught on an issue he could not let go of, and his Presidency would fail in his second term. There have been several subsequent editions, most recently in 2009.

7. I do not necessarily agree with all of Barber's descriptions of the personality types or how he categorizes all presidents. For example, I would add Gerald Ford to the list of "passive–positives." Barber also categorizes Abraham Lincoln as an "active–negative," which would offend the tendency to Lincoln-worship. Lincoln is apparently so categorized because he suffered from depression and because of his autocratic behavior toward northerners who opposed the conduct of the Civil War and the courts. I would take issue with an "active–negative" characterization because he filled his cabinet with Republicans who opposed his nomination in 1860, he had a sense of humor about himself, and he seems to have meant it when he proclaimed "With malice toward none and charity for all." However I might take issue with some of Barber's generalizations, this book is not the place to take them on. Moreover, I consider his framework to offer a useful way of understanding the personal behavior of presidents in office.

Chapter Two

From Umbrella Parties to Polarized Parties in American Politics

Donald Trump was elected president after an unusually bitter election campaign. The national unity that commonly appears, even if temporarily, around the inauguration of a new president, was not there for Mr. Trump. In his early days in office, at this writing, President Trump has an unusually low approval rating for a new president. But neither the bitterness nor the low approval ratings are just about Trump, or even primarily about him. Congress suffers from much lower approval ratings than the new president, and a majority of Americans continue to believe that the country is headed in the "wrong direction." Moreover, polling evidence indicates that Americans have lost confidence generally in most of their public institutions, and no longer had confidence that their democracy is working for them. War, terrorism, the great recession, increasing economic inequality, and a sense of declining opportunity all weigh heavily in the public consciousness. Government seemed unresponsive, paralyzed by policy gridlock, frozen by partisan conflict. The electorate seems not only discouraged, but angry, and afraid, even if voters may be divided on what they are angry and afraid about.

How did we get here? This chapter will address one factor, a very fundamental change in the American two-party system, the rise and fall of umbrella parties and their replacement after the middle of the twentieth century by polarized parties. This chapter will focus on the ideological realignment of political parties in presidential politics. Party polarization in Congress will be addressed in chapter 5.

UMBRELLA PARTIES IN A TWO-PARTY SYSTEM

From its earliest development, the American party system has been a two-party system, and a multifactional system, at the same time. Historically, the two major parties have not been defined by clear ideological distinctions between them, although differences on issues, often minor but sometimes major, could be found across election cycles. But the relative stability of a two-party system in the United States invites interesting comparisons with party systems in advanced parliamentary democracies. Understanding how unique the American party system is is an important step toward understanding the meaning of change in our political parties in recent decades. That discussion takes us to broader issues of political culture, constitutional and legal structure, and social structure.

The central reality about the American party system is that it is a *two-party system*, not a *multiparty system*. There is no parliamentary democracy where a two-party system is so secure. Multiparty systems are much more common. In some parliamentary democracies, such as the United Kingdom, Canada, or Germany, governing authority tends to shift with elections between two dominant parties, but even there, coalition governments involving partnerships with more minor parties are not that unusual. Moreover, regardless of party system, in every national legislature in parliamentary democracies, seats are always held by more than two parties. In the United States, the two major parties often occupy all of the seats in both houses of the Congress. Today, independents hold only two of the one hundred seats in the U.S. Senate, and of necessity they caucus with one of the major parties. Meanwhile, as usual, Republicans or Democrats occupy all 435 seats in the House of Representatives.

One commonly cited reason for a two-party system in the United States is the winner-take-all, first-past-the-post electoral arrangement. Senators and Representatives win seats by securing the most votes, and there is no proportional representation, as in many European parliamentary systems. That, along with a combination of state laws concerning ballot access, discourages minor parties (Duverger 1972; Riker 1982). However, the United Kingdom, for example, also has a first-past-the-post system, and parties beyond the top two still always win seats in the House of Commons. There are other, perhaps more important explanations for a two-party system.

One explanation of the consistency of a two-party system in the United States will be particularly relevant to our discussion of party change over the past half century. In America, there simply is not that much space along the ideological spectrum. American political culture is a classic liberal culture. The political philosophy of John Locke is inherited in both the Declaration of Independence and the Constitution of the United States. In America, classic liberalism, a belief in individual liberty, private property, and limited republican government, is almost a public religion, rather than a competing political ideology.[1] The debates about the divisive issues of the day, including ratification of the Constitution, national authority versus states' rights, slavery, and free markets versus government intervention in the economy, have always been conducted within the this ideological framework.[2] Both major parties have fit within these ideological limits, and today they continue to support the premise of individual liberty, limited government, private property, and capitalism.

The very limited degree of class consciousness in American culture contributes to the historically nonideological basis of our party system. Viewing themselves as individuals, most Americans have, at most times in our history, not identified themselves as members of social classes with social-structural limits on their life chances (Aronowitz 1992; Centers 1949; Lane 1962; Paulson 1985; Schlozman & Verba 1979). American political parties historically have not been able to count on assembling stable majorities based on doctrinaire appeals to a narrow social class base.

In a two-party system within such ideological limits, both parties have to appeal to the center in the effort to win elections (Downs 1957; Scammon & Wattenburg 1970). By comparison, party systems in other advanced democracies offer the voters choices of much greater ideological diversity. Even where classic liberalism is deep in the culture, parties based on varieties of socialism, classic conservatism, communism, and fascism might be competitive.

Of course, in one sense, American political parties were always very ideological. They have been instruments of political socialization to the American experience, with Lockean classic liberalism as the unifying ideology. But for something more than a century after the first appearance of mass-based umbrella parties, ideology was not a consistent defining ingredient of electoral competition.

The constitutional and legal structure of government in the United States also reinforced a nonideological, two-party system. Federalism contributed to the building of state parties, and electoral competition aimed at state electorates, rather than a consistent orientation by national parties to national issues. Indeed, it was to the advantage of party leaders seeking to build and maintain national coalitions to avoid polarizing national issues, such as slavery before the Civil War, and race thereafter. In addition, state laws written by legislators from the major parties, tended to discourage access to the ballot for anyone but the major parties. Members of state legislatures and Congress have been elected from single member districts, winners of pluralities taking all, thus encouraging the major parties whose candidates might win, and discouraging competition from minor parties.

Finally, the constitutional arrangement of the separation of powers, with staggered elections to the Presidency, Senate, and House, discourage electoral competition based on a national policy agenda, as is more likely to be found in a parliamentary system with unitary and party government, such as the United Kingdom. In fact, since 1789, the United States has never had the sort of national general election that the British hold at least every five years.

Thus, historically, American political parties have been patronage-oriented more than issue-oriented. Winning and retaining control of government and delivering for their supporters have been the main goal of party leaders.

Of course, a two-party system does not mean that there are just two sides of the political fence. With many issues on the agenda, coalitions are multi-dimensional. Indeed, the effort to structure and discipline otherwise scattering votes in Congress between supporters of the Washington administration and Hamilton on the one hand (Federalists), and supporters of Jefferson and Madison on the other (Anti-Federalists or Democratic-Republicans) led to the early elite-based founding of the first American political parties (Aldrich 1995, chapter 3). Moreover, even when social consensus is strong, it cannot disguise the diversity of American society. Thus, both of our major parties are best understood as factional systems, and our two-party system should be considered as a multifactional system of interests. Indeed, until the late twentieth century, both major parties contained under their umbrellas interests spanning the American ideological spectrum.

FROM UMBRELLA PARTIES TO POLARIZED PARTIES

Both the Democrats and Republicans were umbrella parties, with factions representing competing interests across the ideological spectrum from their earliest development in the nineteenth century until the middle of the twentieth century. Then, both parties went through decisive internal factional struggles that resulted in ideological polarization of the party system.

The Democrats' Umbrella

The Democratic Party, the oldest continuously functioning political party in the world, was born as a North-South alliance and evolved in the twentieth century into the multifactional system it remains today, featuring reformers, party regulars, and the South.

Martin Van Buren of New York took the lead after the 1824 election to assemble a coalition of North and South, replicating the earlier alliance among Jefferson, Madison, and Aaron Burr of New York, to elect Andrew Jackson to the presidency in 1828 and 1832. Elected president himself in 1836, Van Buren was defeated for reelection in 1840 after the financial panic of 1837. The uneasiness of the North-South alliance was revealed in 1844 when Van Buren failed to win renomination for president after opposing the annexation of Texas. By 1860, subject to the same split over slavery that divided the union, the Democrats failed to unite on any nominee for president, and Northern and Southern Democrats had to nominate candidates of their own, facilitating the election of Republican Abraham Lincoln as president, and hastening the Civil War.

After Reconstruction the Democrats recovered as a major party, remaining an uneasy North-South alliance. The Solid South was the base of the Democratic electoral coalition until the 1960s, and Southern Democrats remained an active faction of the party well beyond that. For three decades after William Jennings Bryan won the Democratic presidential nomination in 1896, Democratic factionalism was shaped by his rural, populist supporters and his opponents based in cities of the Northeast. Thereafter, with the emergence of the New Deal party system, Northern Democrats became the stronger influence in the party, although they were divided themselves between the party regulars supported by urban machines, labor, and working-class voters, and the more middle-class reform faction.

The Solid South

The South offered Democrats their electoral base in national elections from the end of Reconstruction until the middle of the twentieth century. The Democrats carried all eleven states of the old Confederacy in all ten presidential elections between 1880 and 1916, lost Tennessee in the record Republican landslide of 1920, lost five states of the rim south in 1928, when Alfred E. Smith, a Roman Catholic, was the Democratic nominee for president, then swept the South again in the four elections of Franklin D. Roosevelt. Not until the Dixiecrat revolt in 1948 did the Democrats fail to win a Southern state again. Across a total of seventeen presidential elections between 1880 and 1944, the Democrats lost a total of six states in two elections in the South.

The effective one-party system allowed the South to build and maintain a legal system of white supremacy protected from national interference. The Supreme Court decision in *Plessy v. Ferguson* (1896) facilitated the push for white supremacy in general, and the denial of the right to vote to African Americans in particular. In the decade after the election of 1896, the voter turnout in the South was reduced by more than half, reflecting the disappearance of Southern blacks from the electorate (Burnham 1970).

The development of primaries, a progressive era reform, was particularly convenient to the one-party system of the South. The one-party system did not dictate unity, as Democrats there, as elsewhere, were factionalized. The factions were less likely to be ideological, and more likely to be clientelistic and personal, as Southern Democrats were for or against, for example, Huey Long in Louisiana, or Herman Talmadge in Georgia, or Harry F. Byrd in Virginia. Primaries were also an additional vehicle for the denial of the right to vote on racial grounds. In some states, African Americans might have a de jure right to vote in general elections, but the real decisions about public office were made in Democratic primaries, where the Democratic Party was treated as a private club, able to deny membership and voting rights by race.[3]

In addition to the Solid South's one-party system itself, two political institutions served to protect the South from national intervention that might have threatened white supremacy. First, there was the two-thirds rule at Democratic National Conventions, which gave the South effective veto power over nominations for the national ticket, and was an invaluable bargaining chip on matters of national policy. Second, there was the seniority system in Congress that still exists today. So long as the South was solidly Democratic, Southern Democrats who kept getting reelected to the House and Senate had the seniority to claim committee chairs, which put them in a strong position to influence policy, particularly when opposing legislation. Thus, Southern Democrats were often willing to support national tickets in the name of winning Democratic majorities in Congress.

Rural Populism vs. the Urban North

In the early twentieth century, Democratic factionalism was deeply influenced by support of, and opposition to, William Jennings Bryan. Bryan won the Democratic presidential nomination in 1896 after his "Cross of Gold" speech. Thereafter, he became the voice of populism in the Democratic Party. In four out of five Democratic National Conventions starting in 1896, Bryan was decisively powerful, winning renomination in 1900, winning the nomination again in 1908, and shifting his support to Governor Woodrow Wilson of New Jersey in what proved to be the turning point of the long nomination contest at the 1912 convention.

On most issues, William Jennings Bryan was a progressive Democrat, supporting free silver and economic egalitarianism. His populism represented the interests of the rural community and the farmer against the industrializing economic elite of the east. On foreign policy, like the economy, Bryan had views similar to today's liberal Democrat, opposing the war in the Philippines at the turn of the twentieth century, and resigning as Secretary of State in the Wilson administration over the country's drift toward entering World War I.

On cultural issues, Bryan shared a belief in traditional values with many Western and Southern Democrats. A Christian fundamentalist, Bryan supported prohibition, a position widely considered to be "progressive" at the turn of the century. More famously, Bryan opposed social Darwinism, considering it to be an economic rationalization of class exploitation in modern society (Koenig 1971).[4] He tolerated the Ku Klux Klan, and he represented the prosecution in the Scopes Monkey Trial of 1925. He lived long enough to be considered conservative or even reactionary, losing influence in the Democratic Party in his final years. Today, the Republican Party would be the much more fertile home to the sorts of beliefs in cultural traditionalism that Bryan harbored.

The opposition to Bryan was urban and Northern, and in the early years of the twentieth century, more conservative. To win his first nomination, Bryan displaced the supporters of President Grover Cleveland who supported a solid gold standard. Alton B. Parker of New York was the only Northern, urban candidate to interrupt Bryan's string of presidential nominations. But, starting with the Wilson administration and into the 1920s the urban faction of the Democratic Party became decidedly less conservative, even as Bryan was becoming more so.

The Democratic National Convention of 1924 illustrated the internal strife between urban and rural Democrats, and the power of the South, just as the factions within the party were about to shift (Murray 1976). The leading candidates for the Democratic presidential nomination were former Treasury Secretary William Gibbs McAdoo, whose base of support was rural, Southern, Western and relatively conservative, and Governor Alfred E. Smith of New York, the more liberal Democrat, whose support was Northern and urban. With the two-thirds rule, neither could secure the nomination, and it took 103 ballots, a record, to nominate John W. Davis of West Virginia.

The real battle at the 1924 convention was over the minority report to amend the platform to condemn the Ku Klux Klan. Support for the Klan came mostly from the South and West, while support for the minority report was based in the North. The vote was the closest convention roll call in history, as the convention voted against condemning the Klan, 543.15 to 542.35 (Murray 1976, 161). It was the last convention in which conservative Democrats were the winning faction, however narrowly.

By 1928, Democrats seemed more concerned with avoiding a repeat of the factional combat of 1924, than with asserting the interests of any one faction of the party. When Governor Smith won the Democratic presidential nomination, it was with only limited opposition at the convention, and it transferred power among Democrats toward the North, and cities. It proved to be a decisive step in the urbanization of the Democratic Party.

The New Deal Democrats

The seeds of today's factions of the Democratic Party were being planted with the emergence of the New Deal party system. Alfred E. Smith was seeking renomination for president, with the support of most party regulars and urban machines, including Tammany Hall. House Speaker John Nance Garner was in the running, hoping to carry the banner of both the South and West. Unfortunately for Garner, a rural faction uniting the South and West was already in decline, and for most Southern Democrats the priority was to stop Al Smith. The beneficiary of that priority was Governor Franklin D. Roosevelt of New York, the candidate of the growing reform wing of the party. As Governor, Roosevelt had alienated Tammany with his investigations of Mayor James J. Walker of New York. But Roosevelt emerged as the front-runner in the primaries, added the support of most of the South, went to the convention with a majority of the delegates in his corner, and won the Democratic presidential nomination on the fourth ballot. The deal was completed, in the name of a renewed North-South alliance, when Garner was added to the ticket as Roosevelt's running mate (Davis 1994; Ritchie 2007).

Franklin D. Roosevelt was elected to four terms as president, leading the country through depression and war. Promoting the New Deal, FDR also made efforts in enhance the fortunes of liberal Democrats within his party. In 1936, with his renomination unopposed, Roosevelt's supporters took the lead to abrogate the two-thirds rule at Democratic National Conventions. The move to make convention decisions a matter of majority rule was approved by the Rules Committee, and faced no opposition on the floor, thus depriving the south of its historic veto power in party affairs.

Emboldened by his record landslide in 1936, FDR moved not only to exercise his role as president and leader of his party, and but also as the factional leader of liberal Democrats. First, he attempted to pack the Supreme Court, encountering opposition not only from Republicans, but also from conservative Democrats, including Vice President Garner. He failed to pack the court, but he won the wider conflict, as the court reversed itself after 1937 on the issue of government regulation of the economy (Schwartz 1993).[5]

FDR was less successful in his electoral adventures as a factional leader for liberal Democrats. In 1938, he violated decorum to campaign against conservative Democrats in the midterm primaries for the Senate. He met with little success, as his candidates lost more than they won. When FDR won renomination on his way to reelection to a third term in 1940, he successfully pressured the convention to nominate Henry A. Wallace, his Secretary of Agriculture and a liberal Democrat, for vice president. But four years later, with FDR much more ambiguous about his choice of a running mate, liberal Democrats were unable to deliver renomination to Vice President Wallace, who lost his place on the ticket to Senator Harry Truman of Missouri. It proved an important convention decision, as Truman became the thirty-third president of the United States when FDR died the following year.

Thereafter, liberal Democrats would gain more decisive power in party ranks in two waves: First, with the push for civil rights and racial equality, and second, with the factional conflict among Democrats about the Vietnam War and party reform.

Civil Rights and the Not-So-Solid South

Despite the presence of the Southern faction for white supremacy within its ranks, the Democrats would decide as a national party to favor civil rights at their 1948 convention. With the passage of the 24th Amendment to the Constitution banning a poll tax, the Civil Rights Act of 1964, and the Voting Rights Act of 1965, the Democrats came to be identified by much of the electorate as the party of racial equality (Black & Black 1992; Carmines & Stimson 1989; Lawrence 1997; Paulson 2007).

It is ironic that Harry S Truman, having been used by conservative Democrats as a vehicle to stop Henry A. Wallace in 1944, would be used by liberal Democrats as a reluctant vehicle for promoting an endorsement of civil rights reform in the party's platform. In fact, President Truman had already made a commitment to civil rights, well before the convention, ordering desegregation of the military, and advocating an antilynching bill in Congress. But the partisan electoral issues involved in the civil rights issue were difficult for national party leaders. On the one hand, the growth of the African-American population and vote in the urban areas of states in the North with large blocs of electoral votes offered a strategic argument for supporting civil rights. On the other hand, the New Deal Democratic coalition was an alliance of working-class whites of the North, Southern whites, and blacks, which could be threatened by putting civil rights on the policy agenda. In the postwar social atmosphere, having beaten fascism and moving into cold war against communist totalitarianism, public sympathy for racial equality was growing, at least in the North.

On balance, President Truman and the national convention's platform committee, hoping to maintain party unity, favored a moderate plank on civil rights.[6] The Texas delegation, proposed a substitute to the committee's platform plank, instead opposing civil rights and favoring states' rights. The southern plank was defeated by a vote of 924 to 310.[7] Then the pro–civil rights substitute, proposed on behalf of Americans for Democratic Action, and supported in a dramatic speech by Mayor Hubert H. Humphrey of Minneapolis passed by 651.5 to 582.5. In the balloting on the ADA substitute, most of the leaders of big city machines united with reform liberal Democrats in support of civil rights. Delegates from the eleven states of the old Confederacy voted in opposition. The 1948 platform debate on civil rights demonstrated how clearly power at Democratic National Conventions had shifted to the North since the 1924 convention decision not to condemn the Klan.[8] See figure 2.1.

Scattered delegates from the Deep South bolted the convention in the "Dixiecrat" revolt, later forming a third party to oppose civil rights and nominate Governor J. Strom Thurmond of South Carolina for president. Meanwhile, President Truman won the Democratic nomination, defeating Senator Richard B. Russell of Georgia, a segregationist who remained loyal to the party, by a vote of 926 to 266 on the first ballot.

That November, President Truman was elected in the classic election upset. But the experience of 1948 demonstrated the difficulty Democrats would face in keeping the disparate elements of the New Deal coalition under the same umbrella. Truman carried seven of the eleven states of the South, while Thurmond carried four Deep South states. The South has never again voted solidly for the national Democratic ticket.

After 1948, while liberal Democrats had reason to believe they could deliver majorities at Democratic National Conventions, in the name of party unity, they had to be careful what they did with their advantage. In 1952, for example, there was a convention-floor fight over seating the Virginia delegation, which had declined to take a loyalty oath to the party. Segregationist conservative Democrats, supporting Senator Russell for president, voted to seat the Virginia delegates. Democrats outside the south wanted to preserve party unity but were divided on the strategy for doing so. Generally, reform liberal Democrats, many supporting W. Averill Harriman of New York or Senator Estes Kefauver of Tennessee, insisted on loyalty and opposed seating Virginia.[9] But party regulars, most of whom ended up voting for the eventual nominee for president, Governor Adlai E. Stevenson of Illinois, preferred to finesse the issue and encourage loyalty from the south by seating Virginia. After winning the nomination, Governor Stevenson selected Senator John Sparkman of Alabama, a segregationist, as his running mate.

The 1952 convention was the first of three in a row that would attempt to hold the North-South alliance together by nominating a moderate liberal from the north for president, and a Southerner for vice president. In 1960, when Senator John F. Kennedy of Massachusetts won the Democratic presidential

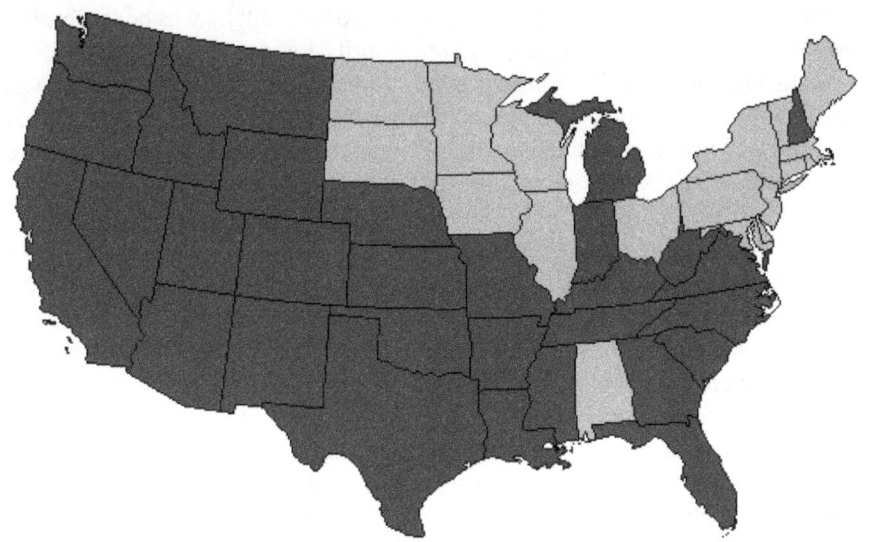

1924. Balloting on Platform Proposal to Condemn the Ku Klux Klan

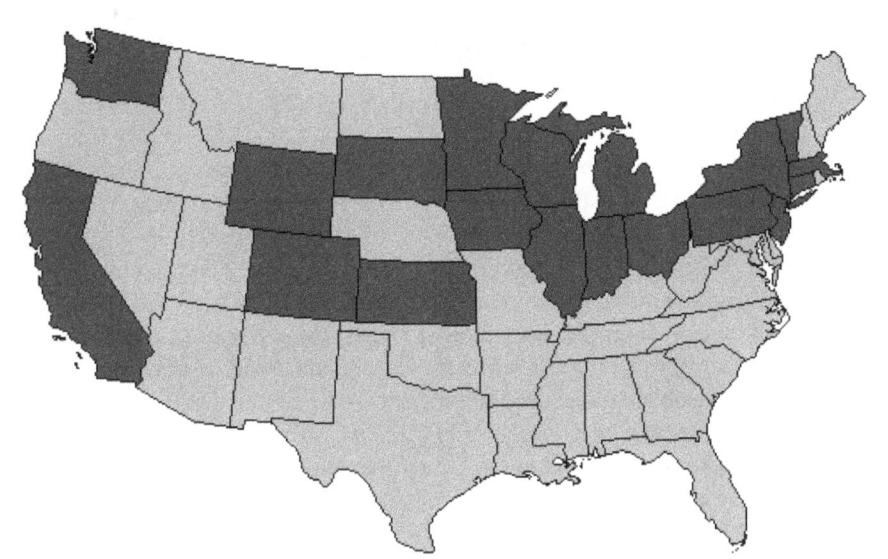

1948. Democratic Convention Balloting on Platform Proposal to Endorse Civil Rights Reform

Figure 2.1 Democratic Convention Balloting on Civil Rights, 1924 and 1948. Dark states represent delegations voting with the majority in each case. In 1924, proposal to condemn the Klan was defeated, 543.15 to 542.15. In 1948, proposal to endorse civil rights reform passed, 651.5 to 582.5.

Source: Maps derived from Dave Leip, www.uselectionatlas.org. Data drawn from National Party Conventions, 1831–1984 (Washington, DC: Congressional Quarterly, 1987): 193 and 202.

nomination, he may have surprised some supporters, but he was not inventing new strategy, when he selected Senate Majority Leader Lyndon B. Johnson, a Texas Democrat, as his running mate. Indeed, the choice of Johnson was essential to the Democratic ticket narrowly carrying the south in 1960. What was just as important to the election of Senator Kennedy was the black vote in the cities of the North, where the electoral votes of New York, New Jersey, Pennsylvania, Michigan, and Illinois proved decisive.

That electoral reality, plus the mounting pressure of the civil rights movement, including the Freedom Riders in 1961, and the march on Washington in 1963, plus Southern violence against civil rights activists, led President Kennedy to introduce the Civil Rights Act. After his assassination, President Johnson pushed for passage of the bill, which was achieved with bipartisan support in the summer of 1964. In Congress, only Southern Democrats cast a majority of their votes against the bill, while Northern Democrats were joined by Republicans in passing it. Nevertheless, after the Civil Rights Act, the Democratic Party was coming to be identified by voters as the party of racial equality.

The Movement Democrats and Party Reform

By 1964, liberal Democrats had emerged as the majority in their national party. What remained, in 1968 and 1972, was a showdown between the Democrats' liberal factions, the party regulars and the reformers. The regulars were party loyalists, mostly products of urban party organizations, with a labor and working-class electoral base. The reformers supported by a younger, more highly educated, more middle-class electoral base, were by comparison ideologues, issue activists who placed policy ahead of party. While both factions of liberals were united on economic issues and civil rights, the reformers were the electoral heart of opposition to the Vietnam War. Moreover, reformers had long been advocates of democratization of the Democratic Party, challenging the power of the regular organizations in party affairs.

In 1968, the antiwar movement led to the most serious challenge to the renomination of a sitting president since 1912. After Senator Eugene McCarthy of Minnesota, an antiwar liberal Democrat, embarrassed President Johnson in the New Hampshire primary, Senator Robert F. Kennedy of New York entered the later primaries. Also antiwar, Kennedy had hesitated about running for president in the name of party unity, but after New Hampshire it was clear to him that the party was hopelessly divided over Vietnam, and that he needed to assert leadership in the battle to come.

Within weeks, President Johnson announced that he would not run again. Soon thereafter, Vice President Hubert H. Humphrey announced his candidacy.

Although he was too late to enter the remaining primaries, Humphrey emerged as the candidate of the Johnson administration and most party regulars.

The result was that Kennedy and McCarthy battled head to head through the primaries. When Kennedy won the California primary, it appeared, literally for a moment in time, that Kennedy had at least won the banner of reform liberal Democrats, and that he would proceed to the convention to challenge Humphrey. However, after declaring victory in Los Angeles, Senator Kennedy was shot by an assassin, and died a day later at the age of forty-two.

While there has been speculation ever since that Robert Kennedy would have been the Democratic nominee in 1968 had he lived, it is not likely. The reformers were probably about to line up for him after the California primary, and he had some support from party regulars.[10] But most party regulars were for Humphrey, and supporters of the Johnson administration were solidly for their vice president. Finally, southern Democrats, loyal to President Johnson, were adding their support to his vice president.

More important, in 1968 there were only sixteen presidential primaries, only seven of them contested between national candidates. In addition, most caucuses and state conventions were not then the participatory contests they are today. Therefore, in most states, party leaders and organizations controlled delegate selection, and in most of those cases the delegates were pledged to Humphrey. Even in that moment after California voted, the nomination of Hubert Humphrey was very likely. When Kennedy died, it became virtually inevitable.

Nevertheless, the Democratic National Convention was a deeply divided event, both in the convention hall, and in the streets of Chicago, where antiwar demonstrators faced the Chicago police. In the hall, reformers challenged the credentials of the regular delegations from Texas, Georgia, and Alabama, losing roll calls on all three. A minority report on the Vietnam War, challenging the policy of the Johnson administration, was defeated after bitter debate. Humphrey won the nomination on the first ballot, soundly defeating McCarthy.

There were important points of unity, even at the embattled 1968 Democratic convention. First, united liberal Democrats, reformers and regulars alike, seated an integrated loyalist delegation from Mississippi and unseated the segregationist delegation appointed by the state party. Second, the delegates banned the unit rule, by which delegations would vote unanimously for the candidate supported by the majority. Finally, the convention established commissions on rules and party structure, which were assigned to reform the delegate selection process for future years. The McGovern-Fraser Commission, named for cochairs Senator George McGovern of South Dakota and Representative Donald M. Fraser of Minnesota, would establish rules which would fundamentally change the process of presidential nominations, ultimately in both parties.

The party reforms were based on the cornerstone principles of participatory democracy and proportional representation (Crotty 1983; Polsby 1983; Ranney 1975). No longer would party leaders or committees appoint delegates or quietly hold caucuses among themselves. The delegate selection process in the states would be open and public, and it would result in the election of delegates reflecting voter preferences. Delegates would also reflect the demographics of Democrats in the population. In states where the process ended with a state convention, local caucuses would be scheduled with public notice, and the delegates at each level would proportionately represent the candidates who received at least 15 percent of the vote. The rules encouraged the proliferation of presidential primaries. See chapter 3 for a more detailed discussion of the McGovern-Fraser reforms and their consequences.

The McGovern-Fraser rules would have immediate impact on the Democrats in 1972. While in 1968 there were seventeen primaries electing 49 percent of the convention delegates, in 1972 there were twenty-four primaries electing 67 percent of the total delegates. The strategy of seeking a presidential nomination without entering the primaries, as Hubert Humphrey had done in 1968, was no longer viable.

The leading beneficiary of party reform in 1972 was Senator McGovern, an antiwar liberal Democrat. The reforms opened the process to issue activists previously limited in their access to party affairs, and McGovern, from his role in the reform process, understood the implications of the new rules better than his rivals, particularly the necessity of organizing on the ground, everywhere and early (Miroff 2007; White 1973).

McGovern and Governor George C. Wallace of Alabama, a segregationist, emerged as the strongest early contenders by unifying the support of their factions of the party. Meanwhile, it took Senator Humphrey, who was seeking renomination for president, too long to eliminate Senator Edmund S. Muskie of Maine in the battle for the votes of moderate Democrats and party regulars. When Wallace was severely wounded in an assassination attempt, he had to suspend his campaign. McGovern remained as the front-runner, with Humphrey his only serious opponent. When he won the hotly contested California primary, McGovern virtually clinched the nomination, and he made it final when his supporters defeated the challenge to the credentials of the California delegates at the convention. Ironically, the California delegation elected winner-take-all in the presidential primary, was unanimous for McGovern. It was Humphrey delegates and other moderate Democrats who challenged their credentials, hoping to impose the McGovern-Fraser principle of proportional representation on the California delegation, only to be fought off by the supporters of Senator McGovern.

Since 1972, liberal Democrats have won contested presidential nominations, except when moderates united against a divided field of liberals (Carter in 1976 and Bill Clinton in 1992), or when a moderate Democrat was the incumbent president (Carter in 1980), or the heir apparent (Gore in 2000 and Hillary Clinton in 2016).

Ironically, it took the nomination of a moderate Democrat for the presidency to consolidate the power of the liberals in their party. In 1976, former Governor Jimmy Carter of Georgia won the Democratic presidential nomination by defeating a divided field of liberal Democrats in the primaries, while eliminating George Wallace in the South. Carter's victories over Wallace in the South, which fueled his momentum in the North, were made possible by the 24th Amendment to the Constitution, outlawing the poll tax, and the Voting Rights Act of 1965. With the addition of African Americans to the electorate across the South, moderates and liberals began to defeat conservatives and segregationists in Southern primaries with greater frequency, promoting the emergence of Democrats like Carter, Albert Gore, and Bill Clinton. It also promoted the disappearance of candidates like George Wallace, who was the last segregationist to make a serious bid for the Democratic presidential nomination. For four decades now, the Democrats are the more liberal or progressive of the two major parties, everywhere across the country, including the South.

The Republicans' Umbrella

The Republican Party historically has a simpler factional structure than the Democrats. While the Democrats have always been a multifactional system, the Republicans have been closer to a bifactional system.[11] This is for three reasons. First, the Democratic umbrella has always covered more diverse interests than the Republican umbrella. The Republican Party has always been generally white, Anglo-Saxon, Protestant, and middle-class. Both of its factions have been electorally based in the middle class, and its elites have represented competing sectors of capital. Second, while Democratic National Conventions maintained a two-thirds rule until 1936, allowing a minority faction, the South, to veto the majority. The Republicans made their decisions in national conventions by majority rule, winning coalitions were assembled earlier at or before Republican conventions, discouraging a multiplicity of factions. Finally, at least until the passage of the Civil Rights Act and the nomination of Barry Goldwater for president in 1964, the South was never an autonomous faction among the Republicans, as it was among the Democrats.

While ideological loyalties have shifted, factional conflict in the Republican Party has usually matched the party establishment against the insurgents, whoever they were. The factional divisions within the GOP were intense enough that they contributed to the impeachment of one president and the assassination of another.

At the birth of the Republican Party, there was conflict between two antislavery factions, the abolitionists who wanted to ban slavery, and moderates who thought containing slavery would strangle it. After the assassination of President Abraham Lincoln, there was the showdown between the radical Republicans in Congress who were for occupation of the South and aggressive reform for racial equality, and those who supported Lincoln's reconstruction policy. That battle led to the impeachment of President Andrew Johnson.

For more than a decade thereafter, the Republicans were embattled by the factionalism between the party regulars, who came to be known as the "stalwarts," and the reformers. In 1872, reformers bolted the party and founded the short-lived Liberal Republican Party to nominate Horace Greeley to run against President Ulysses S. Grant, whose administration was mired in scandal. Grant was reelected by a landslide. Nevertheless, the factional battles continued, leading to deadlocked Republican National Conventions and compromise candidates in 1876 and 1880.

In 1880, Senator Roscoe Conkling of New York, widely recognized as the leader of the stalwarts, tried to return Grant to the presidency. When the effort fell short, the convention settled on Representative James A. Garfield of Ohio on the 36th ballot. An ally of Conkling's, Chester A. Arthur of New York, was nominated for vice president. The ticket was narrowly elected.

During his first year in office, President Garfield was assassinated by a disappointed office seeker who was a low-level stalwart loyalist. The battle between the stalwarts and the reformers led past the assassination of the president to a civil-service system, when as president, Chester Arthur broke ranks with Conkling and pushed successfully for the Pendleton Act. He paid for his leadership, however, when he lost the nomination in 1884 to his secretary of state, James G. Blaine. Blaine, in turn, suffered from the party discord, as Republican reformers known as "mugwumps" deserted the party to endorse Democrat Grover Cleveland for president. Cleveland was narrowly elected, the first Democrat to win the White House since before the Civil War.

Wall Street versus Main Street

The two persistent factions of the Republican Party in the twentieth century were labeled *Wall Street* and *Main Street* by Nelson Polsby (1978), terms which, even if oversimplified, are instructive, and remain helpful in understanding Republican factionalism today. These two factions matched the party establishment against insurgents, but were more defined by geography and conflicting policy interests. The *Wall Street* faction represented the interests of big business, monopoly, and international capital, with its electoral base in the Northeast, and at least until 1964, remained the party establishment. The *Main Street* faction was the more insurgent and issue activist, with its electoral base in the heartland and West. While the two factions consistently represented the above interests, their relative positions on the ideological spectrum were not static. Until the New Deal, the Wall Street faction was the more conservative, Main Street the more progressive. During and after the great depression and World War II, the Wall Street faction became more internationalist and liberal, while the Main Street faction, always nationalist or isolationist, became more conservative. Ideological change within the Republican Party after the New Deal is well explained by the multifactional framework offered by Nicol Rae, which will be discussed in detail below.

The confrontation between the Wall Street and Main Street factions of the Republican Party took shape after the election of 1896, which was historic in two of its related effects. First, the election of 1896 was a realigning election, introducing an era of Republican electoral majorities and control of the Presidency and Congress. It also introduced the progressive era, with a policy agenda set as much or more by Democrat William Jennings Bryan and Republican President Theodore Roosevelt, as by the leaders of the Republican Party.

Over more than three decades after 1896, the Republicans produced six presidents, five of them from the *Wall Street* faction: William McKinley, William Howard Taft, Warren G. Harding, Calvin Coolidge, and Herbert C. Hoover. The first three were all products of the Ohio Republican establishment. These "old-guard" Republicans and their allies generally stood in their turn for the gold standard, opposition to the League of Nations, "normalcy," and free markets.

The more progressive Main Street faction produced one president, Theodore Roosevelt, who came to office only because of the assassination of McKinley. He promoted government regulation of industry, was so active in both domestic and foreign policy as to introduce the modern presidency, and was elected to a full term in 1904 by a landslide. Other Republican insurgents who made historic names for themselves, including Robert M. LaFollette, Hiram Johnson, George W. Norris, and William E. Borah, were perhaps even more committed to the progressive agenda.

The big factional fight of the progressive era came in 1912, when former President Roosevelt challenged his old friend, President Taft for the Republican presidential nomination.[12] Roosevelt had wished he never promised he would not run again after being elected in his own right in 1904, and had retired from office at the politically young age of forty-nine. Moreover, President Taft had, in the view of his supporters, been far too cooperative with the Republican old guard, and too ineffective in defending Roosevelt's policy agenda. In 1910, Roosevelt returned from a trip to Africa, progressive Republicans made impressive gains in the midterm Congressional elections, and the stage was set for TR to announce that his hat was "in the ring."

In the contest that followed, Roosevelt nearly swept the primaries, being used nationally for the first time in delegate selection, a product of progressive reform (Cowan 2016). He won every primary he contested against Taft, including Taft's own Ohio, except for Massachusetts, which he lost by only 3,000 votes. But President Taft maintained control of the party organization, controlled rules and credentials at the convention, and won renomination on the first ballot, as Roosevelt's supporters bolted the party. Roosevelt was the nominee of the Progressive Party, referred to as the "Bull Moose," and the split in the Republican vote caused the election of the only Democratic president between Grover Cleveland and Franklin D. Roosevelt. Governor Woodrow Wilson won by a large plurality of the popular vote, Roosevelt ran second, and Taft third. By 1916, Roosevelt was campaigning for the Republican ticket, and by 1920, both control of party affairs and occupancy of the presidency had been restored to the Republican old guard, where it would remain into the New Deal period.

Republicans After the New Deal

An understanding of Republican factionalism in the New Deal era, and carrying through the conservative takeover of the party with the nomination of Barry Goldwater in 1964, is enhanced by supplementing Polsby's Wall Street versus Main Street description with the later analysis offered by Nicol Rae (1989). According to Rae, the Republican Party historically has been composed of four factions, from ideological left to right: the progressives, moderates, stalwarts, and fundamentalists. Before the New Deal, the progressives stood alone on Main Street against the party establishment on Wall Street. After the New Deal, the more liberal Wall Street faction contained the progressives and moderates, while the more conservative Main Street faction contained the stalwarts and fundamentalists. While the moderates of Wall Street and the stalwarts of Main Street emphasized party loyalty, the progressives on the left and the fundamentalists on the right prioritized ideology over party.[13] Main Street, particularly the stalwarts, had real power among Republicans in Congress, but contests for Republican presidential nominations in the New Deal era seemed to follow another script: Senator Robert A. Taft of Ohio, beloved and considered "Mr. Republican" by stalwarts, ran as their candidate three times, losing to a moderate or liberal at the convention each time.

In his subsequent essay, Rae (1998) simplified his framework for postwar Republicans to a bifactional analysis, matching the "liberals" and the stalwarts.[14] The later nomination of Goldwater for president happened only after fundamentalists gained autonomous power within the Republican Party.

In 1932, in the depths of the great depression, the Republicans lost the Presidency and Congress to Franklin Roosevelt and the Democrats. When FDR was reelected by a record landslide in 1936, Republicans recognized that their party was in crisis. Impressive Republican gains in the midterm elections of 1938 yielded some evidence of new blood in the party. But by 1940, the Republicans had been in opposition for eight years and the New Deal was for the most part accomplished reality. When France fell to Hitler's troops in the European war just before the Republican National Convention, the demand for new party leadership was all the more clear.

The front runner for the Republican presidential nomination as the 1940 convention approached was District Attorney Thomas E. Dewey of New York. Dewey, at the age of thirty-eight, was young and charismatic, famous as a U.S. Attorney, as well as D.A., for his prosecutions of organized crime. He was the Republican nominee for governor in 1938, losing very narrowly to Governor Herbert Lehman, the incumbent Democrat. His impressive showing at the polls at once advanced his candidacy and because of the defeat, required that he sweep the contested presidential primaries in 1940, which he did, effectively eliminating Senator Arthur Vandenburg of Michigan. Dewey was a moderate Republican, moderately isolationist on foreign policy before the war, and willing to accept the New Deal as a fact of life in domestic policy.

Senator Taft, the candidate of conservative Republicans, was making his first run for the presidency in 1940. He entered only his home state Ohio primary, won it unopposed, and went to the convention with the second largest bloc of delegates.

The candidate of the hour as the Republican convention opened was Wendell L. Willkie of New York, who as a private businessman without previous experience in public office, and a Democrat-turned-Republican, reminds us in some ways of Donald Trump (see chapter 1). Willkie announced his availability but did not enter any primaries. But he campaigned with increasing activity, opposing government regulation of business, but supporting social aspects of the New Deal, and taking a decidedly internationalist position in foreign affairs. His appearance on *Information Please*, the radio quiz show with intellectual appeal, plus his article, "We the

People," which appeared in *Fortune* magazine, advanced his name recognition. His candidacy was promoted by Henry Luce and Russell Davenport at *Time-Life*, Dorothy Thompson at the *New York Herald Tribune*, and Arthur Krock at the *New York Times*. His public support mounted in the Gallup Poll, from 1 percent among self-identified Republicans in April, to 17 percent just before the convention in late June, to 44 percent in a poll taken during the convention (Neal 1989, 78 and 108). The fall of France only increased demand for an internationalist candidate. As the convention opened in Philadelphia, Willkie had emerged as the candidate of "progressive" or liberal Republicans.

In the convention voting, Dewey led on the first ballot, but his support did not hold. Taft ran second, and Willkie third. As Dewey's totals declined on subsequent ballots, most of his support went to Willkie, as Willkie and Taft both gained among delegates previously pledged to favorite sons. By the fourth ballot, Willkie led, with Taft running second. By the fifth ballot, the contest was narrowed to Willkie and Taft. With the galleries chanting, "We Want Willkie," he won the nomination on the sixth ballot (Parmet 1968; Peters 2005).

Willkie lost the general election to FDR by 55 percent to 45 percent, carrying ten states, an impressive recovery for the Republicans from their landslide defeat of 1936. But the 1940 campaign does not represent Willkie's contribution to the development of the Republican Party as much as his crusade for internationalism which climaxed in his failed bid for renomination for president in 1944. His rejection of party orthodoxy and party leaders, his support for Lend-Lease, his representation of the Democratic president in visits to world leaders, all led to his not being invited to a Republican conference on the postwar world at Mackinac Island, Michigan in 1943. Nevertheless, the conference overcame the opposition of isolationists including Taft to pass a resolution calling for "participation by the United States in a postwar cooperative organization." Willkie called it a "step forward . . . when one measures against what we could have gotten a few years ago, it seems absolutely amazing" (Neal 1989, 284).

In 1944, Dewey, now Governor of New York and running for president again, enjoyed some support from conservatives, who were committed to stopping Willkie. Adding that to his base among moderates, Dewey eliminated Willkie in Wisconsin, emerged as the front-runner in the primaries, and won the Republican presidential nomination without organized opposition on the first convention ballot. By the time of his nomination, Governor Dewey had taken on a clearly internationalist position. He ran a strong race against FDR, and emerged after the election as the party leader for internationalists and moderate-to-liberal Republicans. Senator Vandenburg, like Dewey an isolationist before the war, led Republican internationalists in the Senate in cooperating in the construction of a bipartisan foreign policy.

Robert Taft would seek the presidency twice more, and both times Dewey and the Wall Street combine of moderate-to-liberal Republicans would frustrate him. In 1948, former Governor Harold E. Stassen of Minnesota, a liberal Republican who had been an early supporter of Wendell Willkie, mounted an insurgent campaign and won early victories in the Wisconsin and Nebraska primaries. But Stassen had virtually no support within the party establishment.

When Dewey beat him in the Oregon primary, after a nationally broadcast radio debate, Stassen was effectively finished. Dewey went to the convention as the front-runner, ahead of Taft, and won renomination for president on the third ballot. Thereafter, of course, Dewey was defeated by President Truman in an upset of historic proportions.

Ike

With Dewey having suffered two defeats in presidential elections, Senator Taft seemed to be the front-runner for the Republican presidential nomination 1952, particularly after scoring a come-from-behind landslide reelection to a third term in 1950. Once again, Taft would be frustrated, but moderate-to-liberal Republicans would require a peculiarly strong candidate, General Dwight D. Eisenhower, to beat him.

Although Ike was hesitant to run for president, Dewey, Senator Henry Cabot Lodge of Massachusetts, and Representative Hugh Scott of Pennsylvania mounted a draft movement for him and entered him in the New Hampshire primary, which he won. Thereafter, General Eisenhower resigned his NATO command in Paris, and announced his candidacy, although he did not return from Paris until late in the preconvention campaign.

Nevertheless, Eisenhower won primaries in New Jersey, Massachusetts, Pennsylvania, and Oregon, while Taft more than held his own, winning primaries in Wisconsin, Nebraska, West Virginia, and Ohio, before narrowly defeating Eisenhower in South Dakota. Taft went to the convention as the front-runner, short of a majority, but with a small lead in the delegate count. Stalwarts supporting Taft also had control of the Republican National Committee, and the convention organization, including the Rules and Credentials Committees. Taft forces could deliver a majority on credentials, but not two-thirds, which proved to be important.

The Eisenhower forces, led by Dewey, Lodge, and Scott, had a strategy. They would challenge the credentials of Taft delegates elected in disputed caucuses in Texas, Georgia, and Louisiana, and also propose a change to the rules, what they called the *Fair Play Amendment*, which would deny challenged delegates the right to vote on convention roll calls, unless they had been approved by two-thirds of the Credentials Committee, or until they were formally seated by the convention. The Eisenhower campaign prevailed on the rules and credentials challenges, with the support of delegates pledged to two liberal Republican favorite sons, Governor Earl Warren of California, and Harold Stassen of Minnesota, and took effective control of the convention.

On the first ballot for president, the convention voted 595 for Eisenhower, 500 for Taft, 81 for Warren, 20 for Stassen, and 10 for General MacArthur. When the Minnesota delegation switched to Eisenhower after the roll call, he secured the nomination, finishing with 845 votes. General Eisenhower went on to win election as president by a landslide.

While the Eisenhower presidency papered over the divide, the split in Republican ranks, aggravated by the 1952 convention, simmered and sometimes bubbled over during the life of his administration. Not an ideologue himself, President Eisenhower had a philosophy of government that he called *modern Republicanism* and liberal Republicans were its most enthusiastic supporters (Eisenhower 1965, 375). He did little to reverse or advance the legacy of the New Deal, but he did promote the role of the federal government in the economy with the passage of the Federal Highway Act in 1956. He appointed Earl Warren as Chief Justice of the United States, and while he did not actively endorse the Supreme Court decisions in *Brown v. Board of Education* (1954 and 1955), he believed in the rule of law, and he enforced them, and *Cooper v. Aaron* (1958) by using federal troops to desegregate Little Rock High School (Eisenhower 1965, 148–76). Thereafter, he was proud, as president and the leader of the party of Lincoln, of the passage of the Civil Rights Acts of 1957 and 1960.

Other than deciding to run for reelection in 1956, after recovery from his heart attack the previous year, President Eisenhower did little to intervene in party affairs. He did not, for example, take on Senator Joseph R. McCarthy (R-Wisconsin) directly and publicly. Many moderate-to-liberal Republicans, like Senator Margaret Chase Smith of Maine, who circulated a "Declaration of Conscience" signed by six colleagues, would have wished that he had. However, Eisenhower believed that public confrontation would only serve McCarthy's purposes, and chose to work indirectly and behind the scenes to stop him (Ambrose 1984, 58–66; Greenstein 1982, 155–227; Nichols 2017; Smith 1972).

The heir apparent to President Eisenhower was Vice President Richard M. Nixon, who had appeal across factions of the party. Governor Nelson Rockefeller of New York, a liberal Republican, explored a campaign before

1960, but announced he would not run when he concluded the Nixon was the unified choice of party leaders. Nixon was unopposed in the primaries and had the Republican presidential nomination clinched well in advance of the convention.

But even a convention without a real contest exposed lingering factionalism. Rockefeller, less than satisfied with the platform, summoned Nixon to New York for a private meeting, even as the convention met in Chicago, and the two negotiated what became known as the "Compact of 5th Avenue," adding planks for a stronger national defense and civil rights legislation. At the convention, conservative Republicans rebelled, revealing the growth of a fundamentalist faction in the GOP. They pushed Senator Barry Goldwater of Arizona to challenge Nixon, which Goldwater declined to do, although his name was placed before the convention. In his withdrawal remarks to the convention, Goldwater he admonished his would-be supporters, "Let's grow up conservatives! If we want to take this party back, and I think we can, some day, let's get to work! (White 1965, 89)."

Coup From the Right

After the very narrow defeat of Vice President Nixon by Senator John F. Kennedy (D-Massachusetts) in the presidential election of 1960, Republicans debated the diagnosis of defeat and the prognosis for victory. While liberal Republicans maintained that Nixon should have made a more serious effort to win several large industrial states he lost by narrow margins, conservative Republicans argued that he should have gone after several Southern states he lost in close races. The debate, however, was not as much about strategy as it was about ideology (Novak 1965, chapter 2).

Indeed, a conservative movement that should be considered "fundamentalist" in ideological terms had been percolating through the Eisenhower years, and was now preparing to make its bid for power within the Republican Party (Perlstein 2009). In 1961 and 1962, F. Clifton White, a New Yorker who had once worked for Thomas E. Dewey before becoming active in Young Republicans, held a series of meetings in Chicago that organized a Draft Goldwater movement down to the precinct level across the country (Perlstein 2009, chapter 10; White 1965, 94–100).

That grassroots organization proved decisive in 1964. Senator Goldwater held his own in the primaries, winning against weak opposition in Illinois, Indiana, and Nebraska, while Ambassador Henry Cabot Lodge won the New Hampshire primary on a write-in vote, and Rockefeller won the Oregon primary. Meanwhile, Goldwater activists were taking over the party in precinct caucuses in states where delegates would be chosen at state conventions.

In most of those states, Goldwater supporters were elected in caucuses to county conventions, where they secured seats to Congressional district and state conventions. Usually, it was not until the Republican state convention, where Goldwater would win all or most of the national convention delegates, that party leaders recognized that they had lost control of the party apparatus to conservative insurgents. When Goldwater narrowly defeated Rockefeller in the California primary, he effectively clinched the Republican presidential nomination. The eleventh-hour candidacy of Governor William W. Scranton of Pennsylvania in an effort to stop Goldwater proved to be much too little, and much too late.

Nevertheless, there was bloodletting of a divided party at the Republican National Convention, in the form of debate over challenges to the proposed platform. First, debates reminiscent of the roll call on the Klan at the 1924 Democratic convention, rejected two minority reports condemning extremist groups, and a minority report on civil rights. The minority reports on extremism were decided in standing votes, while the civil rights plank was settled on a roll call. The platform committee, controlled by Goldwater delegates, had offered a plank promising to enforce the new Civil Rights Act, passed only weeks before the convention. Senator Goldwater had voted against the act. Now, liberal Republicans proposed a minority report proclaiming much more vigorous support of civil rights and racial equality. In a roll call reflecting the balloting for president to come, the convention rejected the minority report, 897 to 409.

On the first and only presidential ballot, Goldwater won the nomination with 883 votes to 214 for Scranton, 114 for Rockefeller, and 97 scattering mostly among favorite sons. Figure 2.2 compares the nominating coalition for Eisenhower in 1952 with the nominating coalition for Goldwater in 1964. The northeast, the base of majorities for Willkie, Dewey, and Eisenhower at conventions between 1940 and 1952, remained the base for liberal Republicans, but was isolated by 1964. The majority for Barry Goldwater was assembled across the South and West, and most of the Middle West. After his landslide defeat at the hands of President Johnson, Goldwater's nomination was widely treated as the act of an agonized party leading to an electoral accident. But four years later, Richard M. Nixon appealed to fundamentally the same conservative coalition to win the Republican presidential nomination. Moreover, the 1968 convention votes for Nixon and Governor Ronald Reagan of California, when combined, revealed and almost identical coalition to the one that nominated Barry Goldwater in 1964, while the vote for Rockefeller at the 1968 convention came from almost the same states as the combined vote for Scranton and Rockefeller in 1964.

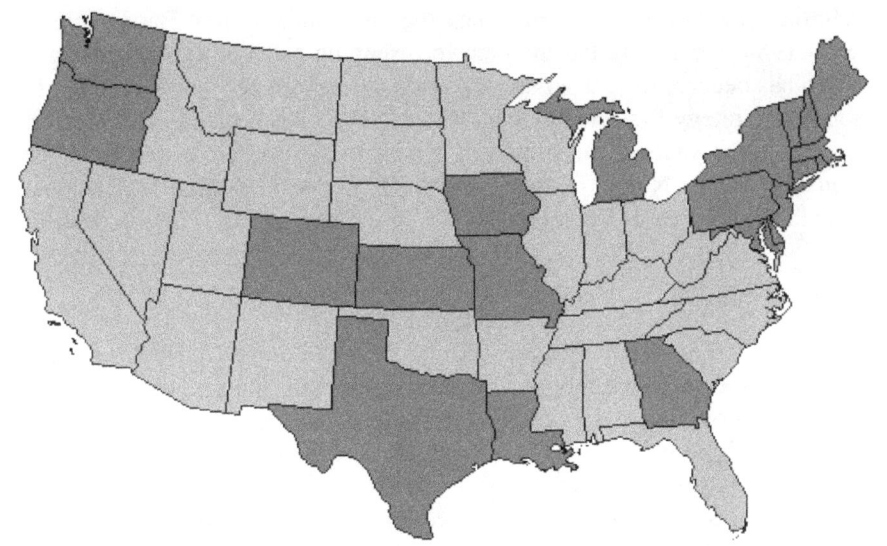

1952 1st Ballot for Republican Presidential Nomination

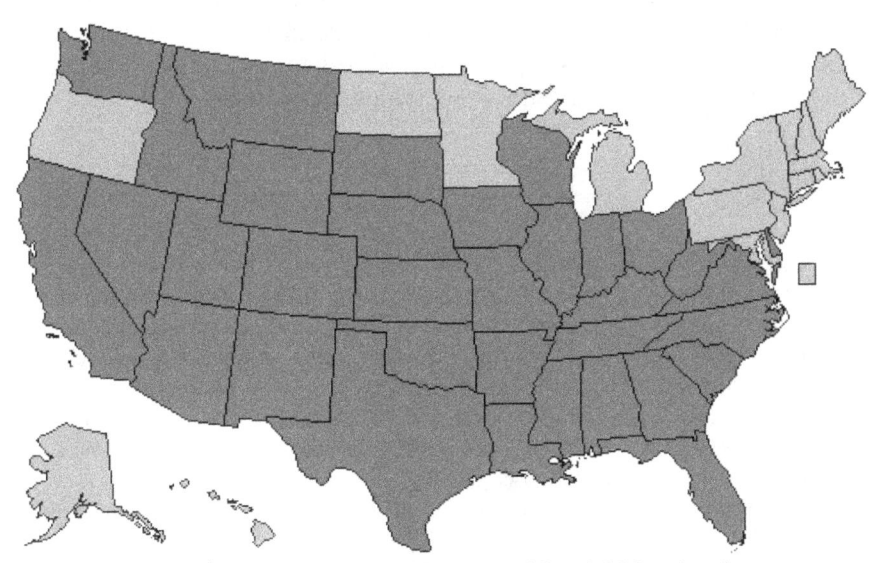

1964 1st Ballot for Republican Presidential Nomination

Figure 2.2 Balloting for president at Republican National Conventions, 1952 and 1964. Dark states represent delegations casting a majority of their votes with a majority of the convention in each case: For Eisenhower in 1952, and Goldwater in 1964.

Source: Maps derived from Dave Leip, www.uselectionatlas.org. Data drawn from National Party Conventions, 1831–1984 (Washington, DC: Congressional Quarterly, 1987): 205 and 208.

In recent years, it has become clear that the nomination of Barry Goldwater in 1964 was a defining moment in reshaping today's Republican Party, which has become the conservative party in American politics. Moreover, the Southern strategy first tried by Goldwater in 1964 has brought more electoral success in the years since, providing a base to the coalitions that have subsequently put for Nixon, Reagan, George H. W. Bush, George W. Bush, and Donald Trump in the White House.

CONCLUSION

The umbrellas of both major parties have historically spanned the ideological spectrum, providing cover for factions among the Democrats and Republicans. Indeed, multifactionalism is as much a cornerstone of American electoral politics as is the two-party system itself. Electoral and party change are promoted as much or more by decisive factional struggles within parties as by change in voting behavior in the electorate at large. Between 1964 and 1972, for the first time, factional struggles in both major parties, won by conservative Republicans and liberal Democrats, reached virtually simultaneous turning points. The result was an ideological realignment between the parties that gave birth to the polarized party system we have today.

NOTES

1. This ideological unity around classic liberalism in American life is one of the foundations of theories of "American exceptionalism." The theory, often referred to incorrectly in today's public discourse, traces back to Alexis de Tocqueville, *Democracy in America*, Harvey C. Mansfield and Delba Winthrop, eds. (Chicago: University of Chicago Press). Tocqueville wrote the classic in two volumes during and after his travels in America in the 1830s. See also Louis Hartz, *The Liberal Tradition in America* (New York: Harcourt, Brace & World, 1955) for his then timely presentation of classic liberalism as an unopposed ideology in American culture.

2. Even during the Civil War, both sides proclaimed themselves to be the defenders of liberty and private property.

3. The Supreme Court declared this form of denial of voting rights unconstitutional in *Smith v. Allwright* 321 U.S. 649 (1944).

4. On William Jennings Bryan, see also Robert W. Cherry, *A Righteous Cause: The Life of William Jennings Bryan* (Boston: Little, Brown, 1985); Michael Kazin, *A Godly Hero: The Life of William Jennings Bryan* (New York: Anchor, 2007); Lawrence W. Levine, *Defender of the Faith, William Jennings Bryan: The Last Decade, 1915–1925* (New York: Oxford University Press, 1965); David J. Nordloh, *William*

Jennings Bryan (Bloomington: Indiana University Press, 1981); Donald K. Springen, *William Jennings Bryan: Orator of Small Town America* (Westport, CT: Greenwood Press, 1991).

5. For the "switch in time that saved nine," see *Schechter Poultry Corporation v. U.S.* 295 U.S. 495 (1935), which overturned the NRA, and *West Coast Hotel Co. v. Parrish* 300 U.S. 379 (1937), *NLRB v. Jones and Laughlin Steel Corporation* 301 U.S. 1 (1937), and *U.S. v. Darby* 312 U.S. 100 (1941), which effectively reversed the policy impact of *Schechter*. Chief Justice Charles Evans Hughes, who had been the Republican nominee for president in 1916, wrote for the court in the first three cases, couching the latter two opinions in sufficiently narrow legal terms to uphold the precedent and reverse the effect of *Schechter*. See Bernard Schwartz, *A History of the Supreme Court* (New York: Oxford University Press, 1993): 236–45.

6. For an excellent history of the 1948 election, including discussion of the Democrats and the civil rights issue, see Andrew E. Busch, *Truman's Triumphs: The 1948 Election and the Making of Postwar America* (Lawrence: University Press of Kansas, 2012). For the discussion of factionalism in both parties, including the civil rights debate within the Democratic Party, see chapters 3 and 4.

7. Unless otherwise noted, data from national conventions are drawn from *National Party Conventions 1831–1984* (Washington, DC: Congressional Quarterly, 1987).

8. Perhaps the classic study of southern politics remains V. O. Key, Jr., *Southern Politics in State and Nation* (New York: Knopf, 1949). Key's study is all the more interesting because it was published the year after the civil rights showdown at the 1948 Democratic National Convention, just as the Democratic Solid South was starting to unravel. For an excellent discussion of the south as a faction of the Democratic Party, see Nicol Rae, *Southern Democrats* (New York: Oxford University Press, 1994).

9. Supporting Kefauver for president, his home state Tennessee delegates voted to deny seats to the Virginia delegates, opposing the rest of the south on the issue.

10. Many his younger, more ideological antiwar supporters took note of Robert Kennedy's ties to both the antiwar movement and the party establishment by referring to him as "the good Bobby and the bad Bobby." See Chester, Hodgson & Page, 1969, 105–26.

11. This does not mean to discount the work of Nicol Rae, who has treated the Republican Party as an evolving multifactional system. Rae's analysis will be discussed below.

12. For a dramatic portrayal of the relationship between Roosevelt and Taft, and their contest in the 1912 primaries, see Doris Kearns Goodwin, *The Bully Pulpit: Theodore Roosevelt, William Howard Taft, and the Golden Age of Journalism* (New York: Simon & Schuster, 1913).

13. The "fundamentalists" defined by Rae should not be confused equated with the Christian right of more recent years. Although the Christian right can be considered part of the fundamentalist faction, the fundamentalism Rae refers to is ideological, not religious.

14. Rae traces the inheritance of the liberal Republicans back to the progressives, and even sooner, to the mugwumps. However, in my view, the progressive

Republicans of the early twentieth century should not be confused with the liberal Republicans on the left of the party during the New Deal and post–World War II era. The latter group was, like their moderate counterparts, more oriented to the eastern and big business establishments, or in Polsby's language, the Wall Street faction. Therefore, I will usually refer to Republicans on the left from about 1940 on as *liberal* Republicans, while using Rae's term, *moderates* to refer to more centrist if left-of-center Republicans. See my discussion of Wendell Willkie and Thomas E. Dewey below, for example.

Chapter Three

Trumping the Republicans and Berning the Democrats

Post-Reform Presidential Primaries and the Case of 2016

The current system of presidential nominations emerged from two related processes of party change dating back a half century: 1) Ideological realignment reaching critical proportions within and between the major parties, which was the subject of the previous chapter, and 2) Reforms in delegate selection and campaign finance. Both factors have combined since 1972 to produce the post-reform system of presidential nominations. This chapter examines the post-reform party system and the 2016 presidential primaries in historical perspective.

PARTY REFORM AND PRESIDENTIAL NOMINATIONS

Deeply divided by the Vietnam War and party politics, the 1968 Democratic National Convention sought to rebuild party unity and legitimacy by authorizing a Commission on Party Structure and Delegate Selection, chaired by Senator McGovern and Rep. Donald M. Fraser of Minnesota. More than any other single source, the McGovern-Fraser Commission provides the foundation of what would become the post-reform system of presidential nominations (Crotty 1983; Norrander 2010; Paulson, 2000, 2007; Polsby 1983; Ranney 1975; Steger 2015). The McGovern-Fraser Commission produced rules that would directly shape the nominating politics of 1972 and beyond, and with subsequent reform commissions, shape the modern Democratic Party as it stands today.

Under the McGovern-Fraser guidelines, delegate selection would be timely, open, public, participatory, and literally democratic. No longer would a governor or party committee select delegates well in advance of the election year; delegates would be selected by public processes during the election year. Proportional representation would be introduced to the system. Candidates who earned at least 15 percent of the vote would be awarded delegates according to their support from voters in primaries and caucuses. Finally, there would also be at least roughly proportional demographic representation, by sex, race, and age, an affirmative action program for delegates.

Once the McGovern-Fraser rules were used as models for state legislation on presidential primaries and delegate selection, they became contagious and influenced the presidential nomination process in the Republican Party, as well. The most immediate impact, for both parties, was a proliferation of presidential primaries. State legislatures commonly found primary laws as the most convenient method of adhering to delegate selection rules. The number of primaries increased from fifteen in 1968, to the upper twenties a decade later, to between thirty-five and forty now. In 1968, about 40 percent of delegates were elected in primaries, compared with 70 or 80 percent now.

Along with the proliferation of primaries came an expansion of candidate fields, with almost all of the candidates running in almost all of the primaries. The result, at least initially, was a much less party-centered and much more candidate-centered contest for presidential nominations.

These reforms and their outcomes in the early post-reform period led to counter reforms (Norrander, 2010). The nominations of insurgent Democrats in 1972 and 1976, and the growing power of issue activists in nomination politics led Democratic Party leaders to add "superdelegates" to the process in 1984, in what amounted to the reintroduction of party officeholders as ex-officio delegates, a practice at least implicitly banned by the McGovern-Fraser rules. The superdelegates made a difference in favor of Walter Mondale in 1984, and their presence in the process has been a continuing controversy ever since, as it was in 2016.

Two more counterreforms, related to the scheduling of primaries and caucuses, were added almost simultaneously in the 1980s. First, prior to the 1988 campaign, Southern moderate Democrats, hoping to nominate a candidate who could appeal to centrist voters, carry their states, and win general elections, arranged across their states to schedule a "Super Tuesday" featuring fourteen primaries in the South and border states. They were hoping a moderate Democrat would win most of those primaries, emerge with a big lead in delegates, and go on to the nomination. Their plan did not work in 1988, mostly because moderate-to-conservative Democrats could not unite on one candidate across the South, but "Super Tuesday" lives on as a factor in presidential nominations to the current day.

Second, starting in the 1970s and advancing with Super Tuesday in 1988, front-loading of scheduled primaries and caucuses became a characteristic of the nominating system (Mayer & Busch, 2004). In many states there was a perception that momentum was an important factor in presidential nominations that would give states early in the delegate selection calendar an outsize role. There have been efforts to mitigate front-loading, including the Republican delegate selection rules for 2016, but state contests and the number of delegates selected are now weighted much earlier in the election year than they were before reform.

Campaign Finance

Reform in the delegate selection process for presidential nominations was accompanied by reform in the campaign finance infrastructure coming from the Campaign Finance Reform Acts of 1971 and 1974, the latter of which created the Federal Election Commission. Key provisions limited total candidate spending on nomination campaigns ($10 million in 1974, adjusted for inflation), limits on contributions by individuals ($1,000) and political action committees ($5,000), and federal matching funds for the first $250 for donations for candidates who could raise $5,000 or more in increments of $250 or less in twenty states or more. The 2002 Bipartisan Campaign Reform Act raised the limits that individuals could contribute, while restricting "soft" money not covered in the campaign finance legislative scheme (Corrado 2012; Steger 2015).

If campaign finance legislation was generally designed to create equitable campaign funding, its impact was also to turn presidential campaigns into functional corporations by requiring a financial infrastructure that would predate the election year and persist beyond it.

Of course, there have been countermeasures on campaign finance reform, as well, in the form of case law, which has rendered federal matching funds in presidential nomination contests functionally voluntary. *Buckley v. Valeo* (1976) and *Citizens United v. FEC* (2010) extended the right of individuals and advocacy groups to spend money for or against candidates and made it a practical choice for well-financed campaigns to eschew federal matching funds and avoid spending limits. The effect was not immediate after *Buckley v. Valeo*. John B. Connally rejected matching funds in his campaign for the Republican presidential nomination in 1980 so he could dump money into South Carolina for his challenge to Ronald Reagan. His failure discouraged a repeat performance anytime soon thereafter. But Steve Forbes ran a competitive campaign in the Republican primaries without federal matching funds in 1996, and in the same year Robert Dole found himself short of cash after clinching the Republican presidential nomination because he had accepted federal matching funds. The overwhelming success of Governor George W. Bush of Texas in his privately financed campaign of 2000 opened the door. Howard Dean did not take federal matching funds in his campaign for in Democratic primaries in 2004, and his opponent, Senator John Kerry of Massachusetts, followed suit on his way to the nomination. Since then, while accepting federal matching funds is still an option, the default position of well-financed campaigns has been to reject them for the advantages of private financing and unlimited spending.

The balance of this chapter will discuss the development of the structure of post-reform presidential nomination contests, then evaluate the 2016 presidential primaries for evidence of stability and change in the post-reform system.

THE IRONY OF REFORM

Early post-reform contests for presidential nominations provided surprises that reflected the instability and party change of the time. Insurgents upset the party establishment with the nominations of Democrats George McGovern in 1972 and Jimmy Carter in 1976. Major challenges to incumbent presidents (one in each party) followed in the primaries of 1976 and 1980. Watergate added to the impact of party reform and ideological realignment on the presidential nominations of both parties. Starting in 1980, however, order was restored, and party elites regained much of the power they had lost, albeit in an altered party system.

Reform and Disorder: Challenging the Presidents

The unique combination of ideological realignment within and between the major parties, reform of party processes weakened party leaders in the early post-reform period. With the Watergate scandal added to the mix, unusual presidential nominations and elections were all the more likely. Historically simultaneous challenges to the nominations of two presidents were mounted by the more ideological, majority or plurality faction in each party, the conservative Republicans in 1976 and liberal Democrats in 1980. The result in each case was similar: The president won the nomination, holding off his party's ideologues, but had to make concessions at the national convention. In both races, the challenging faction consolidated its power within the party, while the incumbent president was defeated in the general election.

Challenging President Ford

Gerald Ford became the 38th president of the United States only because of Watergate and the resulting resignation of President Nixon in 1974. In fact,

Ford was vice president when Nixon resigned only because Vice President Spiro T. Agnew had to resign the year before.

Prior to his appointment as vice president, Ford had been Minority Leader in the House of Representatives, where he maintained a stalwart conservative voting record. Ford considered himself a conservative on economic issues, a moderate on social issues, and a liberal on foreign policy (Ford 1979, 66).[1] Ford had always allied himself with moderate-to-liberal Republicans in party affairs, supporting Wendell Willkie, Arthur Vandenburg, Dwight D. Eisenhower, and George Romney, each in their turn, for the Republican presidential nomination.

When Ford became president, conservative Republicans already did not consider him one of their own. When, as president, he appointed Nelson Rockefeller as vice president, and created a commission to offer pardons to Vietnam War–era draft resistors, opposition from the right within the GOP mounted.

President Ford did not enjoy the normal advantages of incumbency. He did not have a national organization as he assumed office, his supporters had never taken over the party in a presidential nomination contest, and he had not been elected in his own right. Thus, when they were lining up behind former Governor Ronald Reagan of California, conservative Republicans did not consider their rebellion to be an act of disloyalty to the party (Witcover 1977).

The result was the stiffest challenge to the nomination of a president since the Republican contest of 1912 between Roosevelt and Taft. President Ford almost clinched the nomination when he won early primaries in New Hampshire, Florida, and Illinois. Reagan recovered by winning in North Carolina, and made it an even race by adding victories in Texas the Indiana. Ford ended the primary season as the front-runner with a victory in Ohio.

During the period between the primaries and the convention, the Reagan campaign was looking for a way to win over uncommitted delegates and steal some Ford delegates. They thought they found a way: Before the convention, Reagan selected Senator Richard Schweiker of Pennsylvania, a moderate-to-liberal Republican, as his running mate for vice president. The ploy did not work, because it was based on a major miscalculation. Most uncommitted delegates in the preconvention period were conservative Republicans, torn between their ideology and their president. Placing Schweicker on a ticket with Reagan simply neutralized the consideration of ideology. Thus, instead of stealing delegates from Ford, the Schweiker selection drove uncommitted conservatives into the Ford camp, leaving little doubt about his nomination.

In convention, President Ford won the Republican nomination on the first ballot, by a vote of 1,170 to 1,087. The important result for the future of the Republican Party was not so much that the president won, as it was that the conservative challenger had come so close to beating him. The swing delegates at the convention were conservative Republicans, which explains why the Ford forces did not mount a serious challenge to anti-abortion language in the party platform, and conceded the point on a pro-Reagan minority report on foreign policy, avoiding a roll call which might have pulled uncommitted delegates back to the Reagan camp.

The Reagan challenge almost certainly cost Ford the election in November. One might expect that the party would exact a severe price from the insurgent who waged such a campaign against an incumbent president. But when Ronald Reagan announced his candidacy for the Republican presidential nomination in 1980, he was the candidate of his party's conservative majority, and treated as the presumptive front-runner. Reagan had to battle through the primaries in 1980, but he defeated George H. W. Bush of Texas, Representative John B. Anderson of Illinois, and the rest of a crowded field, to win the Republican presidential nomination with relative ease. After he won thirty-one out of thirty-five primaries in 1980, Reagan faced no eleventh-hour preconvention challenge from liberal Republicans, as Barry Goldwater had sixteen years before. Recognizing the demise of liberals in the GOP, Anderson ran for president as an independent. The post-reform system was becoming one in which the candidate of the majority faction of the party who became the front-runner would clinch the nomination with little opposition. Moreover, the Republican Party was now established as America's conservative party.

Challenging President Carter

In 1976, former Governor Jimmy Carter of Georgia won the Democratic presidential nomination only because liberals in his party were divided against him. Carter emerged as the front-runner by winning the crowded New Hampshire primary, then effectively eliminated Governor George C. Wallace of Alabama, the segregationist conservative Democrat, by winning the Florida primary. Representative Morris K. Udall of Arizona ran ahead of other liberal Democrats in the early primaries, but was unable to win any of them. Even as Senator Frank Church of Idaho and Governor Jerry Brown of California scored victories in the later primaries, it was too late for liberal Democrats to unite on either one. Meanwhile, Carter won primaries in Pennsylvania and Ohio, which proved decisive. That November, Carter was elected president because he benefitted from a peculiar combination of circumstances: Watergate, including the courageous act of President Ford to pardon Richard Nixon;[2] the split in Republican ranks; and the fact that Carter was a Southern moderate Democrat who could carry ten states of the south.

Like President Ford before him, President Carter could not claim leadership of the majority faction of his party. During his term, he faced a second wave of oil shocks and a recession starting in 1979. Moreover, his economic policies were considered too austere by many liberal Democrats, who supported a challenge to his renomination in 1980 by Senator Edward M. Kennedy of Massachusetts. Like Ford four years before, Carter almost clinched the nomination early, with victories in the New Hampshire and Illinois primaries, but Kennedy stayed in the race by winning New York. The two battled the rest of the way to the convention, Carter winning a series of primaries before the finish. When Carter won the Ohio primary in June, it was enough to solidify his lead, even while Kennedy was winning in New Jersey and California. Kennedy's effort to open the convention with a rule releasing all delegates from their pledges proved futile when the proposal was defeated in a roll call on the convention floor. President Carter then won renomination decisively on the first convention ballot.

But Carter's convention strategy indicated that he knew it was not his party. In a situation not unlike the Republicans' in 1976, the uncommitted delegates were liberal Democrats torn between their policy preferences and their president. Carter allowed Kennedy to address the convention, with an eloquent speech that promised liberals that "the dream shall never die." (Broder 1980). The delegates then approved platform planks on economic policy proposed by Kennedy, including counterrecession fiscal policy prioritizing jobs and unemployment over inflation. It is not likely that the resulting platform could have pleased liberal Democrats more, even had Senator Kennedy been the nominee.

Presidential Primaries in the Post-Reform Order

Starting in 1980, a semblance of stability and the power of parties in presidential nominations was revived. Ideological realignment has led not only to ideological polarization between the parties, but also ideological homogenization within the parties. The scope of the umbrella covering each party has shrunk so that the ideological differences among the factions in within each party have decreased. The factions within the Democratic Party are more or less liberal, and the factions within the Republican Party or more or less conservative. The result has been a general decrease in factional conflict, and a general recovery of the power of party elites. While factional contests for presidential nominations persist, settling the nomination and achieving party unity are likely to occur sooner rather than later. Sometimes, in fact more often than not, a clear front-runner for the nomination emerges even before the voting starts.

The Invisible Primary

The requirements of campaign finance and the front-loaded delegate selection schedule have combined to highlight the importance of the "invisible primary." Between the midterm Congressional elections and the start of the voting during the presidential election year, prospective candidates for presidential nominations set up exploratory committees, raise money, seek endorsements, and try to establish their standing in public opinion polls (Buell 1996; Cohen, Karol, Noel & Zaller 2008a, 2008b; Hadley 1976; Mayer 1996, 2003). The invisible primary is particularly important for who is eliminated: The winnowing process is now well under way before the first vote is cast in a primary or caucus.

Beyond that, a decisive front-runner is often determined during the invisible primary. William G. Mayer (1996, 2003) developed a model that predicted that the leader in public opinion polls and fund-raising would be the nominee. Between 1980 and 2000, the model worked in every contested presidential nomination where there was a front-runner who led in both coming out of the invisible primary. The model did not accurately predict defeats of early front-running Democrats Howard Dean in 2004 or Hillary Clinton in 2008, but it did rebound to predict the nominations of Republican Mitt Romney in 2012 and Democrat Hillary Clinton in 2016. Altogether, since 1980, the Mayer model has correctly predicted nomination outcomes in nine of the eleven cases in which one candidate was the front-runner at the end of the invisible primary in both fund-raising and public opinion polls.

The less-than-perfect (even if impressive) performance of the Mayer model can be explained by three recent trends in presidential nomination campaigns. First, with more candidates declining federal matching funds, a practice accentuated by the *Citizens United* decision, it is often the case that while many candidates fall by the wayside, more than one candidate in a campaign is in very sound financial condition. In 2008, Hillary Clinton entered the year with about $116 million in net contributions, which led the Democrats and was much more than any candidate in any previous year (FEC 2016). But Barack Obama had raised over $102 million, also much more than any candidate in any previous year, and more than enough to survive a protracted contest for the nomination, which, of course, came to pass. Second, the increased involvement of political action committees and private individuals outside the campaigns, also fed by *Citizens United*, reduces the usefulness of internal campaign finance data in measuring the financial health of or popular support for a campaign. In 2012, Newt Gingrich lingered in his campaign for the Republican presidential nomination much longer than he would have before *Citizens United*, because of the financial intervention of Sheldon Adelson on his behalf. Finally, while presidential nomination campaigns remain much more candidate-centered than they were in the pre-reform period when national conventions were doing the nominating, they have become somewhat more party-centered than they were immediately after reform.

Nevertheless, the early front-runner, if one can be identified, is most likely to be the nominee. In addition to polls and finances, Cohen, Karol, Noel, and Zaller (2008a, 2008b) have persuasively reminded us of the importance of endorsements from party elites. Since 1976, the consensus choice of party elites (when there was one) has won the nomination in eleven out of twelve cases, the only exception being the defeat of Senator Clinton by Senator Obama in 2008. This represents a better prediction rate than is earned by either showing in the polls or campaign finance, or for that matter, both combined. Certainly, a front-runner who has advantages in fund-raising, the polls, and endorsements by party elites, is likely to have the money, organization, and base of support to survive an early upset. That upset usually happens, but a surprise winner who is not already well funded no longer has the time in the front-loaded schedule to build the momentum and resources to keep winning and competing in a long contest. The front-runner rebounds to win the nomination. This front-runner advantage has generally served to further shorten the contest in the primaries and enhance party unity once the nomination is settled. Table 3.1 lists the leading candidates in polls, fund-raising and party endorsements at the end of the invisible primary since the Campaign Finance Reform Act of 1974.

Table 3.1 Front-Runners for Presidential Nominations: Polls, Campaign Finance, and Party Endorsements after Invisible Primary (Nominees in bold.)

Campaign (Party)	Polls	Finance	Endorsements
1976 Republicans	**Ford**	**Ford**	**Ford**
1976 Democrats	Humphrey	Wallace	(No clear favorite)
1980 Democrats	**Carter**	**Carter**	**Carter**
1980 Republicans	**Reagan**	Connally	**Reagan**
1984 Democrats	**Mondale**	**Mondale**	**Mondale**
1988 Republicans	**Bush**	Robertson	**Bush**
1988 Democrats	Hart	**Dukakis**	(No clear favorite)
1992 Democrats	**Clinton**	**Clinton**	**Clinton**
1996 Republicans	**Dole**	**Dole**	**Dole**
2000 Democrats	**Gore**	**Gore**	**Gore**
2000 Republicans	**Bush**	**Bush**	**Bush**
2004 Democrats	Dean	Dean	(No clear favorite)
2008 Republicans	Giuliani	Romney	(No clear favorite)
2008 Democrats	Clinton	Clinton	Clinton
2012 Republicans	**Romney**	**Romney**	**Romney**
2016 Democrats	**Clinton**	**Clinton**	**Clinton**
2016 Republicans	**Trump**	Carson	(No clear favorite)

Sources: http://www.fec.gov/press/campaign_finance_statistics.shtml, accessed July 12, 2016; http://www.gallup.com/poll/10120/history-shows-january-frontrunner-often-does-win-democratic-nomination.aspx, accessed July 12, 2016; Cohen, Karol, Noel, and Zaller (2008a and 2008b); Mayer (1996); Steger (2015).

Of course, the question of whether there is a party favorite before the voting starts is an important one. More often than not, the invisible primary anoints a front-runner, who will usually be the nominee. Sometimes, no clear front-runner emerges, but even then, the invisible primary winnows the field by eliminating candidates who would at one time have contested the nomination at the convention, and the front-runner who emerges in the primaries wins the nomination.

Typologies of Presidential Nomination Contests

However, while these patterns emerge consistently, not all contests for presidential nominations are the same. presidential nomination contests differ according to whether there is an early front-runner, how many candidates enter the race, and the degree of divisiveness or party unity the contest produces.

In the early days of the post-reform period, before the decline of conventions was clear, William R. Keech and Donald R. Matthews (1977) classified presidential nominations according to party unity or divisiveness. Nominations could either be "consensual," when a front-runner established a lead and maintained it to win the nomination of a unified party; or "non-consensual," when there was a factional battle for the nomination that remained divisive even at the finish; or "semi-consensual," when a contested nomination usually confirmed the early front-runner and resulted in party unity around the winner.[3] See table 3.2. At the time they wrote, while both parties were still undergoing factional realignment, non-consensual nominations were unusually frequent, as in 1972 (when the Democrats nominated McGovern), 1980 (when the Democrats renominated President Carter over Ted Kennedy), or 1976 (when the Republicans nominated President Ford over Ronald Reagan).

Since then, the nonconsensual nomination disappeared through 2004, even after hot contests, such as between Democrats Walter Mondale and Gary Hart in 1984, or between Republicans George W. Bush and John McCain in 2000. All of those contests presented relative ideological harmony and party unity at the finish.

Open competition among more candidates in more primaries has made the consensual nomination rare. The only contested nomination of the post-reform period that might be classified as "consensual" would be in 2000, when Albert Gore eliminated Bill Bradley by Super Tuesday without losing a primary or caucus. The default rule for the post-reform period is that contested presidential nominations have become semi-consensual: The primaries and caucuses are actively contested, but the outcome produces a de facto nomination before the convention, accompanied by party unity. Non-consensual nominations reappeared in 2008 and 2016, but even those

Table 3.2 Typologies of Contested Presidential Nominations (Keech and Matthews Model)

Consensual	Semi-Consensual	Non-Consensual
1936 Republicans		
	1940 Democrats	1940 Republicans
	1944 Democrats	
	1944 Republicans	
	1948 Democrats	1948 Republicans
	1952 Democrats	
	1952 Republicans	
	1956 Democrats	
1960 Republicans	1960 Democrats	
1964 Democrats	1964 Republicans	
	1968 Republicans	1968 Democrats
1972 Republicans	1972 Democrats	
	1976 Democrats	1976 Republicans
	1980 Republicans	1980 Democrats
	1984 Democrats	
	1988 Democrats	
	1992 Democrats	
	1996 Republicans	
2000 Democrats	2000 Republicans	
	2004 Democrats	
	2008 Republicans	2008 Democrats
	2012 Republicans	
	2016 Democrats	2016 Republicans

Keech and Matthews sorted presidential nominations going back to 1936, when the Gallup Poll was introduced, measuring party consensus during what we would now call the "invisible primary" using the Gallup Poll of public opinion and party county chairs (Keech & Matthews, 1977). I have shown their sorting for 1936–1972, and have applied their theory to sort post-reform nominations.

contests were resolved before the convention, which would not have been the case before ideological realignment and party reform.

Larry Bartels (1988) offered a more useful classification of contested presidential nominations for the post-reform era. Bartels sorted nomination contests as featuring "two major candidates," "one major candidate," and "no major candidates." In addition to "two major candidates," I find it more accurate to refer to the latter two categories descriptively as "front-runner against the field" and the "crowded field." See table 3.3.

When there are *two major candidates*, each one leads a faction of the party, and their combined support is strong enough to saturate the electorate. One is usually the early front-runner, but the second candidate has sufficient support and resources to compete through most or all of the primaries. The classic cases are the Republican contest between President Ford and Ronald Reagan

Table 3.3 Typologies of Campaigns in Post-Reform Presidential Primaries, 1972–2016 (Bartels Model)

Two Major Candidates	Front-Runner vs. the Field	Crowded Field
		1972 Democrats
1976 Republicans		1976 Democrats
1980 Democrats	1980 Republicans	
	1984 Democrats	
	1988 Republicans	1988 Democrats
	1992 Democrats	
	1996 Republicans	
	2000 Republicans	
	2000 Democrats	
		2004 Democrats
	2008 Democrats	2008 Republicans
	2012 Republicans	
2016 Democrats		2016 Republicans(?)

Bartels (1988) classified the presidential nomination contests between 1976 and 1984. I have applied his method to classify the previous and subsequent contests. See below for a discussion of the Trump campaign in 2016, which might reclassify that contest.

in 1976, and the Democratic contest between President Carter and Senator Edward M. Kennedy of Massachusetts in 1980. Although unexpected, the 2016 race between former Secretary of State Hillary Clinton and Senator Bernie Sanders of Vermont for the Democratic presidential nomination also fits the mold. In all three of these cases, the competition carried throughout the primary season.

Democrats Walter Mondale in 1984, Bill Clinton in 1992, Albert Gore in 2000, and Hillary Clinton in 2008 and Republicans Ronald Reagan in 1980, George Bush in 1988, Robert Dole in 1996, George W. Bush in 2000, and Mitt Romney in 2012 were all *front-runners against the field*. All nine of these candidates were front-runners in the polls and in party endorsements at the end of the invisible primary; seven of the nine led in fund-raising. All except Clinton in 2008 won the nomination. Clinton lost that contest after Senator Barack Obama succeeded relatively early in turning the contest into a two-candidate race (see above). All of the early front-runners who won the nomination except Gore were front-runners against multicandidate fields who had to recover from early defeats to regain their front-runner status. Gore had only one opponent in 2000, former Senator Bill Bradley of New Jersey. What distinguishes Gore from the winners of two-candidate contests is that Bradley was never able to build enough of a challenge to claim leadership of a faction opposing Gore; and what distinguishes Gore from the other front-runners against the field is that Gore maintained his lead from start to finish without losing a primary.

When the invisible primary winnows least, the result is a *crowded field* without a front-runner. What follows is usually a relatively extended contest among candidates and factions for the nomination. Often, the early primaries are elimination contests within factions. The first candidate to emerge as front-runner from the crowded field goes on to the nomination, as was the case with Democrats Jimmy Carter in 1976, Michael Dukakis in 1988, and John Kerry in 2004 and Republican John McCain in 2008.

The End Game in Presidential Primaries

The issue of when a presidential nomination is effectively settled has long been a matter of debate. For example, William Gamson (1962) offered the generalization that when the front-runner reaches 41 percent of the total delegates, the opposition will collapse. Collatt, Kelley, and Rogowski (1981) offered a more complex "gain-deficit ratio" for predicting the end of a nomination contest.[4] Focusing on presidential nominations since 1980, Barbara Norrander (2000, 2010) divided the field of candidates into "office-seekers" and "advocacy" candidates.[5] She concluded that the best estimate of when the nomination is clinched is when the front-runner achieves a lead equaling 25 to 30 percent of the delegates needed for the nomination. The "advocacy" candidates may linger, but the opposing "office-seekers" will withdraw. The important point is that in the post-reform period, the standard for withdrawing from the race has been markedly reduced, and the front-runner has usually clinched the nomination well in advance of the convention. See table 3.4.

Table 3.4 "Agenda-Seekers" Who Extended Presidential Nomination Campaigns (Using Norrander Model)

Year/Party	Front-Runner	"Office-Seeker"	"Agenda-Seeker"
1988 Republicans	George Bush	Robert Dole	Pat Robertson
1988 Democrats	Michael Dukakis	Albert Gore	Jesse Jackson
1992 Republicans	George Bush		Pat Buchanan
1992 Democrats	Bill Clinton	Paul Tsongas	Jerry Brown
1996 Republicans	Robert Dole	Steve Forbes	Pat Buchanan
2000 Republicans	George W. Bush	John McCain	Alan Keyes
2004 Democrats	John Kerry	John Edwards	Dennis Kucinich
2008 Republicans	John McCain	Mitt Romney Mike Huckabee	Ron Paul
2012 Republicans	Mitt Romney	Rick Santorum Newt Gingrich	Ron Paul

See Barbara Norrander (2000, 2010). Candidates listed are he front-runners who in each case went on to the nomination, "office-seekers" who either were runner-up in the delegate count, or who were the last "office-seekers" to withdraw, and "advocacy" candidates who extended the campaign by remaining in the race long after their chances for the nomination, if they ever had any, were gone.

Discussion

In a way, post-reform presidential nominations seem to have come full circle to a *status-quo ante*. Although more candidate-centered, the "invisible primary" is nothing new. Cohen, Karol, Noel, and Zaller have underscored the revival of parties and party elites and their endorsements in the setup to the primaries. Indeed, while the post-reform process is much more participatory, its outcomes have become similar to the pre-reform period. The tendency of early front-runners to win presidential nominations can be verified with polling data going back to 1936 (Cohen, Karol, Noel & Zaller, 2008b; Hadley, 1976; Keech & Matthews, 1976). When there is a consensus within the party, its early choice is most likely to be the nominee. Consensus is facilitated by ideological homogenization within the political parties of our polarized party system. Reform of the rules of the game, particularly front-loaded primaries, often seems to be given too much credit for the fact that presidential nominations tend to be settled before the convention, while not enough credit is assigned to ideological polarization between and ideological homogenization within the major parties. If nomination contests today involved factions supporting Republicans Eisenhower and Taft, or Goldwater and Rockefeller, or Ford and Reagan, or Democrats McGovern, Humphrey, and Wallace, or Carter and Kennedy, the fight would still go to the convention floor, front-loading notwithstanding. Ideological homogenization within today's polarized parties seems to guarantee that the losing factions in the nomination struggle will prefer their party's nominee to the opposing party, making consensus easier to build, and the emergence of a "presumptive nominee" before the convention almost certain.

THE PRESIDENTIAL PRIMARIES OF 2016

There were certainly plenty of surprises during the 2016 presidential primaries. Both party establishments were shaken seriously, and one was clearly beaten before the national conventions. There was evidence that electoral, political, and policy change is in the offing in years to come. But the 2016 presidential nominations may have offered less change and more stability than meets the eye. Tables 3.5 and 3.6 below provide recent historical perspective, showing patterns of support among ideological factions in the Republican and Democratic presidential primaries across four decades of the post-reform system, from 1976 through 2016.

Trumping the Republicans

The biggest surprise of the 2016 presidential primaries was, of course, Donald Trump winning the Republican presidential nomination. It seemed that virtually no one (journalist, academic, or general public) believed what was happening at each stage of the process until after it happened, and then we remained incredulous.[6] Trump's emergence as the front-runner, and then his nomination, led to broad speculation that his candidacy represented a fundamental change in our political parties (certainly the Republican Party) and in the rules of the presidential nomination game. This conclusion certainly may yet prove accurate.

But there has been little emphasis on how much the rules of the post-reform presidential nomination system persisted in 2016. Perhaps there is not enough appreciation of how much the outcomes of the 2016 Republican presidential nomination contest reflected transitory political behavior that was unusual, but not necessarily system changing or even unprecedented. Despite the differences from previous cycles, many of the patterns of post-reform presidential nomination contests were followed by the Republicans in 2016.

The Republicans' Invisible Primary

We expect the invisible primary to at least shape the field of candidates who will be competing in the primaries for the presidential nomination, and often to anoint an early front-runner, based on standings in the polls and fundraising, and endorsements from party elites. Before Trump announced his candidacy on June 16, 2015, the field was crowded, with former Governor Jeb Bush of Florida, Dr. Ben Carson, Senator Marco Rubio of Florida, Senator Rand Paul of Kentucky, Governor Scott Walker of Wisconsin, former Governor Mike Huckabee of Arkansas, and Governor Chris Christie of New Jersey each taking a turn or more at leading in public opinion polls of Republican voters earlier in the year.[7] Mr. Bush was the front-runner when Trump announced, and he looked like a reasonable choice for the party establishment. Mitt Romney was even persuaded by Bush's apparent support not to seek renomination for president in 2016. But Bush's poll numbers, even as he led, were usually under 20 percent, and never measured up to even the unimpressive invisible primary showing of Romney before the 2012 primaries, when Romney was the apparent establishment choice. Thus, party elites never finally settled on Bush or any other candidate during the invisible primary. As it turned out, they never developed a consensus (or at least a positive consensus) during the primaries, either.

Within two weeks of his announcement, Trump had seized the lead in the polls and he seldom relinquished it thereafter. Both Bush and Walker faded, while Carson gained ground with the support of ultraconservative Republicans, the ideological "fundamentalists." When Carson challenged for the lead in the fall of 2015, increased media attention exposed his own carelessness in describing his biography, and he faded fast. As we now know, Trump would survive multiple worse missteps throughout the campaign.

In November, polls of Republican voters revealed a decisive pattern that would persist into and through the primaries. Trump was the clear front-runner, and his leading opponent was Senator Ted Cruz of Texas, who had emerged as the candidate of conservative Republicans.

By the end of the invisible primary, then, Trump was the clear front-runner in the polls. Carson led in fund-raising, but as we have discussed, the increased financial power of independent PACs has decreased the usefulness of campaign finance data in measuring candidate strength. Moreover, despite his finances, Carson's free fall in the polls had already effectively eliminated him as a real possibility for the nomination. Meanwhile, the party establishment remained without a candidate.

Even in the absence of elite consensus, if there was a front-runner before the voting started, it was Donald Trump. To a degree not appreciated at the time, Mr. Trump had succeeded in turning the race from a crowded field to a match of front-runner against the field, and the results of the invisible primary would be ratified by the voting in the presidential primaries to follow.

The Republican Presidential Primaries

Mr. Trump solidified his front-running status in the early primaries, rebounding from a loss in the Iowa caucuses to win the New Hampshire and South Carolina primaries, then winning Massachusetts, Vermont, and most of the South on Super Tuesday. Trump's victories in the North and South, and exit poll data, indicated that his support stretched across the ideological spectrum. According to the exit polls (table 3.5), Trump enjoyed pluralities among moderates and conservatives alike. But this did not mean the end of factional conflict. Senator Cruz strengthened his claim as Trump's leading opponent by winning the Iowa caucuses, followed by victories in the Texas and Oklahoma primaries on Super Tuesday. But only Republican voters who called themselves "very conservative" provided Cruz with a plurality over Trump. Governor John Kasich of Ohio placed second in New Hampshire, Massachusetts, and Vermont, drawing his support from moderate-to-liberal Republicans. But even among those voters, Kasich could only place second to Trump. Among the other candidates, only Senator Rubio survived beyond

Table 3.5 Exit Polls in Republican Presidential Primaries, 1976–2016

	Liberal	Moderate	Conservative	National
1976				
Ford	**64**	**60**	41	**53**
Reagan	36	39	**56**	46
National	10	53	37	100
1980				
Reagan	34	**45**	**66**	**51**
Bush	31	33	27	31
Anderson	**35**	15	7	14
National	10	58	32	100
1988				
Bush	**55**	**57**	**54**	**55**
Dole	31	31	22	26
Robertson	6	6	16	12
National	7	38	55	100
1992				
Bush	**68**	**71**	**65**	**68**
Buchanan	27	25	31	29
National	9	34	57	100
1996				
Dole	**48**	**51**	**49**	**50**
Buchanan	15	14	27	22
Forbes	22	22	16	18
National	8	30	62	100
2000				
George W. Bush	37	41	**64**	**53**
McCain	**58**	**56**	29	42
National	12	34	54	100
2008				
McCain	**55**	**52**	32	**40**
Romney	18	22	**35**	29
Huckabee	13	13	25	21
National	10	28	62	100
2012				
Romney	**34**	**47**	**38**	**40**
Santorum	21	20	30	27
Gingrich	18	15	23	21
Paul	20	14	8	10
National	6	26	68	100

(continued)

Table 3.5 Continued

	Liberal	Moderate	Conservative	National
2016				
Trump	34	41	38	41
Cruz	18	14	31	27
Kasich	21	25	12	14
Rubio	10	14	13	13
National	3	22	75	100

	Moderate/ Liberal	Somewhat Conservative	Very Conservative	National
2016				
Trump	40	44	37	41
Cruz	14	23	42	27
Kasich	25	15	7	14
Rubio	14	15	10	13
National	25	42	33	100

Figures represent percentages of the vote in presidential primaries. Data derived from exit polls weighted to state results and proportioned to national outcomes. Sources: For exit polls, 1976–2004, International Consortium for Political and Social Research (ICPSR). For 2008–2016 exit polls: the *New York Times*, MSNBC, CNN, or Fox News, accessed throughout the primary season. Results of presidential primaries drawn or derived from *Presidential Elections 1789–1996* (Washington, DC: Congressional Quarterly, 1997), pp. 186–227; Since 2000, from www.thegreenpapers.com. Only primaries held in the "competitive phase" are included. Mayer (2008) conceptualizes the "competitive phase" and identifies when contests going back to 1976 end, while Norrander (2010) offers an empirical estimate of when nomination contests end. For 2016, there were not enough liberal Republicans to amount to a statistically significant sample in most states. Respondents were sorted as "very" or "somewhat" conservative and moderate. The first reporting of the 2016 exit polls combines "very conservative" with "somewhat conservative" respondents and derives the vote of liberals for the purpose of maintaining a comparison with the ideological divisions in exit polls for primaries in previous years.

Super Tuesday, placing second in South Carolina, Georgia, and Virginia. But Rubio could not stake a claim to any faction of the Republican electorate as a base of his own, and was effectively eliminated long before he or his supporters recognized reality.

Using the initial classification of Republican factions offered by Nicole Rae (1989), Trump led among progressives, moderates, and stalwarts; Cruz led among fundamentalists; and Kasich was battling Trump, albeit unsuccessfully, for the support of progressives and moderates. This pattern of support persisted throughout the Republican primaries, to the finish.

Rae (1998) offered a revised vision of Republican factions that enhances our understanding of Trump's triumph in the primaries. Rae described four factions emerging in the 1990s, recognizing that virtually all Republicans were conservatives of one brand or another. This framework of Republican factionalism seems to supplement, rather than replace Rae's previous description. He called the party establishment the "traditional" Republicans, the rough equivalent of the "stalwarts." The "religious right" is at home among the "fundamentalists."

The "supply-side libertarians" emphasize economic issues, and could even be considered "fundamentalist" on the free market, but relatively moderate on social issues. Finally, Rae identified the "populists," who voted for Pat Buchanan in the 1992 and 1996 Republican primaries, and would become Trump's base in 2016. Rae described the populists as generally culturally conservative, nationalist, protectionist on trade, and anti-immigration. Their support of big government solutions on trade and jobs makes them appear less conservative than the other factions on economics, but more conservative than the stalwarts or libertarians on social issues. Thus, Trump's lead in the primaries among voters almost all the way across the ideological spectrum did not represent unity, so much as it did pluralities from an eclectic coalition with a populist base.

As Trump made his claim as the front-runner in the primaries, party elites were finally developing a consensus, but only a negative one: They were against Trump, but unwilling or unable to settle on an alternative. Many were leaning toward Rubio, despite his almost hopeless situation. Mitt Romney called on Republicans to vote for favorite sons in upcoming primaries in their home states, Kasich in Ohio and Rubio in Florida. Meanwhile there was no settling on an alternative to Trump, even within factions, as moderate Republicans failed to endorse Kasich, while conservative Republicans failed to endorse Cruz.

Two weeks after Super Tuesday, Trump won four out of five primaries across the south and Midwest: Florida, North Carolina, Illinois, and Missouri. Gov. Kasich scored his only victory, in his home state of Ohio, while Rubio withdrew after his defeat in his home state of Florida. Cruz hung on by finishing second in three states.

Cruz then benefitted from one of Trump's streaks of gaffes before the Wisconsin primary. Mitt Romney joined conservative Republicans in Wisconsin to call on voters to support Cruz, who won the state. For the moment, the Wisconsin primary created a last gasp of hope for Trump's opponents.

The Republican Endgame

Nevertheless, the end was at hand. The primaries in April would all be in the Northeast corner of the country. While Cruz was enjoying some momentum off his victory in Wisconsin, he had little or no appeal in the Northeast, and while Kasich may have had potential there, his third-place finish in Wisconsin deflated his campaign. The result was that Trump won his home state of New York, plus Pennsylvania, Rhode Island, Connecticut, Delaware, and

Maryland, all with impressive majorities. This was the first time Trump had won any primaries with majorities of the vote, but the result put him very close to the nomination.

At this point in the race, the endgame seemed normal. After winning the Pennsylvania primary, Trump had 36 percent of the delegates, just short of the 41 percent that William Gamson (1962) predicted a front-runner needed to clinch the nomination. Trump's delegate lead over Ted Cruz amounted to 27 percent of a majority, right about at the point at which Barbara Norrander (2000, 2010) indicated that serious "office-seekers" would concede the race to the front-runner.

Cruz made one last stand, in the Indiana primary. Desperate to change the narrative, he publicly selected Carly Fiorina as his running mate, and the two campaigned together for a few days. But it was too late. Trump crushed Cruz in Indiana by 53 percent to 36 percent. Now, Trump had 42 percent of the delegates and a lead equaling 39 percent of a majority, satisfying both of the above predictions for when a nomination would be decided. As would be expected, although Trump had not yet surpassed an actual majority of the delegates, both Cruz and Kasich withdrew, although neither was prepared to offer an endorsement of the front-runner.

The Republican Convention: Party Unity?

Party leaders, including House Speaker Paul Ryan, who would chair the Republican National Convention, hesitated about endorsing Trump, although Republican National Chairman Reince Priebus proclaimed the front-runner to be the presumptive nominee.

The Republican National Committee had adapted rules long before the primaries that were intended to ensure that the front-runner (who they then assumed would be the favorite of party elites) would not face a contest at the convention. Candidates had to have majorities in eight delegations to have their names placed in nomination at the convention, and some state parties had a rule that only active candidates could receive votes at the convention. These rules discouraged the emergence of a preconvention candidate who had not entered the primaries, and forbade Kasich, who enjoyed only the support of Ohio, to have his name placed before the convention. Cruz could have had his name placed in nomination, but did not.

Neither Trump's claim on the nomination nor these rules could hide the presence of displeasure with Trump. Both living Republican former Presidents (Bush) announced they would not attend the convention, and neither did Governor Kasich, who would have been expected to host of the convention in Cleveland. And there was the "Never Trump" movement (if it could be called that), flailing away aimlessly in their efforts to stop Trump.

The political behavior of the Trump campaign and of the Never Trump opposition in the immediate preconvention period and at the Republican National Convention illustrated how much the culture of the presidential nominating process has changed in the post-reform era. The shared assumption that nominations are settled before the convention is so widely accepted that most party leaders seem to be unable to even hold contested conventions anymore.

"Never Trump" Republicans still hoped to stop Trump at the convention by amending the rules to allow delegates to "vote their conscience" at the convention and release them from their commitments to candidates. Their expectation was that with such an amendment, Trump might at least be stopped on the first ballot, creating a free for all thereafter. But Trump forces prevailed on a voice vote in the Rules Committee, and on a voice vote not to amend the rules on the floor. The failure of the "Never Trump" crowd even to obtain a count of votes in the Rules Committee prevented them from presenting a specific rules amendment on the floor, or obtaining a roll call vote on the rules.

With the nomination effectively settled, the closest thing to drama on the presidential roll call was the dispute over the rules and vote of the Alaska delegation. Alaska was one of those states that had a rule requiring that votes be distributed among "qualified" candidates. On the floor, Alaska delegates followed the result of their Republican State Convention to cast their 28 votes as 12 for Cruz, 11 for Trump and 5 for Rubio. Because of the rule, the chair announced and recorded all 28 for Trump. When the Alaska delegation objected, the chair of the convention upheld its own interpretation of the rule requiring all votes for Trump. The Alaska delegation disagreed with the interpretation but did not formally challenge it.

Neither the Trump nor "Never Trump" forces were prepared for a contested convention. The Trump campaign did not act like a majority that could confidently count the votes and defend their ground without alienating opponents. Instead, they seemed the bully their way on the rules to be sure no one could interfere with Trump's nomination, thus irrationally standing in the way of the unity of their own party. The "Never Trump" campaign, such as it was, had no coherent strategy to challenge Trump. Before the convention "Never Trump" had no state-by-state strategy for backing selected candidates against the front-runner in the primaries. They might have vigorously backed Cruz and Kasich in selected states, to earn enough delegates to stop Trump short of a majority, but failed to do it. At the convention, they had no coherent strategy on the rules, either in committee or on the floor, and did not present the challenges they might have. This failure to fight where the opportunity presented itself is a product of the culture of uncontested conventions that has developed in the post-reform era. Before ideological realignment and reform, we might have expected opposition to the front-runner in the later primaries, and challenges on rules and credentials at the convention. At the 2016 Republican National Convention, the nomination of Donald Trump was effectively treated as inevitable, even by those who most opposed it.

In the absence of presenting an effective opposition, all the "Never Trump" people could do was shout. Even then, they were shouted down. When Senator Cruz addressed the convention and pointedly declined to endorse the nominee, he was booed off the stage.

Throughout the general election campaign that followed, the "Never Trump" people generally became "Maybe Trump" people. While most Republican leaders supported their party's nominee, there certainly was fluctuation, particularly around the time of the *Access Hollywood* drama. Despite the temptation to resist, Republicans were accommodating themselves to the reality of Donald Trump.

Berning the Democrats

Even the Democrats were surprised in the 2016 presidential primaries, by the challenge of Senator Bernie Sanders of Vermont, an independent-turned-Democrat and a self-declared democratic socialist, against former Secretary of State Hillary Rodham Clinton.[8]

The Democrats' Invisible Primary

Ms. Clinton was the clear early front-runner by every measure. She led in public opinion polls among Democrats all the way from the start of the invisible primary, through the primaries, to the convention. Throughout 2015, Clinton enjoyed support from majorities of Democrats, with leads of nearly fifty points. Before Sanders became a factor, the coming contest looked like a front-runner against the field. Clinton's leading potential opponents were Senator Elizabeth Warren of Massachusetts, the apparent darling of liberal Democrats, and Vice President Joseph Biden. Neither one entered the race. Former Senator Jim Webb of Virginia, former Governor Lincoln Chafee of Rhode Island, and former Governor Martin O'Malley of Maryland all entered the race but trailed badly. Chafee and Webb withdrew during the invisible primary, and O'Malley withdrew immediately after the Iowa caucuses.

When Senator Sanders announced his candidacy on April 30, 2015, he stood at single digits in the polls. Immediately his support began to grow, slowly at first, but soon he was established as Clinton's leading opponent. By the time the voting was about to start in Iowa, Clinton had settled at about 50 percent, and she enjoyed a lead of about 3–2 over Sanders. In addition to her lead in the polls, Hillary also had by far the most endorsements from party elites, and she had raised the largest sum of money. Moreover, it was clear that she would have the support of almost all of the superdelegates who held their convention seats by virtue of public office or party position, giving her a big head start in the delegate count. She could claim a clear victory in the invisible primary.

But Bernie could also claim a successful invisible primary. He was between 30 and 40 percent in the polls, and had raised "huge" sums of money in small contributions. If he could be competitive in the voting, he had more than enough resources for the long haul. While Clinton was still the clear front-runner and favorite of the party establishment, Sanders had turned the contest from a front-runner against the field into something more like a one-on-one race between two major candidates.

The Democratic Presidential Primaries

Iowa and New Hampshire firmed the shape of the race as a one-on-one contest. Clinton barely won the Iowa caucuses, while Sanders won the New Hampshire primary with 60 percent of the vote. Clinton remained the front-runner in the national polls, although her lead had shrunk to single digits. But she looked ahead to primaries across the south on Super Tuesday as a firewall against the Sanders advance, and she got it.

Hillary won the South Carolina primary by almost 3–1. On March 1, Super Tuesday, she swept the south by margins of 2–1 and 3–1, permanently taking the lead in the delegate count. More important for her, she narrowly won the Massachusetts primary, where the Sanders campaign had hoped that regional loyalties and support from liberal Democrats would carry the day for him. Nevertheless, Sanders survived. His victory in the Vermont primary was expected, but he also won Oklahoma by ten points, an unexpected victory that demonstrated Bernie's potential with working class voters.[9] A week later, Sanders added a narrow but important victory in the Michigan primary.

Michigan gave those "feeling the Bern" hope, but five primaries on March 15 appeared to give Hillary an insurmountable lead. She won all five. She won Florida and North Carolina in the South by large margins, and Missouri and her native Illinois in the Midwest by very narrow margins. Her most impressive and decisive showing came in the Ohio primary, where she won with 56 percent of the vote.

Yet, Sanders hung on. On April 5, he won a handsome victory in the Wisconsin primary. It was no surprise, since insurgents and liberal Democrats have historically made a habit of winning primaries in Wisconsin. But it gave Bernie some momentum to challenge Hillary in her home state (and his native state) of New York.

The Democratic Endgame

Clinton had been elected to the Senate from New York twice, and the state hardly seemed to be the place for the Sanders campaign to stage a major challenge. But Clinton's lead in the delegate count was so large that something dramatic had to be done to turn around the outlook. Sanders needed at least a close race yielding a respectable share of the state's 291 delegates, but it wasn't to be. Clinton beat Sanders, 58 percent to 42 percent.

A week later, Clinton won four out of five primaries in the Northeast, including Pennsylvania. The result left Clinton with 37 percent of all the delegates to be selected, and a lead that amounted to 22 percent of a majority. She was just short of achieving margins that Gamson (1962) and Norrander (2000, 2010) projected as being decisive in presidential nomination contests.

Before that would happen, Sanders added victories in Indiana and West Virginia. Then, on May 17, Clinton won the Kentucky primary while Sanders was winning in Oregon. She now had 46 percent of all delegates to be selected, more than the 41 percent Gamson considered to be decisive, and a lead amounting to 27 percent of a majority, about what Norrander considers decisive.

But Sanders persisted still, to the end and perhaps beyond. Even when Clinton won the New Jersey and California primaries at the end of the schedule in June, Sen. Sanders maintained that he would take his campaign to the convention.

The battle through the primaries had been vigorous, and while Sanders' showing was impressive, the results nationally were not particularly close. Across the country, Clinton polled 57 percent of the vote in the Democratic primaries, to 42 percent for Sanders. According to exit polls of Democratic primary voters (table 3.6), Clinton won almost all the way across the ideological spectrum. Among voters who called themselves "somewhat liberal," Hillary won by almost exactly the same margin as her total national vote. She won among moderate-to-conservative Democrats by 2–1. Bernie won only among voters who called themselves "very liberal," and even among them by less than a percentage point.

Table 3.6   Exit Polls in Democratic Presidential Primaries, 1976–2016

	Liberal	Moderate	Conservative	National
1976				
Carter	29	41	41	38
Brown	17	16	10	15
Wallace	6	12	22	12
Udall	19	9	6	11
Henry Jackson	8	8	10	8
Church	8	5	3	5
National	29	55	16	100
1980				
Carter	40	53	58	51
Kennedy	45	36	29	37
National	23	58	19	100
1984				
Mondale	34	41	37	38
Hart	36	37	35	36
Jesse Jackson	26	15	15	18
National	28	50	22	100
1988				
Dukakis	37	41	32	37
Jesse Jackson	37	25	23	28
Gore	9	17	25	17
Gephardt	5	8	10	8
Simon	5	5	5	5
National	27	49	24	100
1992				
Clinton	42	53	49	48
Tsongas	29	26	26	27
Brown	21	14	14	16
Kerrey	2	2	3	2
National	34	44	22	100
2000				
Gore	67	75	69	72
Bradley	29	22	27	26
National	51	40	9	10
2004				
Kerry	58	54	43	54
Edwards	22	28	31	25
Dean	6	5	6	6
Clark	3	4	4	4
National	47	38	15	100

(continued)

Table 3.6 Continued

	Liberal	Moderate	Conservative	National
2008				
Clinton	47	**50**	47	48
Obama	**49**	42	44	47
National	47	39	14	100
2016				
Clinton	53	62	66	57
Sanders	46	36	24	42
National	62	32	6	100

	Very Liberal	Somewhat Liberal	Moderate/ Conservative	National
2016				
Clinton	49	**56**	65	57
Sanders	**50**	43	34	42
National	25	37	38	100

Figures represent percentages of the vote in presidential primaries. Data derived from exit polls weighted to state results and proportioned to national outcomes. Sources: For exit polls, 1976–2004, International Consortium for Political and Social Research (ICPSR). For 2008 and 2016 exit polls: the *New York Times*, MSNBC or CNN, accessed throughout the primary season. Results of presidential primaries drawn or derived from *Presidential Elections 1789–1996* (Washington, DC: Congressional Quarterly, 1997), pp. 186–227, for 1976–1996. For presidential primaries since 2000: www.thegreenpapers.com. Only primaries held in the "competitive phase" are included. Mayer (2008) conceptualizes the "competitive phase" and identifies when contests going back to 1976 end, while Norrander offers an empirical estimate of when nomination contests end. For 2016, there were not enough conservative Democrats in most states to amount to a statistically significant sample. Respondents were sorted in the exit polls as "very" or "somewhat" liberal and moderate. The first reporting of the 2016 exit polls combines "very liberal" with "somewhat liberal" respondents, and derives the vote of conservatives, for the purpose of maintaining a comparison with the ideological divisions in exit polls for primaries in previous years.

Bernie barely won among whites, while Hillary carried the black vote by 3–1 and Latinos by 2–1. It is an important consideration for the future of the Democratic Party that Bernie Sanders won among young voters by 2–1.

While Sanders won most of the caucus states, Clinton won about 55 percent of all elected delegates. She won by a comfortable margin, and she did not even need her claim to over 90 percent of the superdelegates to win the nomination.

So why didn't Bernie Sanders withdraw? It is important to remember that Sanders is not a liberal Democrat, indeed, not a liberal at all, and until he ran for president, not a Democrat at all. His focus when he began his campaign was on issues, and it was still on issues at the end. He was, in the classifications of Barbara Norrander (2000, 2010), an "advocacy" candidate, even as his showings in the primaries gave him chance to win. There was no reason to expect him to withdraw as his chances for the nomination deflated, and every reason to expect him not to.

The Democratic Convention

Nevertheless, Senator Sanders finally did withdraw and endorse Hillary Clinton for president before the convention. His decision was again based on the issues: The Democratic platform that emerged out the platform committee was one that Sanders could call the "most progressive" in the history of the Democratic Party. It included compromises resulting in a shift toward his positions on economic inequality, the minimum wage, financial access to higher education, single-payer national health insurance, banking reform, and climate change. It was almost the platform that would have been presented had Sanders himself been the nominee. And while the platform did not oppose the Trans-Pacific Partnership, as Sanders supporters would have preferred, Hillary Clinton as the Democratic nominee for president came out against it, despite her role as Secretary of State in the early stages of its negotiation.

There was also a democratization of party rules, with a two-thirds reduction in the number of superdelegates. This did not represent a reversal of the party reforms of 1968–1972. Superdelegates were not added until the 1984 campaign, and their reduction now is a move back in the direction of the original McGovern-Fraser reforms designed to increase the voice of voters in presidential nominations.

Despite the preconvention spirit of party unity, there was still drama at the convention. First, the revelation of e-mails (partly by the hidden hand of the Russians?) showing that leaders of the Democratic National Committee had intervened in favor of Clinton in the recently concluded campaign for the Democratic presidential nomination, and that there had been discussion of personal attacks on Bernie Sanders, forced the resignation of the Democratic National Chairperson, Representative Debbie Wasserman Schultz of Florida. Finding some alliance between Schultz and Clinton should not have been much of a surprise, and is simply a reflection of the fact that Clinton was the favorite of party elites. Indeed, the outrage on the part of colleagues at Wasserman Schultz may have been more staged than genuine. But the party's formal apparatus is expected to be at least formally neutral in a nomination contest, and the personal venom of attacks that might have been directed at Sanders was embarrassing and represented a dangerous threat to party unity.

Second, Bernie Sanders had problems with the "Bernie or Bust" element among his own supporters, who at a preconvention caucus booed his request that they support Hillary Clinton. They wanted to fight, but Sanders had made his call that party unity and a Democratic victory in November was the best way to advance their principles and issue agenda over the next four years. Sanders was graceful and sincere in his motion at the convention to suspend the rules and nominate Clinton, but at least the "Bernie or Bust" delegates among his supporters were inclined to withhold their support from Clinton, and some indicated they would vote for Jill Stein, the Green Party nominee. Like Bernie, at least some of his supporters were progressives first, and Democrats (if at all) second.

The movement for Sanders was a reflection of an even more progressive element growing within the Democratic Party and of the prospect for real factional conflict in years to come. Had the 2016 convention been a pre-reform convention before the days of ideological realignment, that factional conflict may have surfaced in a real contest at the convention. There may have been real challenges on rules and credentials, and those challenges would have been invigorated by something like the e-mail exposure. And there almost certainly would have been a real contest on the presidential roll call at such a convention, although Clinton would have won it.

As it is, we find ourselves with the ideologically realigned Democratic Party in the post-reform culture of uncontested conventions. In 2016, the potential conflict was avoided, and the Democrats put on a well-crafted convention that performed the function of recent post-reform conventions: To sell the party brand. Speeches at the Democratic convention offered a sense of the Democrats' opportunity and reflected an awareness of the party realignment over the past half century that has terminated the Republicans' historic claim to be the "party of Lincoln." President Obama and former Mayor Mike Bloomberg of New York made direct appeals to liberal Republicans-becoming-independents or -Democrats. So did Senator Tim Kaine of Virginia, the Democratic nominee for vice president, whose acceptance speech said as much about the polarized party system as it did the campaign of 2016: "If any of you are looking for that party of Lincoln, we've got a home for you right here in the Democratic Party."

CONCLUSION

Even in the face of the dramatic and surprising campaigns for presidential nominations in 2016, the polarized party system that has emerged in the last half century persists, and with it, the post-reform system of presidential nominations. Granted, the nomination of Donald Trump and the success of Bernie Sanders in the primaries were both initially unanticipated. But the institutional structures and processes of post-reform presidential nominations survived severe strain to remain fundamentally in place. The ingredients of electoral and party change are visible on the horizon, but the 2016 contests did not present the sort of sea change in presidential nomination systems that accompanied the decline of "King Caucus" and the birth of national conventions between 1824 and 1832, or the introduction of presidential primaries in

1912, or the participatory reforms after 1968 that have produced the current system. Moreover, the evidence of at least institutional stability in the presidential nomination process was strong.

First, as has been the rule for more than three decades, both 2016 presidential nominations were decided in the primaries, before the convention. For the Democrats, the process was much more smooth and consistent with post-reform presidential nominations. Hillary Clinton, the early front-runner and favorite of party elites, battled through the primaries against a stiff challenge to clinch the nomination before the convention. While there were important policy differences between the supporters of Clinton and Sanders, the culture of party unity and uncontested conventions prevailed.

For the Republicans, the outcome was the same. Donald Trump clinched the nomination during the primaries, earlier than Clinton did. But opposition to Trump was more pronounced, as the "Never Trump" movement, apparently anchored in the party establishment (such as it was), made public efforts to stop him before the convention. They failed to settle on a candidate during the invisible primary, failed to unite on an alternative during the primaries, and failed even to deliver support to selected candidates (at that point Cruz or Kasich) in the later primaries. And although they might have built a convention strategy around challenging rules and credentials at the convention, no such strategy was forthcoming. While opposition to Trump represented real factional conflict within the Republican Party, the culture of uncontested conventions had become so strong that "Never Trump" leaders simply did not know how to do what they were about, and, in fact, seemed not even to know how to think intelligently about their problem.

Second, neither convention was a decision-making body. As has been the case for most of three decades, both conventions were show biz presentations designed to sell the party brand.

Finally, the polarized party system that emerged at the national level a half century ago, and had spread to the state level by the 1990s, is still with us, perhaps even in exaggerated form. The Democrats, somewhat "Berned" by the experience of 2016, produced a platform and an approach to the campaign that indicated that the more progressive of our two parties is becoming more still more progressive, even as it nominated its more moderate candidate for the presidency. In the next four years, the Democrats may face factional struggles between liberals and opponents who are more progressive, and those struggles may be dramatic, but the underlying glue of party unity when it comes time to do battle with the Republicans seems relatively safe.

The "Trumped" Republican Party remains the much more conservative of the two major parties, a fundamental reality that is unlikely to change, although a matter of degree is still to be settled. Mr. Trump won his electoral support in the primaries across the ideological spectrum, and opposition to him with the GOP also comes from across the spectrum, apparently more tied to his personal approach than to ideology. However, conservative Republicans who oppose Trump are clearly responding not only to his personality, but also to the fact that he is not a reliable conservative. If Trump is to be classified as a moderate however, it is not because he has moderate positions on the issues; rather his place on the spectrum would be a result of a combination of extreme positions, left and right. In addition, he has shown a tendency to favor an economic policy agenda aimed at working class voters, particularly on international trade. That, plus his authoritarian style creates the fear that even if he is a Republican, he is a big government Republican.

Factional struggles within the Republican Party carry the potential for real disruption and party change over the next four years. Even before the Trump candidacy the Republicans were experiencing battles between factions of conservative Republicans in the House caucus that can be understood in Nicol Rae's terms: The stalwarts versus the fundamentalists. The fundamentalists declined to cooperate with then House Speaker John Boehner, deepening gridlock on federal policy. That conflict remains, even as the office of Speaker has passed to Paul Ryan. Ryan's reluctance to endorse Trump was a sign of how deep and wide opposition to Trump remains within the party.

We can expect interesting internal battles within the Republican Party at the state and Congressional district level over the next four years. Trump supporters may span the ideological spectrum, while moderates, stalwarts, and fundamentalists alike will be defending their factional turf in contests for primaries for nominations for the House, Senate, and Governor. In addition, the possibility of a challenge to President Trump in the 2020 primaries cannot be discounted. Moreover, Republican loyalists will be concerned that Trump's populist voters may yet seek expression not only in Republican primaries, but outside the Republican Party.

Whatever factional struggles within the parties can be foreseen, the outlook for the present is that the polarized party system will persist, and with it, policy gridlock. Third-party possibilities aside, the polarized major parties that trace their origin to the 1960s have not changed in concert with a changing world. They remain locked in debates a half-century old, about economics, civil rights, and war and peace. The actual policy issues we face, living as we do in a postindustrial society locked in a global economy, provided the conditions that promoted support for both Trump and Sanders in 2016. These issues demand attention and will not go away. But that attention is likely to prove indecisive and progress marginal at best, at least until one party or the other wins a compelling national landslide at the polls, or until the factional struggles within one or both parties take a turn not currently foreseen.

NOTES

1. Ford was pro-choice, and considered himself a "liberal" on foreign policy because he had always sided with internationalists on foreign policy issues, and particularly with Republican internationalists in Congress and internal party debates.

2. Gerald Ford was recognized by the Kennedy Center with a John F. Kennedy Profiles in Courage Award in 2001.

3. The fact that Keech and Matthews wrote in another era is illustrated by the fact that their chapter on the nomination itself is entitled, "The Convention's Decision."

4. The "gain-deficit" ratio, which claims a nomination is clinched when the front-runner makes gains in the delegate count equaling .36 of the number of delegates needed for the nomination after the gain is just too cute; too complex to offer a simple enough explanation. I prefer to respect "Occam's razor."

5. In her earlier article (2000), Norrander refers to "advocacy" candidates as "agenda-seekers."

6. I remember a conversation with my brother-in-law right after Trump announced his candidacy. My brother-in-law, a venture capitalist, maintained that Trump could not be serious; he was just pushing his brand. I replied that Trump would win the nomination if he emerged as the winner in the primaries, admitting that it was a big "if." And I remained incredulous every time Trump made a gaffe that would have ended most campaigns.

7. All references to public opinion polls in 2016 other than exit polls from the primaries use data from Real Clear Politics: www.realclearpolitics.com.

8. For once, the Republicans had the potential of facing a Democrat who they could call a "socialist" and actually be right!

9. Late polls did show a shift toward Bernie in the state, but historically conservative Democrats have won primaries in Oklahoma.

Chapter Four

The Presidential Election of 2016 in Historical Perspective

The presidential election campaign of 2016 was one of the most unusual, dramatic, and bitter in recent memory. It matched two major party candidates who were about as unpopular as two candidates ever have been in a national campaign. Both were highly controversial and under investigation for suspected scandalous or criminal behavior.

Democrat Hillary Clinton had one of the strongest resumes for a presidential candidate ever: She had been First Lady, U.S. Senator from New York, a previous candidate for the Democratic presidential nomination (2008) and Secretary of State of the United States under president Obama. Now, in 2016, she was being treated, at least by Democrats, as the heir apparent to the presidency. Moreover, she was the first woman to be nominated for president by a major party. But she had been involved in her share of personal controversies (some only by association) during her tenure as First Lady, and now she was involved in a scandal all her own, the product of her use of a private e-mail server in her official role as Secretary of State. She was not only opposed by her political opponents, she was despised by them, and some Democrats did not regard her warmly, either.

Republican Donald Trump was certainly the least experienced presidential candidate ever, probably the least prepared, and possibly personally incapable of holding the office he sought. He had won the nomination over the spirited but ineffective resistance of the leaders of his own party, who continued to vacillate in their support during the general election campaign. There were serious questions about his character and behavior throughout the campaign, along with revelations about previous behavior that only made matters worse.

It seemed that neither candidate could win the election. In a way, neither did. It was unusual, although certainly not unprecedented, that the winner of the popular vote was not elected president. Clinton won the popular vote by 48 percent to 46 percent, while Trump was elected by an electoral vote of 304 to 227. The difference was provided by Pennsylvania, Michigan, and Wisconsin, all three of which had voted Democratic in at least the previous six presidential elections, this time voting Republican, for Donald Trump.

Yet, much in the 2016 presidential election seemed the same as most recent elections. The nation remained closely divided, almost even in the popular vote. The Republicans remained strongest in the South and interior West, while the Democrats remained a coastal party even more so than in recent elections, running strongest in the Northeast and on the West coast. The partisan, ideological, geographic, and demographic structure of presidential elections reflected at least as much stability as change in electoral behavior.

As different as this election felt, evaluating its longer-term meaning requires historical perspective. Providing that perspective on the 2016 election is the purpose of this chapter.

POLITICAL GEOGRAPHY, PARTIES, AND POLARIZATION IN PRESIDENTIAL ELECTIONS

When Donald Trump was elected president by winning a majority of electoral votes without winning the popular vote, it was the second time in five elections that a popular vote winner did not win the presidency. Indeed, while winning the popular vote in four of the last five presidential elections, the Democrats have won the presidency only twice. A study of the popular vote in recent presidential elections, by itself, would lead the observer to conclude that we live in the Democratic electoral age, but that conclusion is not supported when counting actual occupants of the office of president of the United States over the same period of time

These results are a reminder of the importance of states in presidential elections. States are the constitutional building blocks of presidential elections. The people of the states elect the electors who cast the constitutionally decisive electoral votes. Thus, coalitions not only of voters, but of states, decide presidential elections, even when, as is usually the case, the winner of the popular vote is elected.

"As your state goes . . ."

Today, it is common to refer to "red" states and "blue" states in analyzing American elections, the former tending to vote Republican and the latter tending to vote Democratic. There is nothing new about these states voting together mostly as blocs. What is relatively new in historic terms, going back about a half century, is which party these states vote for.

In fact, there has been a remarkably consistent political geography to presidential elections. The same coalitions of states tend to vote together over extended periods of time (Archer, et al. 1988; Archer, et al. 1996; Burnham 1970; Rabinowitz & MacDonald 1986; Reiter & Stonecash 2010; Schantz 1996; Speel 1998; Sundquist 1983). Today's red states in the South and interior West lean heavily toward the Republicans. But prior to the middle of the twentieth century, the South was "solid" for the Democrats, most of the states of the interior West voted Democratic more frequently than they have in the last five decades. Meanwhile, the blue states in the Northeast and down the West coast, today's Democratic base, tended to support the Republicans, the Northeast heavily so. Indeed, parts of New England were as solid for the Republicans as the South was for the Democrats.

This consistent political geography has been marked by a general partisan continuity. The South provided a base of support for the Democratic-Republican Party (see chapter 2), and for the Democrats for about a century and a quarter after their founding in the Jacksonian era. The Northeast was the base for the Federalists, Whigs, and Republicans over the same period of time. As tides in national elections provided victories for one major party or the other, the tendencies of states to provide relatively strong support for one party or the other remained on the whole undisturbed.

Prior to the New Deal age, there was a popular expression that persisted beyond the time of its meaning: "As Maine goes, so goes the nation." It was considered a useful guide, because Maine once held state elections in September, and they were treated as a harbinger for national elections to come in November. It seemed to work, because prior to the New Deal, the Republicans always carried Maine, and nearly always won national elections. Louis H. Bean, who made a name for himself by predicting against all the polls that President Truman would win in 1948, used a method of forecasting based on the relative standing of the states in their support for the major parties. He revised the saying by pointing out that "As your state goes, so goes the nation." His point was that all states generally followed the national curve in their voting behavior, although some were relatively Democratic, and some relatively Republican. Variations of state electoral behavior, when they occurred, could be explained by short-term issues that may make a difference, usually a small one. The data Bean (1948) used extended from 1896 through 1944, and during that period there was very little shifting in the relative patterns of partisan support among the states, even during the New Deal realignment.

There has been one major disruption, a partisan realignment of the states starting in the middle of the twentieth century, reaching a turning point between

1964 and 1972. Since then, today's coalitions have been roughly in place, red states for the Republicans and blue states for the Democrats.

The Political Geography of Electoral Realignment

Realignment theory organizes the history and analysis of elections around the proposition that there is an electoral sea change in American politics about every thirty or forty years. Critical realignment usually results in some combination of a new majority party, new electoral coalitions, a new governing coalition, and a new policy agenda. The literature is rich with the original conceptualizations of realignment (Burnham 1970; Key 1955, 1959; Sundquist 1983), applications of realignment theory (Andersen 1976, 1979; Bartels 1998, 2000; Clubb, Flanigan & Zingale 1990; Reiter & Stonecash 2010; Speel 1998; Wilson 1985), efforts to offer the dealignment alternative (Burnham 1978; Ladd 1978, 1981; Ladd with Hadley 1978; Silbey 1991); to critique the fundamental assumptions and usefulness of realignment theory (Mayhew 2002), or to revive or defend the concept of realignment (Burnham 1991, 1996; Campbell 2006; Paulson 2000, 2007; Stonecash 2006).

The importance of realignment theory to the analysis that follows is the difference between "surge" realignment and "interactive" realignment, conceptualized by Clubb, Flanigan, and Zingale (1990). Surge realignment involves persistent change in aggregate shares of the vote between parties, usually resulting in a new majority party and governing coalition. Surges have defined the most generally recognized electoral realignments in American history, such as when the Democrats emerged as the majority party in the 1830s, or when the Republicans won the presidency in 1860, or when the Republicans claimed majority party status in 1896, or when the Democrats reclaimed the majority in 1932. Interactive realignment involves crosscutting change within the electorate reflecting emerging interests and cleavages in American politics. Interactive realignments may reveal change in electoral behavior along geographic, demographic, cultural, or economic lines, and may or may not result in a new majority party or governing coalition.

This book does not seek to relitigate the debate on realignment theory. But, regardless of one's view of the usefulness of the concept of realignment, or even discounting the reality of periodic electoral realignment in American politics, there has been at least one compelling realignment in our history which reached a turning point about a half century ago. Often missed, this realignment did not generally involve a persistent aggregate surge, or result in a new majority party. But it was an "interactive" realignment, involving crosscutting electoral change in the relative partisan vote for the major parties in states, regions, and political subcultures. The realigning process itself took almost a half century to complete, starting in 1948, reaching critical proportions in presidential elections between 1964 and 1972, and extending to Congressional elections by 1994. Umbrella parties predated this interactive realignment, while today's polarized party system is the result.

Table 4.1 shows correlations of the vote at the state level in presidential elections, from 1880, the first election after the end of Reconstruction through 2016. These correlations measure the relative partisan standing of the states much more than they do aggregate shifts of support in the electorate toward one party or the other. All elections are correlated with 1896, the realigning election in which Republican William McKinley defeated Democrat William Jennings Bryan; 1932, the first New Deal election; 1964 for the Republicans, the nomination of Barry Goldwater for president; 1972 for the Democrats, the nomination of George McGovern; and the very close elections, a century apart, of 1916 and 2016.[1]

The state level vote for each party is correlated positively for all elections between 1880 and 1944, the last reelection of FDR. The state votes for both parties between 1880 and 1944 are correlated negatively with almost all elections starting in 1964. While correlations would be expected to be temporal, that is, to have declining, if positive correlations as time passes, two observations counter that explanation. First, the positive correlations are reasonably steady across more than six decades. Second, there is a sudden shift focusing on 1964 through 1972, to negative correlations with the 1880 through 1944 elections. From 1964 through 2016, the state votes for both parties in almost all elections are positively, and in most cases strongly correlated.

In 1948, the year of the Dixiecrat revolt, Democratic correlations are negative with all previous elections and with 1952 and 1956, and positive with all but two elections starting in 1960. Meanwhile, Republican correlations between 1948 and 1960 remain positive with 1880 through 1944, and negative with most subsequent elections.

In 1964, for the first time, the state votes of both parties are negatively correlated with 1880 through 1944, and positively correlated with almost all elections after 1964. That patterns persists after 1964, with notable qualifications in 1968, 1976, and 1980. In 1968, the third-party candidacy of George Wallace influences the correlations. With the base of his vote among Southern Democrats, the state votes for Vice President Hubert H. Humphrey looks very much like the liberal Democrats of elections to follow. The Republican vote for Richard M. Nixon, however does not resemble future patterns for Republicans. With Southern Democrats, who would later be "Reagan Democrats" voting for Wallace, Nixon's 1968 correlation with 1964 is negative, and his correlations with most subsequent Republicans positive but low. In 1976, Democrat Jimmy Carter of Georgia gains enough support from South-

Table 4.1 Correlations of Vote by States in Presidential Elections 1880–2016

Democrats					Election	Republicans				
1896	1916	1932	1972	2016		1896	1916	1932	1964	2016
.62	.77	.73	−.58	−.23	1880	.67	.73	.74	−.55	−.48
.63	.79	.78	−.61	−.40	1884	.56	.71	.74	−.48	−.33
.64	.87	.84	−.60	−.31	1888	.68	.86	.86	−.65	−.46
.37	.65	.56	−.47	−.20	1892	.78	.88	.88	−.77	−.33
1.00	.73	.67	−.66	−.47	1896	1.00	.78	.70	−.69	−.39
.82	.94	.86	−.68	−.28	1900	.83	.93	.84	−.72	−.30
.52	.89	.80	−.60	−.11	1904	.61	.90	.82	−.67	−.26
.66	.94	.86	−.66	−.26	1908	.74	.94	.88	−.75	−.36
.53	.92	.86	−.60	−.14	1912	.55	.73	.70	−.62	−.14
.73	1.00	.88	−.68	−.27	1916	.78	1.00	.90	−.75	−.35
.58	.91	.79	−.70	−.21	1920	.67	.90	.82	−.68	−.30
.47	.86	.79	−.64	−.16	1924	.72	.91	.95	−.73	−.40
.47	.80	.77	−.36	−.11	1928	.49	.73	.76	−.56	−.18
.68	.88	1.00	−.60	−.32	1932	.70	.90	1.00	−.72	−.38
.76	.90	.93	−.63	−.24	1936	.75	.89	.94	−.70	−.29
.60	.88	.86	−.60	−.10	1940	.64	.88	.85	−.67	−.20
.57	.89	.84	−.56	−.08	1944	.61	.87	.84	−.65	−.17
−.21	−.41	−.29	.30	.02	1948	.47	.63	.62	−.69	−.17
.29	.59	.58	−.32	.02	1952	.29	.55	.57	−.37	−.12
.41	.51	.64	−.31	−.18	1956	.55	.73	.79	−.66	−.30
−.18	.06	.08	.33	−.39	1960	.26	.48	.49	−.30	.09
−.60	−.75	−.71	.68	.51	1964	−.69	−.75	−.72	1.00	.55
−.66	−.67	−.70	.89	.67	1968	.26	.55	.56	−.23	.17
−.66	−.68	−.60	1.00	.69	1972	−.56	−.66	−.53	.70	.67
−.06	.31	.44	.43	.43	1976	.01	.30	.41	.17	.36
−.15	.27	.30	.40	.50	1980	−.40	−.07	−.02	.40	.61
−.57	−.30	−.20	.82	.74	1984	−.49	−.34	−.18	.49	.67
−.53	−.50	−.37	.87	.69	1988	−.52	−.51	−.33	.62	.85
−.35	−.10	−.03	.69	.73	1992	−.54	−.62	−.61	.75	.73
−.56	−.27	−.24	.76	.82	1996	−.62	−.49	−.45	.67	.75
−.58	−.33	−.31	.72	.88	2000	−.58	−.43	−.40	.62	.85
−.62	−.42	−.42	.81	.93	2004	−.59	−.46	−.43	.62	.87
−.62	−.49	−.51	.78	.94	2008	−.60	−.54	−.52	.63	.91
−.58	−.39	−.41	.74	.97	2012	−.56	−.43	−.42	.59	.92
−.47	−.27	−.32	.69	1.00	2016	−.39	−.35	−.38	.55	1.00

Correlations are Pearson's r calculated by the author. Data drawn or derived from Dave Leip, www.uselectionatlas.org (accessed April 6, 2017).

ern Democrats that he carries ten of eleven Southern states. Even that would not have been possible without the black vote, virtually nonexistent in much of the South before the 24th Amendment and the Voting Rights Act. Thus, Carter's state level vote across the country is positively correlated with elections both before and after 1976, and that pattern holds for 1980. After 1980, consistent negative correlations of the Democratic vote with elections before 1944, and positive correlations with elections starting in 1964 are restored and have remained in place.

Figures 4.1 and 4.2 illustrate the difference between surge and interactive realignment among the states in presidential elections. Figure 4.1 compares the surge realignments of 1896, won by the Republicans, and 1932, won by the Democrats. Each map covers four elections immediately during and after each realignment, and the maps look very different. After 1896, the Republicans carried the Northeast, the upper Midwest and the West Coast, while the Democrats held the Solid South and parts of the interior West. The surge that accompanied the New Deal realignment was much more decisive. In his four elections, particularly the first two of them, Democrat Franklin D. Roosevelt nearly swept the country. He won the Solid South, of course, but also most of the Northeast and West. The only two states that voted Republican more than twice between 1932 and 1944 (indeed all four times) were Maine and Vermont, the only states to vote Republican against FDR in the record landslide of 1936.

The search for interactive realignments for the same periods on figure 4.2 does not reveal the same results. The two maps are very similar. After both 1896 and 1932, the Republicans are strongest in the Northeast, the Democrats in the Solid South, and party strength seems to spread westward, although the West Coast shifts from the Republicans to the Democrats. What makes the difference in majority parties is that electoral results surge about evenly everywhere toward the Democrats in 1932. But even in the face of the surge realignment for the New Deal, there was almost no evidence of a simultaneous interactive realignment among the states.

Figure 4.3 illustrates both the surge realignment and the unprecedented interactive realignment that occurred in the middle of the twentieth century. States are sorted according to which party carried them in most elections during each era. The two periods are comparable because the national results are so similar in each time. Between 1880 and 1944, there were seventeen presidential elections, the Republicans winning nine, and the Democrats eight. Between 1964 and 2012, there were thirteen presidential elections, the Republicans winning seven and the Democrats six. Therefore, figure 4.3 indicates both which party won which states most of the time, and the relative strength of the parties in the states in each era. We see the pattern discussed above: Between 1880 and 1944, the Democrats enjoyed the support of the Solid South and parts of the interior West, while Republicans drew their support from the Northeast, a swath of states across the North, and down the West Coast. Since 1964, Democrats have drawn their support from the Northeast quadrant and the West Coast, while Republicans have

1896–1908

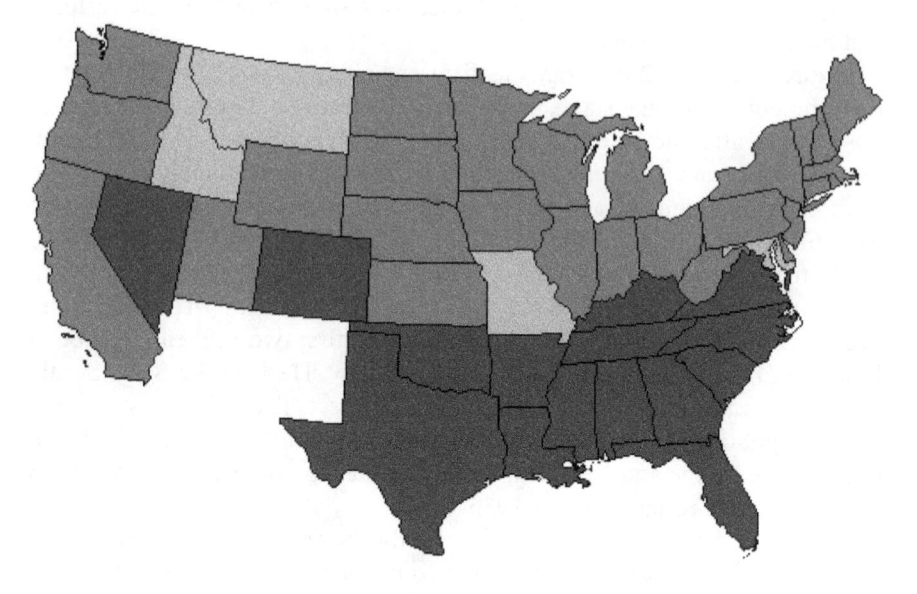

1932–1944

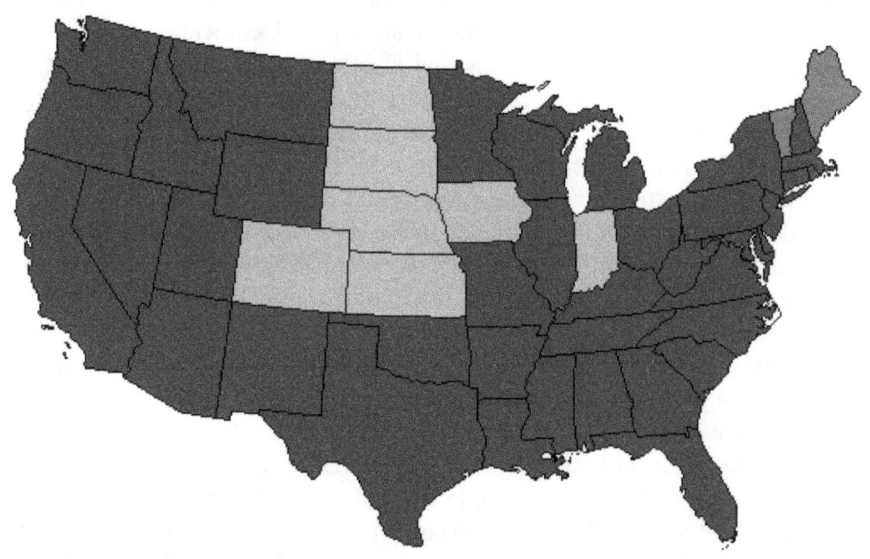

Figure 4.1 Surge Realignment of States in Presidential Elections 1896–1944. Darkest=Democratic, Gray=Republican. States sorted with a party voted at least three times for that party in the era. States voting twice for each party are in the lightest shade.
Derived from Dave Leip, www.uselectionsatlas.org

1896–1908

1932–1944

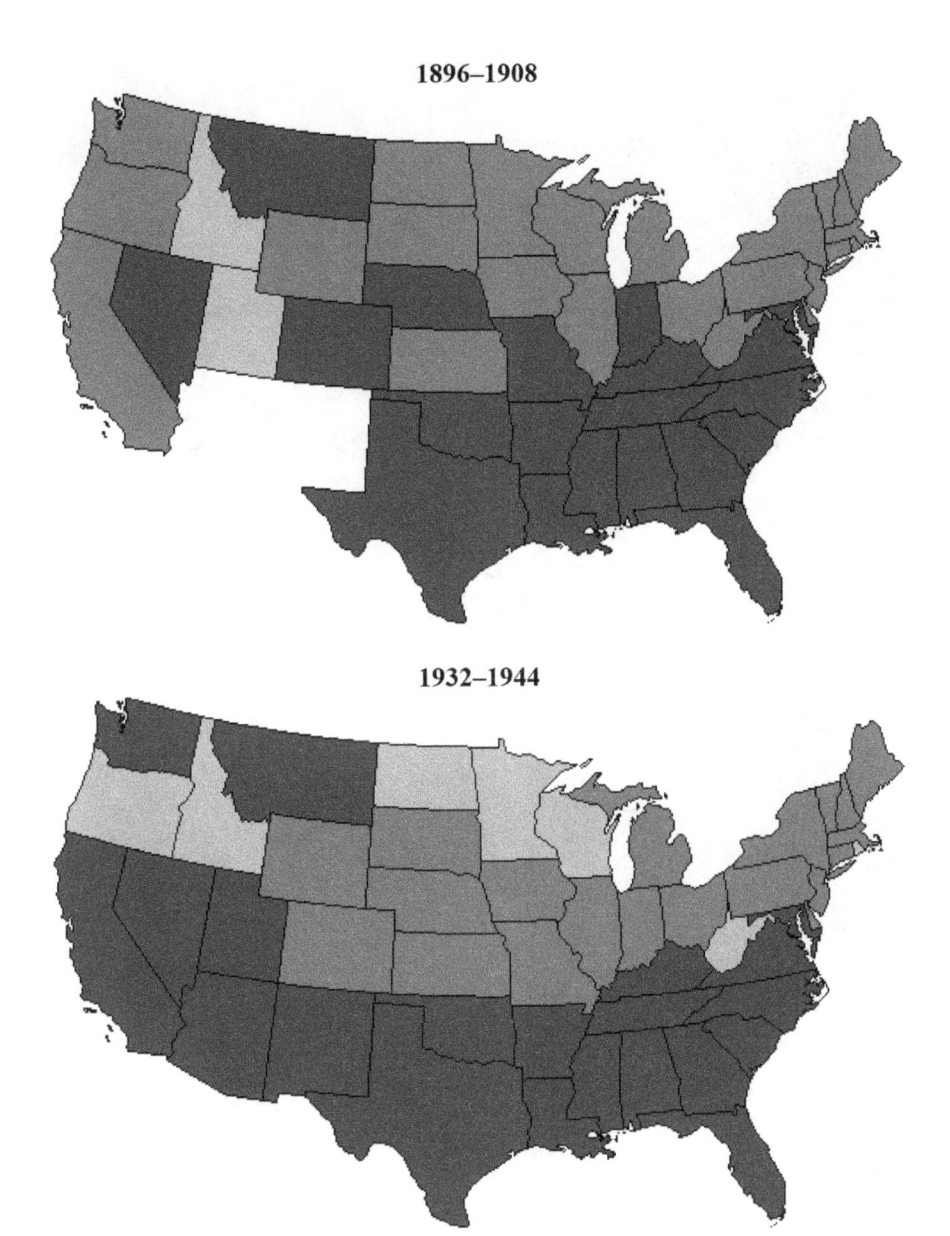

Figure 4.2 Interactive Realignment of States in Presidential Elections 1896–1944. Darkest=Democratic, Gray=Republican. States sorted according to percentages of the vote relative to the national vote. States of the lightest shade voted more strongly for each party, relative to the national vote, twice in the indicated era.

Data drawn or derived from Dave Leip, www.uselectionatlas.org

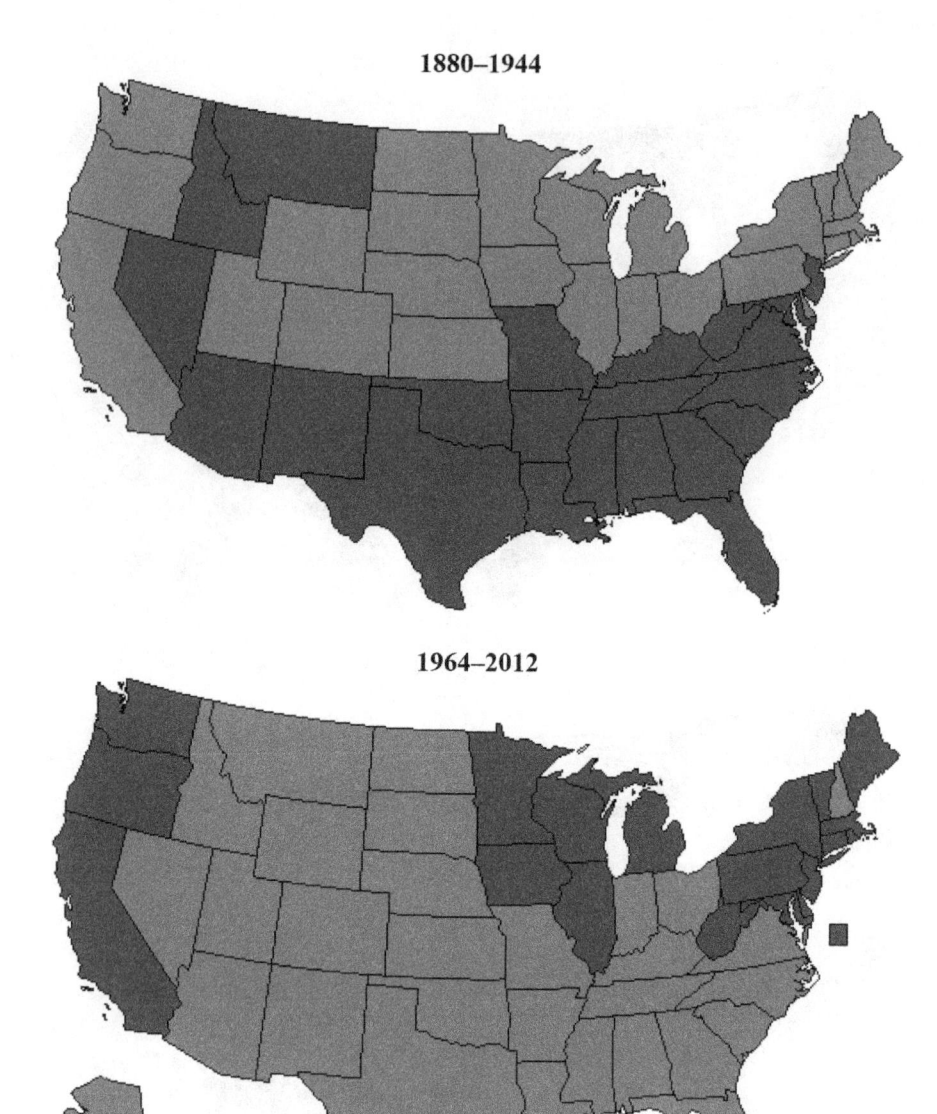

Figure 4.3 Realigning Coalitions of States in Presidential Elections 1880–2012. Darker=Democratic, Lighter=Republican. There are seventeen elections between 1880 and 1944, nine won by the Republicans and eight by the Democrats; and thirteen elections between 1964 and 2012, seven won by the Republicans and six by the Democrats. States shaded according to the party that carried the state in most Presidential elections in the indicated era.

Data drawn or derived from Dave Leip, www.uselectionatlas.org

found their base in the South and interior West. Thus, the dramatic interactive realignment really did not break up the coalitions of states. Instead, the coalitions of states go through a partisan reversal almost intact. The result is that the electoral map of the United States after 1964 is a virtual mirror image of the electoral map prior to 1944.

Polarized Presidential Elections

Since 1964, polarized presidential elections have been the rule, characterized by the interactive realignment among the states discussed above. The elections of 1964 through 1972 were not generally recognized as realigning at the time, for two reasons. First, there was little evidence of a persistent surge realignment favoring either party in presidential elections. Second, the 1964 through 1972 elections have been followed by extensive periods of divided government between the Presidency and Congress (see chapter 5).

However, had it not been for Watergate and its electoral consequences, a critical realignment may have been more evident. Between 1968 and 1988, the Republicans won five out of six presidential elections, and without Watergate, probably would have won all of them. The only exception was 1976, immediately after Watergate. Watergate was, of course, costly for the Republicans, Jimmy Carter was the most centrist candidate the Democrats could have nominated, and the 1976 presidential election was the least polarized of any since 1964, matching two moderates as the major party candidates (Carter versus Ford). Moreover, had President Ford not pardoned Richard Nixon, he may have been elected even under those circumstances.

As it is, Nixon was elected president twice, the second time by a landslide. Ronald Reagan was elected president twice by large margins, the second time by a landslide, and George Bush was elected in 1988. The base of conservative Democrats that voted for George Wallace in 1968 reflected the swing vote for the next two decades, both in the electorate and in Congress. In fact, between John F. Kennedy and Barack Obama, all three Democrats who won presidential elections were Southerners who could appeal to conservative Democrats.

Post-polarization presidential elections have, of course, not been uniform in their results. If the two decades following 1968 was a Republican era, presidential elections have been much more closely contested for these last two decades. Since 1992, the Democrats have won four of seven presidential elections, and have won the popular vote in six out of seven, although it has hardly been a Democratic era. Four of the elections have been very close, two were cliff-hangers, and the election of 2000 took thirty-six days to settle in the Florida controversy (Ceaser & Busch 2001). None of the presidential elections for the past quarter century have been landslides.

Moreover, for most of the last two decades, the Republicans have held majorities in both houses of Congress.

Even in the presence of electoral change, however, the relative strength of the political parties across the states has remained consistent. Figure 4.4 indicates some evidence of surge realignment of the states between the first two decades of the post-polarization era and the second two decades, from the series of Republican victories to much more closely contested presidential elections. But there has not been the same interactive realignment. Across the last half century, the Republicans have run strongest in the South and interior West, while the Democrats have gained their best support from the Northeast and down the West Coast. Today's electoral maps of red states and blue states are not of recent origin. See figure 4.5.

The Polarizing Issues

Nor are the issues that polarize all of recent origin. Related issues of "modern" versus "traditional" values have lingered across time in American politics (Jensen 1978), with remarkably consistent patterns of support reflected in the political geography of American elections. Most of today's most compelling issues, new in their particulars, inherit continuing interests and ideological ingredients from past debates. Race has consistently been the most divisive of American issues, although the particulars have changed from slavery, to segregation versus desegregation, to affirmative action, to police and community relations. National authority versus states' rights has been an issue of contention back to the founding of the republic. Economic issues, from the National Bank to industrialization to free silver to international trade to the welfare state to postindustrial modernization have always carried serious cultural implications.

Table 4.2 offers a general summary of issues across time in American politics and the patterns of support they have generated.

The issues listed on table 4.2 are all issues that are polarizing, or were in their own time. But they were not always both polarizing and partisan as issues are today. Some, such as the National Bank and slavery, had definite patterns of partisan support. President Andrew Jackson hoped to disable the National Bank, for example, with the support of most Democrats. And the Republicans were born as an antislavery party, although they disagreed internally on how to achieve that end. But polarization on most of these issues occurred as much or more within parties among factions as between the major parties. The most pronounced example of intraparty conflict on a polarizing issue, of course, is the Democrats on the issue of racial equality.

Over the past five decades, polarizing issues have become partisan.

1968–1988

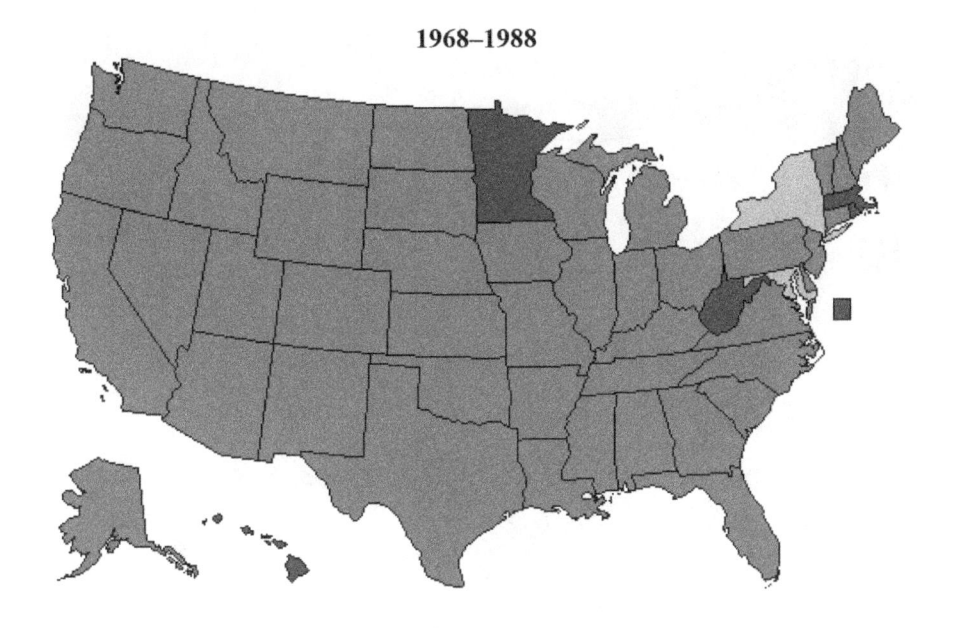

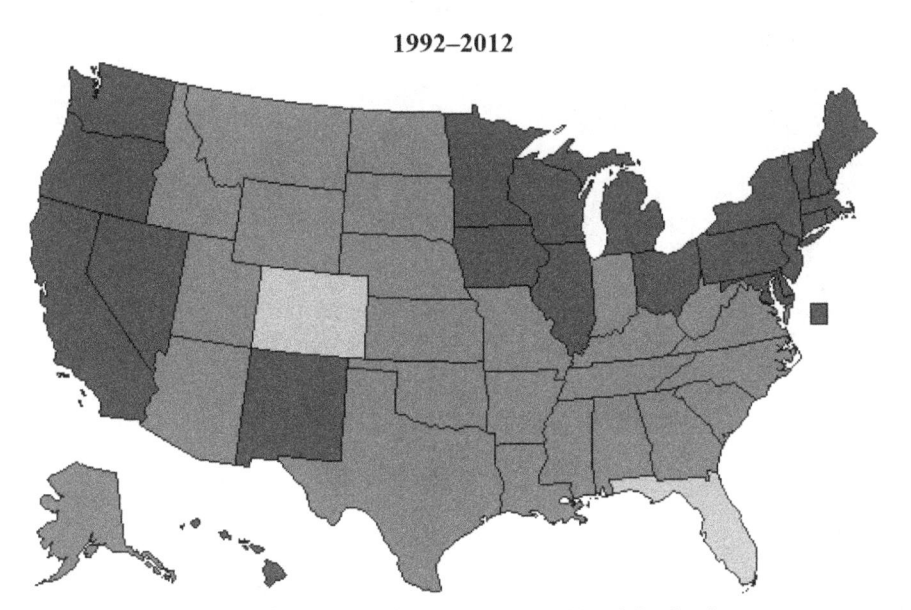

1992–2012

Figure 4.4 Surge Realignment of States in Presidential Elections 1968–2012. Darkest=Democratic, Gray=Republican. There are six presidential elections in each era. States voting for each party an equal number of times are of the lightest shade.
Data drawn or derived from Dave Leip, www.uselectionatlas.org

1968–1988

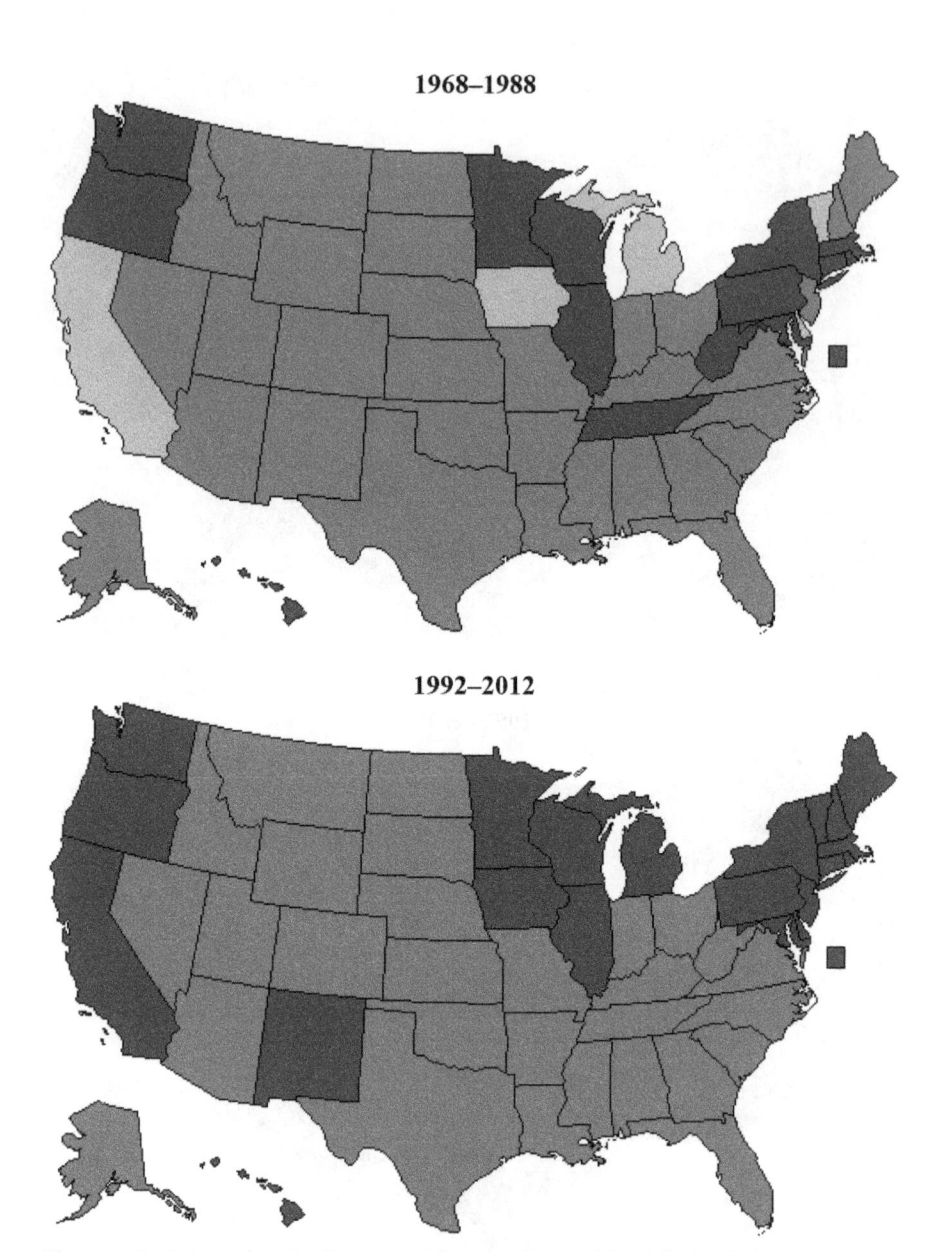

1992–2012

Figure 4.5 Interactive Realignment of States in Presidential Elections 1968–2012. Darkest=Democratic, Gray=Republican. States sorted according to percentages of the vote relative to the national vote. States of the lightest shade voted more strongly for each party, relative to the national vote, three times in the indicated era.

Data drawn or derived from Dave Leip, www.uselectionatlas.org

Table 4.2 "Modern" vs. "Traditional" Values in American Politics

Issue/Alignment	Modern Values	Traditional Values
Geographic Base	Northeast, West Coast	South, interior West
Constitutional ratification	Federalist	Anti-Federalist
Constitutional interpretation	Loose Construction	Strict Construction
Centralization/Decentralization	National Authority	States' Rights
National Bank	For	Against
Slavery	Against	For
Industrialization	For	Against
Free Silver	Against	For
League of Nations	For	Against
Foreign Policy	Internationalism	Isolationism, Nationalism
International Trade	Free Trade	Protectionism
Civil Rights	For	Against
Vietnam War	Against	For
Economy	Government intervention	Free Markets
Welfare State	For	Against
Abortion	Pro-Choice	Pro-Life
Entitlement Reform	Against	For
Iraq War II	Against	For
National Health Insurance	For	Against
LGBT Rights	For	Against
Postindustrial modernization	For	Against
Political Party	Republicans 1854–1910 Democrats 1948–	Democrats 1830–1912 Republicans 1964–

Labels reflect generalizations of support and opposition among political actors at the times of the salience of each issue.

THE PRESIDENTIAL ELECTION OF 2016

As unconventional as the campaign was, and as different as it felt, there was more stability than change in the results of the presidential election of 2016.[2] The country remained closely divided between the major parties, as it has been for most of the last two decades, and the electoral coalitions of the two parties remained largely intact. The popular vote for both parties remained highly correlated at the state level with recent elections (table 4.1). The correlations between 2016 and 2012 was .97 for the Democrats, and .92 for the Republicans. The Democratic coalition of blue states remained based in the Northeast and on the West Coast, while the Republican coalition of red states was based in the South and interior West. See figure 4.6.

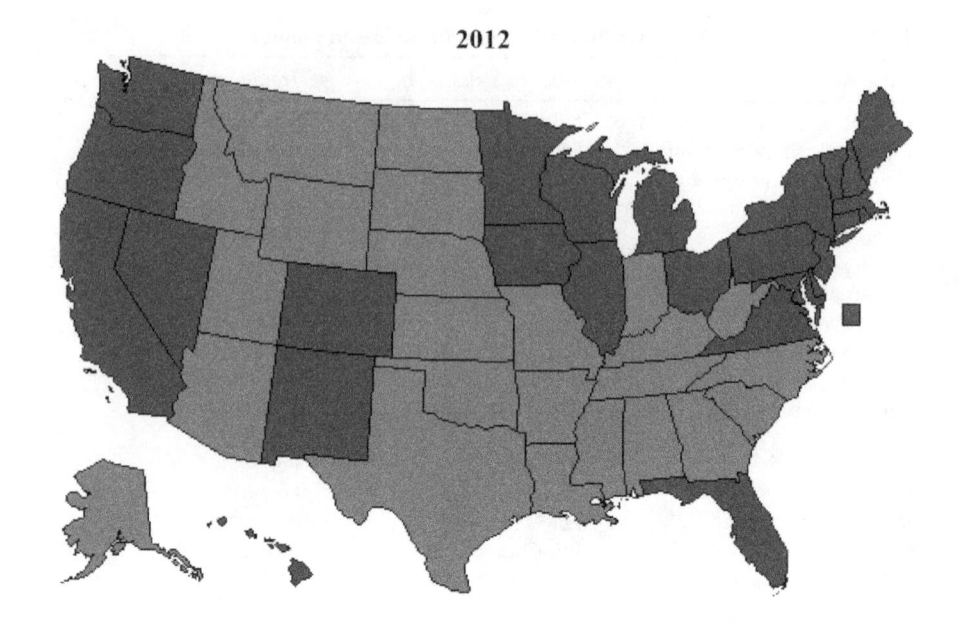

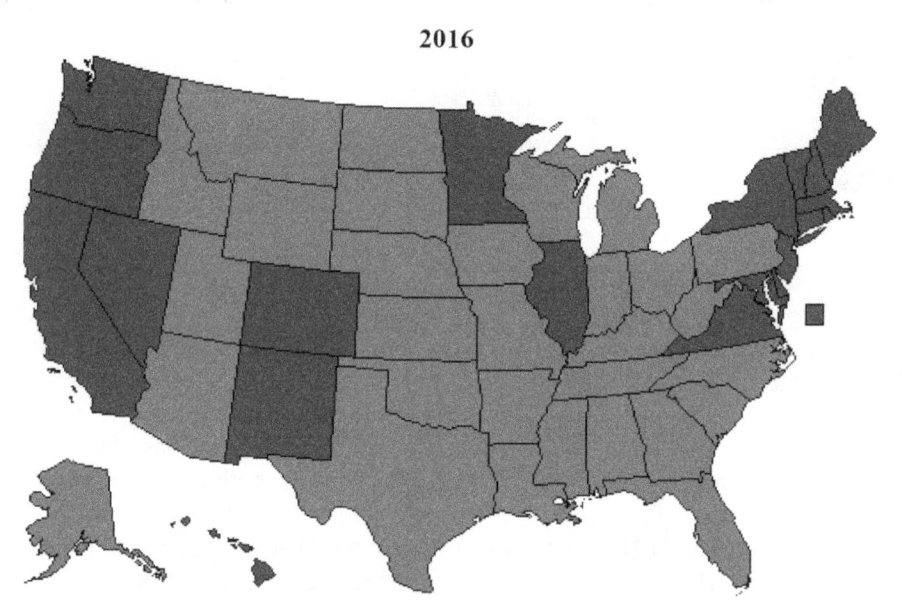

Figure 4.6 States in Presidential Elections 2012–2016. Darker=Democratic, Lighter=Republican.

Data drawn or derived from Dave Leip, www.uselectionatlas.org

Demographic patterns of support for the two parties generally persisted. The racial divide and gender gap remained definitive factors in electoral behavior, as did the split between urban and rural voters. Trump won among whites, particularly white men, and rural voters, while Clinton won among nonwhites, particularly African Americans, women, and urban voters.

Underneath these generalizations, pockets of change caused an unexpected result. However limited the electoral change in 2016, it proved decisive, delivering a victory in the Electoral College to Donald Trump and making him the 45th president of the United States.

States in the 2016 Presidential Election

Democrat Hillary Clinton won the popular vote by 48 percent to 46 percent over Republican Donald Trump in 2016. The result represented a decline of three percentage points of the total vote for the Democrats, and two percentage points of the two-party vote. Trump actually lost a percentage point of the total vote for the Republicans, while gaining one point in the two-party vote.

There were few surprises among the states, as almost all clung to their recent partisan leanings. If states had followed the national curve uniformly, Clinton would have lost three states from among those President Obama carried in 2012: Florida, Ohio, and Virginia. In fact, she narrowly lost Florida and Ohio. She carried Virginia, probably because she selected Senator Tim Kaine of Virginia as her running mate for vice president. Had she lost only Florida and Ohio, she would have won the electoral vote by 285 to 253. Had she lost all three, she still would have won a cliff hanger, 272 to 266.

As it is, six states flipped, all from the Democrats to the Republicans, delivering the election to Donald Trump. In addition to Florida and Ohio, Pennsylvania, Michigan, Wisconsin, and Iowa all voted for Trump after voting for Barack Obama twice. While Florida and Ohio are swing states, Pennsylvania and Michigan had voted Democratic for the previous six presidential elections, while Wisconsin had voted Democratic for the previous seven. Iowa had voted Democratic in six of the previous seven presidential elections. Generally, the most pronounced Republican gains in 2016 are found in areas that have experienced economic decline, disproportionately in rural areas or small cities with a manufacturing or mining base.

Florida provided little surprise in its switch to Trump. In 2012, President Obama carried Florida by less than a percentage point, about 73,000 votes. In 2016, Donald Trump carried Florida by 49 percent to 47 percent, a margin of about 113,000 votes. Florida was following the national trend line, voting slightly more Republican than the country in both elections, providing no extraordinary surprise.

While Clinton's loss of ground in Florida, at three percentage points, was no greater than would be indicated by the shift in the national curve, her losses in the five states across the North that flipped ranged from four points (in Pennsylvania) to ten (in Iowa), generally increasing as one moves West along the Great Lakes and the Ohio River Valley.

Ohio votes close to the national curve, generally following the trend line. In 2012, President Obama carried by Ohio by 50 percent to 48 percent. In 2016, Trump carried Ohio by 51 percent to 43 percent. Republican gains in Ohio were a little stronger than the national trend, as Trump gained three percentage points while Hillary Clinton lost seven. Trump made his most impressive gains along the Ohio River, from Youngstown to Cincinnati, and in the Lake Erie corridor of suburbs between Cleveland and Toledo, both areas where mining or manufacturing were once the base of the economy and have declined.

Michigan, Wisconsin, and Pennsylvania were the three states with very close finishes whose switch from the Democrats to the Republicans provided Trump with the critical electoral votes he needed. All three states had consistently voted Democratic and more Democratic than the country in recent elections, but in 2016, voted Republican and more Republican than the country.

The closest finish among these states came in Michigan, which Trump carried by barely 11,000 votes, 47.3 percent to 47 percent. In 2012, President Obama defeated Mitt Romney here by ten points. In 2016, Trump gained two points, Clinton lost seven. Trump padded the Republican advantage in central Michigan and the Upper Peninsula, but made his biggest gains in the South, around Detroit, where manufacturing has been in decline. For example, Obama carried the blue collar suburbs of Macomb County by four percentage points in 2012. In 2016, Trump carried Macomb County by twelve points. Trump carried the more white collar Oakland County by seven points, about the same margin Romney won the county in 2012. Meanwhile, Hillary Clinton won by large margins in the cities but actually lost ground there, about seven percentage points in Detroit, and twelve points in Genesee County around Flint.

In 2016, Donald Trump carried Wisconsin by 23,000 votes, well under a percentage point. Clinton held her own in around Milwaukee and Madison, but lost ground everywhere else in the state. The North and West of Wisconsin, closely contested in recent elections, voted heavily for Trump in 2016, giving him his narrow victory in the state.

In Pennsylvania, Trump won by 44,000 votes, also less than a percentage point. The electoral map of Pennsylvania for 2016 is consistent with previous years: The Democrats carried Philadelphia and its metropolitan area, and Pittsburgh, while the Republicans carried almost everything else. But the margins differed. Clinton carried both Philadelphia and Pittsburgh by margins similar to Obama's and carried the Philadelphia suburbs by increased margins. But she lost five to ten percentage points generally almost everywhere else, as Trump swept central Pennsylvania. Erie County in the Northwest gave stronger evidence of the trend than most places on the map of Pennsylvania. Around Erie, where manufacturing has been an important base to the economy, President Obama won by fifteen points in 2012; in 2016, while Trump won by two points in 2016. Clinton lost twelve points, while Trump gained seven.

Iowa has drawn less attention that the other states that flipped from Democratic to Republican, partly because it is not as large and has fewer electoral votes, and partly because its finish was not as close. But the vote in Iowa is nonetheless revealing. Donald Trump carried Iowa by 51 percent to 42 percent, Trump gaining about five points over Romney's performance, and Clinton losing about ten points from Obama's. In 2012, Obama carried Des Moines and most of Eastern Iowa, while Romney carried most of the West. In 2016, Clinton carried Des Moines and scattered smaller cities, while Trump carried almost everything outside the Des Moines area.

Thus, Trump's gains in Iowa are more extensive than in any of the other states that switched columns, even though Iowa's economy has not suffered so much, either generally or in the face of international trade. The explanation seems to be that Iowa is more white and rural than the other states that flipped and more white and rural than the country.

According to exit polls, 90 percent of Iowa's voters were white in 2016, compared with 71 percent of all American voters. That difference proved decisive, although Iowa's white voters were not as Republican as the country's. Trump carried the national white vote by twenty points, while winning the white vote in Iowa by fourteen. The composition of the Iowa electorate also differed from the nation with regard to the interaction between race and higher education. Half of the American electorate reported earning a college degree, and voted for Clinton by ten points, while the half that reported no college degree voted for Trump by seven. Nationally, whites with a college degree voted for Trump by three points, and those with no degree voted for Trump by thirty-five points, well over 2–1. In Iowa, 43 percent of voters reported having a college degree, and voting for Trump by two percentage points, while 57 percent reported no degree, and voted for Trump by fourteen points. Meanwhile, 40 percent of all Iowa voters were white with a college degree and voted for Trump by five points, while half of all Iowa voters were white with no college degree, and voted for Trump by twenty points. Thus, Iowa's white voters voted for Trump by smaller margins than national white voters, and even white voters without a college degree yielded smaller margins than the same demographic nationally. But on balance the composition of the Iowa electorate played decisively to Trump's favor.

Perhaps the biggest demographic advantage for Trump in Iowa was its rural vote. According to census data, more than half of all Iowans live in rural areas. According to exit polls, 39 percent of Iowa voters reported themselves to live in rural areas (compared with 17 percent nationally in polling data). Trump won among rural voters in Iowa with 63 percent of the vote.

Trump also added another additional electoral vote, carrying the heavily rural inland Congressional district of Maine while losing the coastal district and the state to Clinton.

Exit Polls: The People

Like the electoral map, exit polls reveal more stability than change in the 2016 presidential election, with continuing evidence of a culture gap in American political life. There were, however, pockets of decisive change. See tables 4.3 and 4.4.

In 2016, voters continued the recent pattern of voting the party line. About 90 percent of Democrats and Republicans alike voted for the nominee of their party. Voters also followed their ideological inclinations, 84 percent of self-identified liberals voting Democratic, and 81 percent of self-identified conservatives voting Republican. Also following the recent pattern, a healthy plurality of moderates voted for the Democrat.

The racial divide, so central to electoral behavior as it is to American life, remained pronounced. With Barack Obama no longer heading the Democratic ticket, African-American turnout was down slightly as a share of the electorate, and the Democratic margin very slightly reduced. The decline in turnout and Democratic margins in Detroit, however, may have been enough to cost Hillary Clinton Michigan. Nationally, she won the black vote with 88 percent, down from 93 percent for President Obama in 2012.

Meanwhile, the anticipated expansion of Hispanic and Latino support for the Democrats, expected because of Trump's reference to Mexican "rapists" in his announcement of candidacy and because of the hard-line positions he took on immigration, did not materialize. Clinton won Hispanics by better than 2–1, but her 36-point margin was down from 47 points for Obama in 2012.

The gender gap remained in place. Women generally have been offering more support to Democrats than Republicans for over three decades, and consistently voting Democratic since 1992. Once again in 2016, women voted Democratic by 12 percentage points, while men voted Republican by 12 points. In 2012, women voted Democratic by 10 points, while men voted Republican by 8. One might have expected a greater gender gap than the one that materialized in 2016, as Hillary Clinton was the first woman to win the

Table 4.3 Exit Polls in 2012 and 2016 Presidential Elections (By Population Characteristics)

	2016 D	2016 R	2012 D	2012 R	2012–2016 Net Change	
White (70)	37	58	39	59	R	1
African-American/Black (12)	88	8	93	6	R	2
Hispanic/Latino (11)	65	29	71	27	R	3
Asian (4)	65	29	73	26	R	5
Female (52)	54	42	55	44	0	
Male (48)	41	53	45	52	R	1
Urban (34)	60	34	62	36	R	1
Suburban (49)	45	49	48	50	R	1
Rural (17)	34	61	41	57	R	6
Age 18–29 (19)	55	37	60	37	R	2
Age 30–44 (25)	50	42	52	45	0	
Age 45–64 (40)	44	53	47	51	R	3
Age 65 + (15)	45	53	44	56	D	2
Under $30,000 (17)	53	41	63	35	R	8
$30,000–$50,000 (19)	51	42	57	42	R	3
$50,000–$100,000 (31)	46	50	46	52	R	1
$100,000–$200,000 (24)	47	48	44	54	R	4
Over $200,000 (10)	47	48	44	54	R	4
Protestant (52)	39	58	42	57	R	2
Catholic (23)	45	52	50	48	R	4
Jewish (3)	71	24	69	30	D	5
White evangelical, born again (26)	16	81	21	78	R	5
None (15)	68	26	70	26	R	1
College degree (50)	52	42	50	48	D	4
No college degree (50)	44	51	51	47	R	6
Married (58)	43	53	42	56	R	2
Single (42)	55	38	62	35	R	5
LGBT (5)	78	14	76	22	D	7

Net change = Change in two-party vote. Numbers in parentheses are percentages of the sample in 2016.
Source: Exit Polls 2012 and 2016, as reported by the *New York Times* https://www.nytimes.com/interactive/2016/11/08/us/politics/election-exit-polls.html and CNN, http://edition.cnn.com/election/results/exit-polls (both accessed April 6, 2017).

nomination of a major political party for the presidency, and Donald Trump displayed a pattern of speech and conduct that, despite his claims to the contrary, displayed disrespect to women. But the gender gap showed only minor expansion, and according to exit polls, the female vote for the Democratic ticket was actually down from 55 percent in 2012 to 54 percent in 2016.

The differences in party support between urban and rural areas drew significant attention in the days after the 2016 election. According to exit polls,

Table 4.4 Exit Polls in 2012 and 2016 Presidential Elections (By Party, Ideology, and Issues)

	2016 D	2016 R	2012 D	2012 R	2012–2016 Net Change	
Democrats (37)	89	9	92	7	R	3
Republicans (33)	7	90	6	93	D	1
Independents, other (30)	42	48	45	50	0	
Liberals (26)	84	10	86	11	0	
Moderates (39)	52	41	56	41	R	2
Conservatives (35)	15	81	17	82	R	1
Country on "right track" (33)	90	8	93	6	R	2
Country "off track" (62)	25	69	13	84	D	13
Approve Obama (53)	84	10				
Disapprove Obama (45)	6	90				
Most important issue:						
Economy (52)	52	42	47	51	R	7
Terrorism (18)	39	57				
Foreign Policy (13)	60	34	56	33	R	1
Immigration (13)	32	64				
Economy excellent (3)	83	16				
Economy good (33)	76	19	90	9	R	11
Economy fair (41)	39	55	55	42	R	15
Economy poor (21)	15	79	12	85	D	4
Immigration:						
Closer to legalization (70)	60	34	61	37	D	2
Closer to deportation (25)	14	84	24	73	R	11
International trade creates jobs (38)	59	35				
International trade costs jobs (42)	31	65				
International trade neutral (11)	63	30				

Net change = Change in two-party vote. Numbers in parentheses are percentages of the sample in 2016.
  Source: Exit Polls 2012 and 2016, as reported by the *New York Times*, https://www.nytimes.com/interactive/2016/11/08/us/politics/election-exit-polls.html and CNN http://edition.cnn.com/election/results/exit-polls (both accessed April 6, 2017).

Clinton won 60 percent of the urban vote, while Trump won 61 percent in rural areas. Trump won a narrow plurality in the suburbs. While issues of economic decline in small towns and rural areas reflect a reality of the American and global political economy, the urban-rural divide follows a long-established pattern, with the difference only slightly increased in 2016.

Younger voters supported the Democrats, and older voters the Republicans in 2016, following the pattern of the previous three elections. The difference between the youngest and oldest voters did not match those of the Obama elections, but surpassed the differences in 2004, when younger voters offered relatively strong support for John Kerry over George W. Bush.

The role of religion in voting behavior was relatively unchanged, remaining a central element of the cultural divide. Protestants have voted Republican as a habit, as 58 percent of them did in 2016. Catholics, swing voters in recent elections, cast 52 percent of their votes for Donald Trump. Jews increased their support for Democrats, to about 3–1. As has often been the case, religiosity seemed to have more to do with the vote than religion itself. Despite behavior that might be offensive to people of faith with deep moral convictions, white evangelicals and "born agains" remained with the party that seems to appeal to most of their values, voting for Trump by 5–1. Meanwhile, voters identifying with no religion voted for Clinton by 68 percent to 26 percent.

Marital status remained an important factor in voting behavior. Married voters cast 53 percent of their votes for Trump, while Clinton won 55 percent of the votes of "singles." Meanwhile, 78 percent of self-identified LGBT voters supported Clinton.

The two noticeable demographic characteristics associated with electoral change decisive in Trump's victory and yielded evidence of his populist support were income and education.

As usual, voters reporting the lowest incomes voted most heavily Democratic, but by significantly reduced margins. About 52 percent of voters with incomes under $50,000 annually voted for Clinton. Trump won among all voters with incomes above $50,000, winning about half their votes and small pluralities at every level of income up the ladder. Moreover, the difference in the vote at the lowest and highest levels of income were greatly diminished in 2016. The Democratic vote among voters with incomes under $30,000 was about six percentage points higher than among voters with incomes over $200,000. This compares with differences in the same comparison of 19 percentage points on 2012, 23 points in 2008, and 25 points on 2004.

This is consistent with the shift among voters toward the Republicans in communities with declining economies, as proved decisive in Pennsylvania, Ohio, Michigan, and Wisconsin.

This evidence of economic frustration combines with the cultural divide in the difference in voting behavior between people who have college degrees and those who do not. In 2016, voters with a college degree cast 52 percent of their votes for Hillary Clinton, while those without a degree yielded 51 percent of the vote for Donald Trump. By comparison, President Obama narrowly won both groups in 2012, with those without college degrees voting slightly more heavily for him than did people with college degrees.

Exit Polls: The Issues

As usual, retrospective voting played an important role in the 2016 vote (Fiorina 1981). See table 4.4. While 90 percent of the voters who felt the country is on the "right track" voted for Hillary Clinton, the two-thirds of the electorate who felt the country is "off track" cast 69 percent of their votes for Donald Trump. A small majority of voters approved of President Obama's performance in office, and 84 percent of them voted for Clinton. The large minority of voters who disapproved of President Obama cast 90 percent of their votes for Trump.

Among those who believed that the economy was in good or excellent condition, about 80 percent voted for Clinton, but among those who reported that they considered economic conditions fair or poor, about 63 percent voted for Trump. Not coincidentally, the proportion of those groups was about the same as the "right track" versus "off track" question. A little under two-thirds were dissatisfied with the economy.

Populism on globalization issues worked for Donald Trump. While Clinton actually won 52 percent of the vote among all voters who identified the economy as the most important issue, immigration and international trade delivered votes to Trump in numbers that matched the feeling during the campaign. Moreover, Trump voters were the more decisive. Those who agreed with Trump on immigration and international trade voted more heavily for him than voters who agreed more with Clinton voted for her. Among the 13 percent of voters who identified immigration as the most important issue, Trump won by 2–1. On immigration, only 25 percent leaned with Trump toward deportation of undocumented immigrants as the solution, but 84 percent of them voted for him. Among the 70 percent who leaned more toward a path to legalization, 60 percent voted for Hillary Clinton. On international trade, among the 42 percent who agreed with him that trade hurts American jobs, Trump won by 34 points, better than 2–1. Among the 38 percent who thought trade produces jobs, Clinton won by 24 points, about 3–2.

The "Inversion of the New Deal Order" Returns?

Crosscutting issues of globalization, particularly immigration, international trade, and the decline of the industrial employment, had the impact of driving working-class voters toward Donald Trump, while attracting upper-middle-class voters to Hillary Clinton. Trump made gains for the Republicans not only in the North central states he took from the Democratic column, but also across the border states, which produced enlarged Republican majorities, and in areas in other blue states, such as on Long Island, in the Hudson Valley, and in upstate New York; in central and South New Jersey; in outstate Minnesota; and in downstate Illinois. Clinton made scattered gains in the upscale suburbs around Philadelphia, Chicago, Los Angeles, and even Houston and Dallas-Fort Worth.

While split-ticket voting has become rare in the polarized party system, these areas of partisan change also produced the most frequent cases of Congressional districts carried by one party for the presidency and the other party for the House. Trump made the obvious appeal for working-class voters in his campaign. At the same time, Clinton made a less observed but nevertheless vigorous appeal for upper-middle-class voters, particularly with the bid for frustrated members of the "party of Lincoln" at the Democratic National Convention.

The election results were not as "unprecedented" as Donald Trump appeared to be. They were more like a copy of what Everett Carll Ladd (1978, 1980, and with Hadley 1978) referred to in the 1970s as the "inversion of the New Deal order," or what Kevin Phillips (1969) called "the emerging Republican majority." The inversion shows working class voters, once referred to as "Reagan Democrats," voting for Trump to flip the string of blue states across the North.

This inversion of class voting, even if it accurately describes electoral behavior in the future, does not necessarily indicate that a Republican majority is necessarily reemerging. The other ingredient of the "inversion of the New Deal order" is the shift of more upscale voters, moved by cultural issues, toward the Democrats. This shift brings to mind not only the identification of a top and bottom vs. the middle coalition by Apter (1964) and Burnham (1978) discussed in chapter 1, but the "postmaterialist" progressivism conceptualized by Ronald Inglehart (1977, 1981). According to Inglehart, "postmaterialist" values emphasized cultural issues, moving beyond the material economic issues of the industrial age. The Clinton campaign certainly offered a more "postmaterialist" perspective than either Bernie Sanders in the primaries or Donald Trump in the general election.

The reemergence of "inversion" may or may not be a long-term factor. Although working class conservatism persisted to some degree after the electoral turning point of 1964 to 1972, policy change including tax cuts, a reduction in government commitments to discretionary social services, and three recessions helped revive class voting in the late twentieth century. The great recession produced a class-based retrospective voting in the election of Barack Obama in 2008. Moreover, the inversion itself reduced rather than erased Democratic advantages among working-class voters in 2016.

Certainly the 2016 election did not produce a new majority party. The Republicans won the presidency and both houses of Congress, but did not win the popular vote for president. While some electoral change from recent elections was notable, it was not clear it would persist, and it did not decisively outweigh evidence of electoral stability. Thus, the results of the 2016 presidential election pose more questions about the future than it offers answers.

LOOKING FORWARD

The characters in the script of the 2016 presidential election focused public attention on the personal rather than the meaning of the election. Is Donald Trump really capable of being president? Does his character merit the office? Is Hillary Clinton really defined by scandal? Were her e-mails disqualifying? Did she lose because of the content and timing of public statements made by FBI Director James Comey? Did the Russians interfere effectively in our election, that is, did they have something to do with altering the result?

These questions are important. Some of them focus on this election and its personalities in particular, although in a globalized world the prospect of international or foreign state actors interfering in national elections is a problem that requires public attention.

But even if Hillary Clinton lost because of Comey's intervention, or because of Russian interference, she also lost for a number of isolated reasons which, if reversed, might have resulted in her election. What if she had not relied on campaigning against the character of Donald Trump and focused more on economic issues? What if she had remembered, as Bill Clinton and she herself once knew, that "it's the economy stupid"? What if she had not made reference to the "basket of deplorables"? What if Hillary Clinton had not made use of a private e-mail server to conduct State Department business at all? Even these questions are asked against the reality that *even so*, Hillary Clinton won the popular vote.

But the meaning of the election, in terms of what it says about American democracy, goes well beyond the fates of Donald Trump and Hillary Clinton, well beyond the next four years, and even beyond the limits of our shores. It is no accident or coincidence that the issues of globalization, immigration, and international trade were also deeply impacting the politics of Europe in 2016, with a similar rise of populism, the plebiscite to withdraw the United Kingdom from the European Union, and several national elections in which crosscutting issues produced some working-class support for nationalism against transnational political institutions. The personalities engaged in these elections, including our own, only serve to dramatize issues of political and economic structure that remain to be resolved.

Chapters 5 and 6 will address two questions about the prospects for American democracy in particular and postindustrial democracy in general.

Chapter 5 will discuss the prospects of governing with polarized parties in the American separation of powers system. We have developed political parties that would fit in a system of parliamentary government, such as we find in other advanced democratic capitalist systems, but ours is not a parliamentary government.

Chapter 6 will discuss outlook for postindustrial democracy in America. Can institutions of government designed in our Constitution in the eighteenth century facilitate public decisions on the issues we face in the twenty-first century?

NOTES

1. Using Pearson's r, I correlated all elections with each other between 1880 and 2016, but for the convenience of presentation selected the chosen elections to be illustrated for their historic purpose. My comments below consider all elections, not just those chosen for illustration.

2. Election data obtained from the *New York Times*, https://www.nytimes.com/elections/results/president and Dave Leip, www.uselectionatlas.org.

Chapter Five

The Irony of Polarization

Parliamentary Parties Without Parliamentary Government

In previous chapters we have examined the rise and fall of umbrella parties, their displacement by polarized parties, and the impact of polarization on presidential nominations and presidential elections. Our focus in this chapter will be on Congressional party polarization in the American separation of powers system.

Polarized party systems are not unusual in today's advanced democratic capitalist systems. Indeed, party systems spanning the ideological spectrum, or polarized parties, are rather common in democracies that link executive powers to parliamentary majorities. But in the United States today, we have polarized parties and policy gridlock. The policy gridlock, however, is not the product of either the separation of powers or polarized parties alone. Rather, policy gridlock in American politics is the product of a combination of the constitutional separation of powers with polarized parties that has emerged over the last half century.

CONGRESSIONAL ELECTIONS AND PARTY POLARIZATION

In the United States, we have a separation of powers system, with staggered elections for the presidency and the two houses of Congress. There is no provision for the sort of party government found in parliamentary systems where a prime minister is the leader of the majority party or coalition. Nevertheless, in the United States, unified control of the executive and legislative branches of government was the rule for most of the two centuries of the republic under the Constitution. Through 1964, thirty-eight of the first forty-five presidential elections resulted in a president whose party enjoyed a majority in both the House of Representatives and the Senate, and unified control of the elected branches was the general rule.[1]

Since 1968, divided government has been the reality more often than not. Since then, the party that won the presidency won both houses of Congress after only six of thirteen presidential elections, losing both houses of Congress on four occasions. The increase in split-ticket voting and divided government, along with declining partisan identification, declining partisan voting, declining voter turnout, was widely interpreted as party decay (Broder 1978; Burnham 1975, 1978; DeVries & Terrance 1972; Jacobson 1990; Ladd 1977, 1978, 1981, 1991; Ladd with Hadley 1978; Silbey 1991; Wattenberg 1990). Elections were becoming less party-centered and more candidate-centered, particularly in elections for the House of Representatives, where incumbents were reelected over 90 percent of the time.

However, split-ticket voting and divided government, growing after the ideological realignment of the parties in presidential elections between 1964 and 1972 (see chapter 4), was not the product of a linear process of party decay. For nearly thirty years after the 1960s, it was better explained by both party decay and party renewal (Paulson 2000, 2007, 2015), namely the decline of umbrella parties along with the development of polarized parties.

Although President Johnson was elected by a landslide that greatly increased Democratic majorities in Congress in 1964, evidence of the sort of split-ticket voting that would prevail over the next thirty years emerged in that election. While the South trended toward Senator Barry Goldwater of Arizona, the Republican nominee for president, the Solid South remained intact in the Congressional elections, with conservative Democrats winning reelection, even in the deep South states carried by Goldwater.

Thus, the advantages enjoyed by virtually all incumbents of both parties in House elections did not have a neutral partisan or ideological impact on Congress. Between 1968 and 1988, the Republicans won five out of six presidential elections, while the Democrats retained control of the House all of the time and the Senate most of the time. The swing voter for most of that period was the Southern conservative Democrat, who would vote for Republicans Richard M. Nixon, Ronald Reagan, and George H. W. Bush for president, while voting for an incumbent Democrat for the House or Senate (Paulson 2000, 2007). James Q. Wilson (1985) called it "realignment at the top, dealignment at the bottom."

Electoral realignment took another turn in 1994, when the Republicans, led by Newt Gingrich and campaigning on a national platform of their "Contract for America," won control of both houses of Congress for the first time in four decades. The Republicans won 230 seats in the House to 204 Democrats, a gain of 54 seats, and 53 seats in the Senate to 47 for the

Democrats. All Republican incumbents running for reelection to the House or Senate, or as Governor, won. Clyde Wilcox (1995) called the election the "latest American Revolution" and Walter Dean Burnham (1996) proclaimed that "realignment lives!"

It was no surprise that the Republicans had gained seats in the House and Senate in 1994. The party out of the White House almost always gains seats at the midterm election. But the magnitude of the victory was stunning. President Clinton had at least modest approval ratings and the economy was performing reasonably well. The "surge and decline" of seat change in midterm elections (A. Campbell 1960; J. Campbell 1985, 1986, 1987, 1993) which argued that losses by a president's party at the midterm are related to the size of the president's election and coattails two years before, would have predicted Republican gains in 1994, but on the much smaller scale. Clinton had been elected two years earlier with a modest plurality, and the Democrats had actually lost ten House seats in 1992.

The 1994 Congressional election was certainly not one in which the "normal" vote prevailed. Indeed, not only had the Republicans won both houses of Congress, they had also won a majority of seats from the once solid Democratic South in both houses. The Southern conservative Democrats who had been hanging on to their seats had slowly disappeared over the years, either by retirement, defeat for renomination in Democratic primaries, or defeat for reelection. The 24th Amendment to the Constitution and the Voting Rights Act had decisively expanded the share of African Americans in the Democratic electorate across the South, to the electoral detriment of conservative Democrats in primaries.

By 1994, electoral change across the South had reached critical proportions, with national consequences. For three decades, Southern conservative Democrats had been a national swing vote, but now their numbers in the electorate and in Congress were depleted. Voters whose demographic characteristics indicated they were Southern conservative Democrats were, by 1994 and thereafter, voting Republican.

What had happened over three decades was not so much "dealignment" as it was a secular realignment in Congressional elections. Coalitions that had emerged in presidential elections in the ideological realignment of 1964 to 1972 had spread to the states, and had persisted over two decades since 1994. Table 5.1 illustrates electoral change in the Republican vote at the state level in elections for the House of Representatives between 1946 and 2014, two Congressional elections in different electoral eras in which the Republicans took over both houses of Congress with impressive midterm gains. The Republicans polled 53 percent of the national vote for the House in 1946, and 51 percent in 2014. Table 5.1 demonstrates that in most states, the change was

Table 5.1 Republican Vote for House of Representatives by State, 1946–2014

State	1946	1948–1962	1964–1992	1994	1996–2012	2014	Net Change
South Carolina	0	5	38	57	58	64	64
Louisiana	6	9	21	**	57	66	60
Georgia	0	10	29	55	58	59	59
Arkansas	2	16	49	52	48	61	59
Alabama	8	10	35	56	58	65	57
Texas	5	13	35	53	55	60	55
Mississippi	0	3	30	42	51	53	53
Florida	19	26	45	51	55	54	35
Tennessee	30	32	44	55	52	62	32
Oklahoma	41	38	42	58	62	70	29
Arizona	33	46	56	61	55	56	23
Virginia	33	32	48	55	52	54	21
North Carolina	39	33	43	54	51	55	16
Utah	52	52	54	63	58	62	10
Wyoming	56	56	59	56	59	66	10
Kentucky	54	41	44	59	58	63	9
Idaho	56	51	55	65	61	63	7
Missouri	52	43	42	48	49	59	7
Montana	49	47	48	46	58	55	6
West Virginia	50	43	34	34	34	55	5
Indiana	55	52	49	57	53	59	4
Kansas	60	56	59	63	61	63	3
South Dakota	63	57	49	38	52	66	3
Ohio	57	53	52	53	51	59	2
New Mexico	48	43	51	58	45	47	−1
New York	45	51	45	51	37	42	−3
Pennsylvania	58	51	48	46	48	55	−3
Nevada	59	44	38	61	53	56	−3
Nebraska	68	60	63	64	69	64	−4
Rhode Island	45	39	42	30	28	39	−6
Colorado	56	49	51	60	51	50	−6
Maryland	48	45	41	51	39	41	−7
Illinois	56	51	48	54	45	48	−8
Iowa	62	57	50	58	53	53	−9
Washington	58	56	44	49	43	48	−10
California	52	49	48	51	42	41	−11
Minnesota	59	50	45	49	43	47	−12
New Jersey	60	53	48	55	46	48	−12
Michigan	61	50	46	52	47	47	−14
New Hampshire	62	59	58	60	52	48	−14
Wisconsin	66	54	48	54	51	52	−14
North Dakota	72	63	47	46	44	56	−16
Connecticut	57	51	47	51	41	39	−18

Table 5.1   Continued

State	1946	1948–1962	1964–1992	1994	1996–2012	2014	Net Change
Delaware	57	51	50	73	60	37	−20
Maine	63	57	54	50	37	39	−24
Oregon	65	53	41	42	40	40	−25
Vermont	64	62	66	48	30	31	−33
Massachusetts	54	47	32	39	19	17	−37

Sources: Jerrold G. Rusk, *A Statistical History of the American Electorate* (Washington, DC: CQ Press, 2001); and the website of the Clerk of the House of Representatives at http://history.house.gov/Institution/Election-Statistics/Election-Statistics (accessed May 27, 2017).
** Louisiana Representatives elected by majorities in a non-partisan primary in 1994.

gradual, but moving in one direction across the years. The states are listed in the order of the net magnitude of Republican gains. Note that the Republicans make their most significant gains in the South. The top nine states in Republican gains are all from the South, and all eleven of the South appear among the top thirteen states on the list. Most of the rest of the states where Republicans gained the most ground are among today's red states in the heartland and interior West, and most of these states were reliably Democratic until the middle of the twentieth century. Note also that most of the states at the bottom of the list are among today's blue states, solidly Republican until the 1960s, where the Democrats have gained ground. It is a reversal of partisan patterns in Congressional elections that mimics the direction of electoral change in presidential elections, albeit at a slower pace.

Since 1994, national electoral coalitions in Congressional elections have almost matched the national electoral coalitions found for the most part in presidential elections since the 1964 to 1972 ideological realignment. Split ticket voting has declined, and partisan voting has revived to the point that about 90 percent of voters nationally vote for the candidates of their party in both Presidential and Congressional elections. In four of the last six presidential elections, the party winning the presidency has also won both houses of Congress. In 2016, every Senate race was won by the party that carried the state in the presidential election.

Incumbency advantages in House elections, enhanced to some extent by House districts gerrymandered in state legislatures, remain a major factor in divided government when it occurs. The Republican gain of 64 seats in the House in the 2010 midterm elections almost guaranteed that the Republicans would retain the House in 2012, even if President Obama were reelected, as was the case.

But the electorate no longer has the partisan and ideological makeup that structurally makes divided government likely, as it did between 1968 and

1994. The swing vote is no longer a large number of conservative Democrats inclined to vote Republican for president. With partisan voters loyal to the party line, today's swing vote is a smaller number of independents, more moderate on the issues. This electorate makes unified government more likely than it was before 1994. Incumbency advantages in House elections aside, when a presidential election produces divided government it is likely to be the product of a small number of ticket splitters in a closely divided electorate.

Evidence of the revival of straight ticket party line voting in presidential and Congressional elections is illustrated on table 5.2, which displays correlations between the vote for President and the House at the state level. The correlations are consistently high from the end of Reconstruction to the middle of the twentieth century. Then, negative correlations appear in 1948, the year of the Dixiecrat revolt, and during the ideological realignment of 1964 to 1972. Thereafter, the correlations are positive again, but low, and do not climb until after 1994. In the last two presidential elections, the state level correlations again reach about .90.

Electoral maps provide the same illustration. The maps featured in figures 5.1 and 5.2 are both constructed according to the party that carried each state more often in each era. Figure 5.1 covers the era that began with the realignment of 1896, and continues through the three decades starting with the New Deal realignment. Figure 5.2 covers the period since the ideological realignment of 1964 to 1972. The same pattern of electoral change discussed in chapter 4 concerning presidential elections emerges again here, with the important wrinkle of split-ticket voting and divided government that occurred for thirty years after the ideological realignment in presidential elections.

At the turn of the twentieth century, and until the 1960s, the Republicans found their electoral strength across the Northern tier of the United States (Speel 1998). The Democrats found their electoral support across the Southern tier, starting with their base in the Solid South, and following migration patterns into the Southwest. The electoral maps of the states for Presidential and Congressional elections in the post-1896 era are almost identical.

Figure 5.1 also illustrates the emergence of a Democratic majority after 1932. But the political geography remains mostly undisturbed. The Democrats still have their base in the Solid South, with their support extending across to the Southwest. While the Democrats gain ground in the North, the Republicans still find the base of their support there, and, as demonstrated in chapter 4, continue to run stronger across the North than they do nationally. Moreover, patterns of support in the states for the two parties in presidential elections continues to be generally consistent with the patterns of support found in Congressional elections.

Table 5.2 State Level Correlation of Vote for President and House, 1880–2016

	Democratic	Republican
1880	.94	.95
1884	.96	.94
1888	.99	.94
1892	.91	.94
1896	.60	.72
1900	.98	.97
1904	.97	.98
1908	.93	.96
1912	.96	.65
1916	.94	.93
1920	.95	.93
1924	.93	.89
1928	.79	.81
1932	.88	.89
1936	.86	.92
1940	.92	.96
1944	.94	.93
1948	–.23	.47
1952	.83	.79
1956	.73	.84
1960	.37	.75
1964	–.19	–.29
1968	–.20	.80
1972	–.04	.02
1976	.59	.61
1980	.31	.22
1984	.45	.45
1988	.32	.30
1992	.20	.14
1996	.47	.68
2000	.65	.69
2004	.50	.72
2008	.65	.62
2012	.89	.93
2016	.90	.86

Correlations are Pearson's r calculated by the author. Data drawn or derived from Dave Leip, www.uselectionsatlas.org. Jerrold G. Rusk, *A Statistical History of the American Electorate* (Washington, DC: CQ Press, 2001); and from the website of the Clerk of the House of Representatives at http://history.house.gov/Institution/Election-Statistics/Election-Statistics.

110   *Chapter Five*

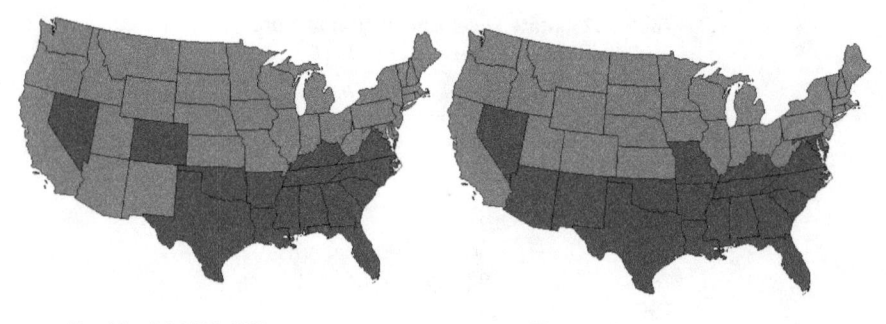

Presidential 1896–1928   **House 1896–1930**

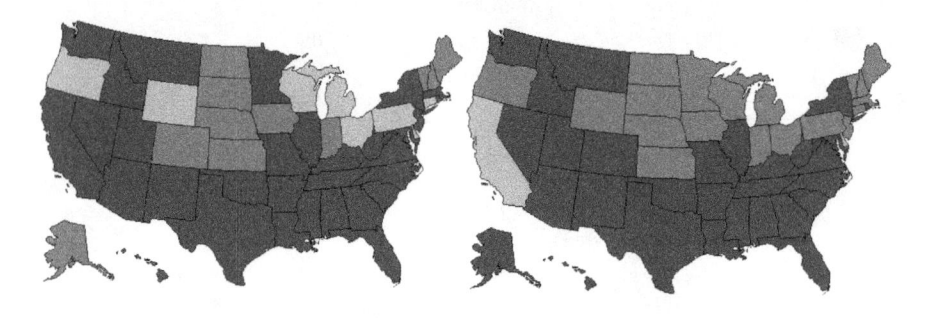

Presidential 1932–1960   **House 1932–1962**

Figure 5.1   States in Presidential and House Elections 1896–1962. States sorted according to party that won total popular vote for the President and House in most elections. Darkest=Democratic, Gray=Republican, and Lightest=states won an equal number of times in the era.

Maps derived from Dave Leip, www.uselectionatlas.org. Data drawn or derived from Dave Leip, www.uselectionsatlas.org, Jerrold G. Rusk, A Statistical History of the American Electorate (Washington, DC: CQ Press, 2001), and from the website of the Clerk of the House of Representatives at http://history.house.gov/Institution/Election-Statistics/Election-Statistics.

Figure 5.2 shows disturbance in the geographic patterns of support after 1964. Starting with the Democratic landslide of 1964, the Republicans gain ground across the South, and take advantage by following a Southern strategy in the decades to follow. The general coalition of states that led to Republican victories in five out of six presidential elections between 1968 and 1988 emerges of the electoral map for the 1964 through 1992 presidential elections. In presidential elections, the Democrats run strongest where their base is developing, in the Northeast. But in Congressional elections, the Democrats still have their base in the Solid South, where incumbent Democrats are winning reelection to the House. The Democratic gains in the Northeast show on the electoral map of House elections, and Democrats retain their share of seats

The Irony of Polarization 111

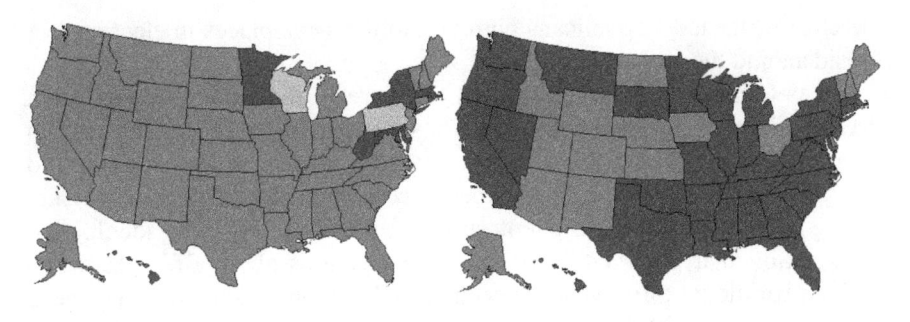

1964–1992 Presidential   **1964–1992 House**

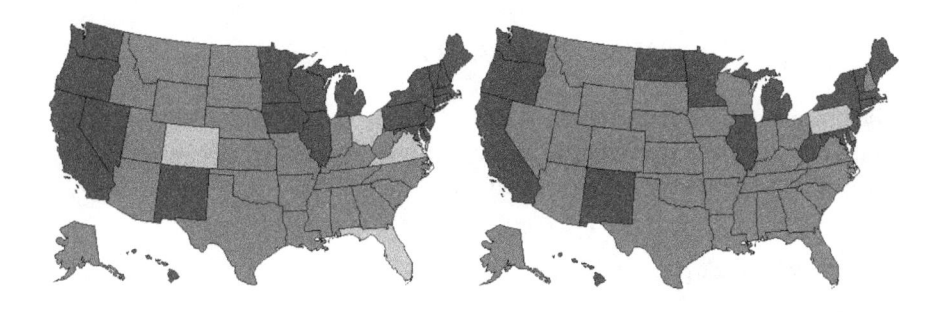

1996–2016 Presidential   **1994–2016 House**

Figure 5.2   States in Presidential and House Elections 1964–2016. States sorted according to party that won total popular vote for the President and House in most elections. Darkest=Democratic, Gray=Republican, and Lightest=states won an equal number of times in the era.

<small>Maps derived from Dave Leip, www.uselectionatlas.org. Data drawn or derived from Dave Leip, www.uselectionatlas.org, Jerrold G. Rusk, *A Statistical History of the American Electorate* (Washington, DC: CQ Press, 2001), and from the website of the Clerk of the House of Representatives at http://history.house.gov/Institution/Election-Statistics/Election-Statistics</small>

in the West, where the Republicans are strongest. There is little resemblance between the party coalitions for president and the House on the maps for 1964 to 1992, which illustrate the pattern that would produce divided government during most of that period.

Convergence between party coalitions in Presidential and Congressional elections has been revived in elections since 1994. The electoral maps of red states and blue states, with which we have become familiar are visible in both Presidential and Congressional elections over the past two decades. The Democrats run strongest in the Northeast quadrant of the country and down the West Coast, while the Republicans run strongest in the South (now nearly solid for the GOP) and in the interior West. Unlike the thirty years after 1964, the Democrats and Republicans both win in the same places in elections for President and the House.

James Campbell (2006) has called this spread of electoral change from Presidential to Congressional elections "staggered realignment." With almost identical electoral coalitions for both parties in Presidential and Congressional elections, we can expect a continued reduction in split-ticket voting, with divided government structurally less likely. The ideological polarization that emerged in presidential elections about fifty years ago took an additional thirty years of secular realignment to spread to the states and Congressional elections, leaving us with today's polarized political parties in a polarized Congress.

THE POLARIZED PARTISAN CONGRESS

The presence of ideological extremes in Congress is nothing new, with polarization on some issues. What is historically new to the American experience is the almost uniform partisanship of ideology.

Ideology and Party Unity in Congress

Although methods of measurement of ideology in Congress differ, studies of voting records yield the observation of a significant increase in both party polarization and ideological polarization in both houses of Congress, as well as an increase in party unity.

For years, Congressional Quarterly measured the presence of the "conservative coalition" in Congress, roll calls on which majorities of Republicans and Southern Democrats would vote on one side of an issue against Northern Democrats. It played a particularly important role on civil rights issues, although most Republicans joined with Northern Democrats in support of the Civil Rights Act of 1964, against the opposition of most Southern Democrats. At the end of the twentieth century, party unity in Congressional voting had advanced to the point that the conservative coalition, as measured at CQ, no longer emerged on roll calls frequently enough to yield useful data (CQ 1999).

Interest group ratings have been commonly used to indicate the ideology of Representatives and Senators. Americans for Democratic Action (ADA), the liberal interest group, has been the most persistent of these groups in terms of longevity. Measurements of support for conservative positions have been conducted by Americans for Constitutional Action (ACA), replaced in recent years by the American Conservative Union (ACU), and there have been numerous other associations whose interests are focused on specialized issues. The ADA has been scoring Congressional voting records on a general range of issues going back to 1947.

While ADA scores are a good indicator of support for liberal positions (and counterindicator of support for conservative positions), they have two drawbacks. First, legislators are scored only on selected roll calls designated as important by ADA. Second, ADA has generally counted an absence on which a legislator is unpaired on an issue the same as a vote against the ADA position.

Over the last three decades, there has been support among academics, and increasingly among journalists as well, for DW-Nominate scores (Poole & Rosenthal 1984, 1985, 1991, 1997) as a valid measurement of the ideology of members of Congress. DW-Nominate scores are calculated on two dimensions. The economic dimension yields the traditional left-right ideological spectrum based on support for government intervention in the economy. The regional dimension measures voting coalitions on issues of historic regional division in American politics. The most important of these is race, but other issues that generated regional polarization are included, such as the National Banks and coinage of silver. The result of DW-Nominate scores is a two-dimensional spatial sorting of legislators which reveals who voted with, or against, whom on a variety of issues.

DW-Nominate scores offer two methodological advantages over ADA scores in assessing a legislator's ideology. First, they are based on virtually all roll calls in the House or Senate over time, rather than specifically picking certain roll calls as indicators. Second, they sort legislators on the two dimensions, based on economic and regional issues. On both dimensions, the DW-Nominate scores scale from -1 (most liberal) to + 1 (most conservative), although most ideological generalizations are based upon the economic left-right continuum.

On the other hand, DW-Nominate scores have two potential drawbacks. First, they are biased toward rating party loyalty. Many roll calls will be procedural and based on party governance in the House or Senate, although they have little to do with a member's ideology. Second, DW-Nominate scores are usually based on a member's entire career, rather than a given year or session. This career measurement is useful, treating the member's "ideal point" of preference in the universe roll call votes, but it also produces a fixed score that does little to measure actual polarization within one session of Congress against another.

However different ADA scores and DW-Nominate scores are, they both provide valid evidence and suggest the same conclusion that party polarization has increased in Congress, to the point that ideology and party unity now are now conflated in roll call voting. Figures 5.3 and 5.4 show the increase in ideological partisans of both parties from 1964, the year the Civil Rights Act passed Congress, and 2015, according to ADA scores. At the time of the Civil Rights Act, the number of Southern conservative Democrats was still substantial. Thus, Republicans collectively were more conservative than the Democrats were liberal. Although moderate-to-liberal Republicans were never as numerous as conservative Democrats, they were much more visible fifty years ago than they are now. Party polarization actually declined slightly into the 1970s, and in 1974, President Nixon was still hoping that a conservative coalition of Republicans and Southern Democrats would save him from impeachment in the Watergate affair. Since about 1980, Congress has become more polarized with the increase in both conservative Republicans and liberal Democrats. Since the Congressional elections of 1994, that increase in polarization has been geometric. Fifty years ago, about half of the members of the House and Senate were ideological partisans, either conservative Republicans or liberal Democrats. Today that number is around 90 percent in both houses. Meanwhile, while the number of moderates in both parties has decreased, both conservative Democrats and liberal Republicans have become virtually extinct.

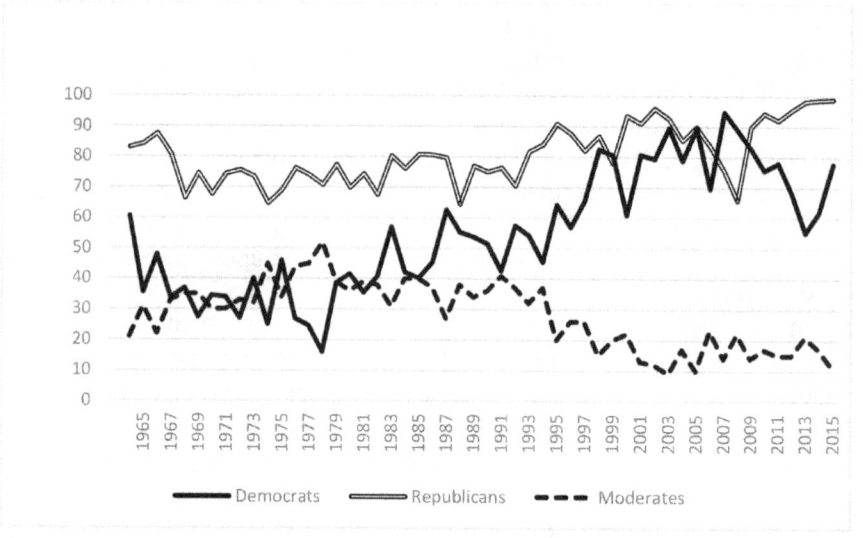

Figure 5.3 Party Polarization in the House 1964–2015 (ADA Scores). ADA scores over 75=liberal, and under 25=conservative. Numbers on the left axis represent percentages of each party who are liberal Democrats or conservative Republicans, and moderates of both parties.

Scores obtained directly from Americans for Democratic Action, and from the ADA website at http://www.adaction.org/pages/publications/voting-records.php

The Irony of Polarization

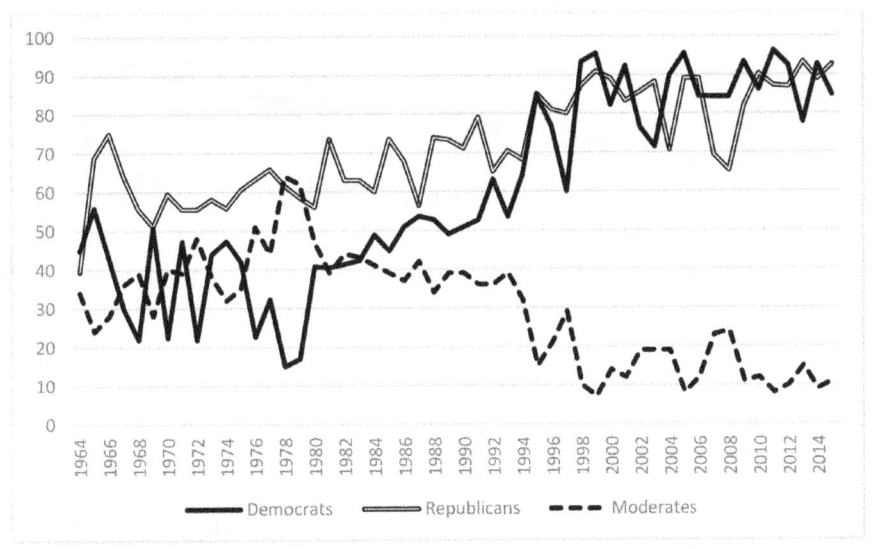

Figure 5.4 Party Polarization in the Senate 1964–2015 (ADA Scores). ADA scores over 75=liberal, and under 25=conservative. Numbers on the left axis represent percentages of each party who are liberal Democrats or conservative Republicans, and moderates of both parties.

Scores obtained directly from Americans for Democratic Action, and from the ADA website at http://www.adaction.org/pages/publications/voting-records.php

The uniformity of party polarization and ideological polarization yields almost compelling party unity in voting in the House and Senate. Figures 5.5 and 5.6 illustrate the increase in both party unity voting in Congress, and party loyalty by the membership, using the party unity scores of *Congressional Quarterly* (Carney 2015). "Party unity" votes occur when a majority of one party opposes a majority of the other party on a Congressional roll call. Party unity votes have increased in frequency from about 50 percent fifty years to ago to about 70 percent in recent years, although the increase has been uneven and halting. The increase in members voting with their party has been steadier and more complete, averaging about 60 to 70 percent about fifty years ago to about 90 percent today.

Party Unity, Public Policy, and Gridlock

Party unity does not necessarily translate into effective government, particularly in the American system. Under the constitutional separation of powers, it would seem that unified party control across the executive and legislative branches would be necessary to productive policy making, and that divided government would frustrate policy making. That may be generally true, but the reality is more complex.

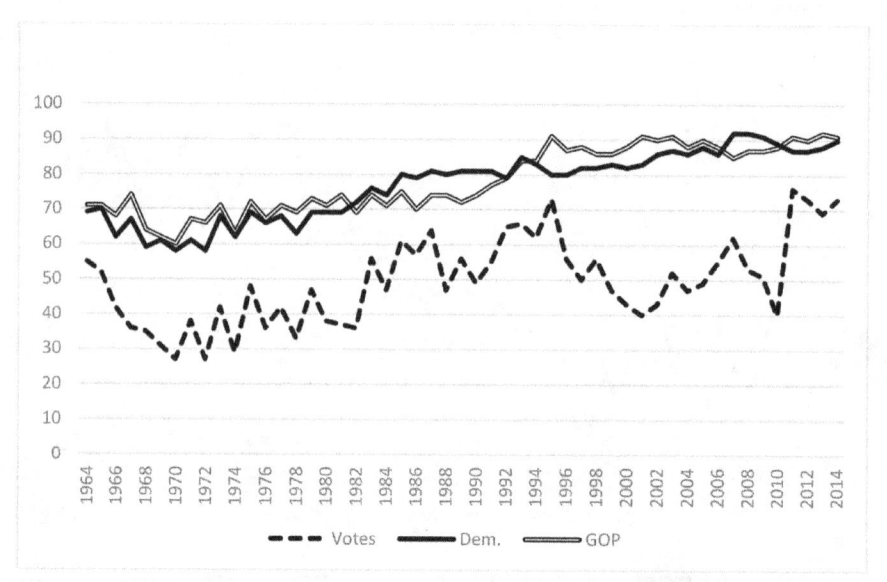

Figure 5.5 Party Unity in the House of Representatives 1964–2014. Numbers on left axis represent percentages of roll call votes classified as "party unity" votes with majorities of one party opposing majorities of the other; and average percentages of Democrats and Republicans voting the party line.
Congressional Quarterly *(Carney 2015)*.

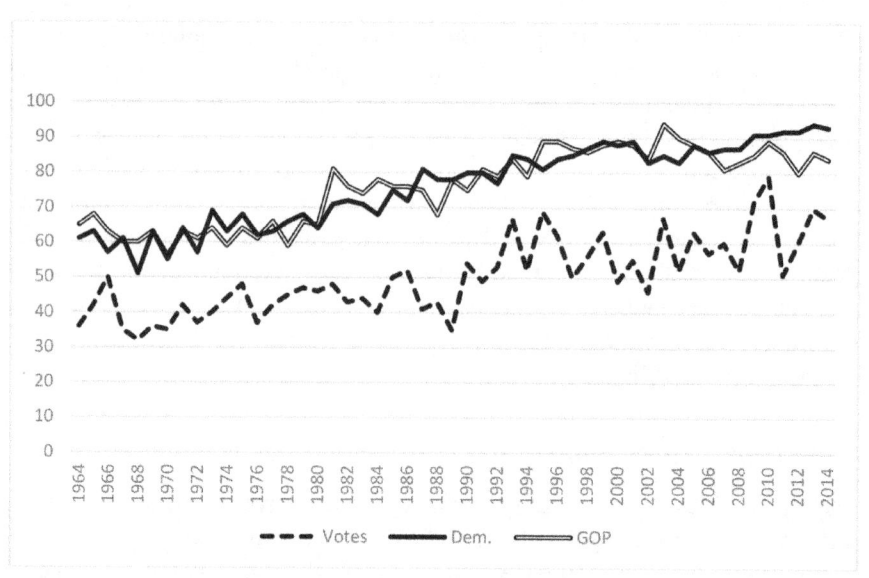

Figure 5.6 Party Unity in the Senate 1964–2014. Numbers on left axis represent percentages of roll call votes classified as "party unity" votes with majorities of one party opposing majorities of the other; and average percentages of Democrats and Republicans voting the party line.
Congressional Quarterly *(Carney 2015)*.

Presidents operating in a system of factionalized umbrella parties occasionally found themselves fortunate enough to have partisan majorities on their side in making policy. Franklin D. Roosevelt enjoyed legislative success with the New Deal and Lyndon B. Johnson with the Great Society after landslides resulted in unified party control of the presidency and both houses of Congress. But at times, presidents were able to use the factions of umbrella parties to produce policy in periods of divided government. For example, Ronald Reagan counted on some support from mostly moderate-to-conservative Democrats to join Republicans in support of tax cuts as recently as 1981.

As political parties in Congress have polarized and unified internally, party control across the branches has become more necessary to policy making, and policy once made has become more vulnerable to reversal when the opposing party wins the presidency plus majorities in Congress. President Clinton pushed an economic program through Congress with Democratic majorities in his first year in office, only have to deal with what effectively became a coalition government after the Republicans won Congress in 1994. While Clinton in the main supported welfare reform as designed by the Republicans, and benefitted from Republican support on international trade, he ultimately only barely survived impeachment in 1999. President Obama was able to narrowly gain the passage of the Affordable Care Act from a Democratic Congress in 2009, and even then, only through the reconciliation process. Republicans campaigned vigorously in favor of repealing the ACA, and in no small part, regained control of Congress on that basis.

However, in the early days of the Trump administration, Republicans who enjoy party control of both elected branches have often been unable to focus on the particulars of legislative packages. In the early days of the Trump administration, Republicans who agree that the Affordable Care Act should be repealed and replaced have been unable to agree on what to replace it with. More recently, President Trump and Congressional Republicans have been successful in passing tax reform legislation, which focuses on about a permanent 40 percent cut in corporate taxes and some personal temporary income tax cuts. The tax reform package also includes a repeal of the individual mandate to buy health insurance under the Affordable Care Act.

On other issues, of course, President Trump has presented an image of executive activity. He has taken stands on issues going back to the 2016 campaign that have built a populist coalition for Trump, but do not necessarily unite Republicans in Congress. There is, for example, little Republican unity on international trade. Most Republicans seem to support his announced withdrawal from the Paris Climate Accords, but they do not provide united support for withdrawal from the Trans-Pacific Partnership, or the renegotiation of NAFTA, or for his approach to NATO. While there may be Republican support for the general direction of Trump administration policy on illegal immigration, the controversies over his executive orders on immigration from selected Muslim countries, whether or not they are "travel bans" and the problems they face in the courts draw attention away from their legislative agenda. Focus on a policy agenda is further eroded by controversies over Trump's personal behavior, his tweets, and most important the Congressional and Justice Department investigations into the Russian interference in the 2016 presidential election, and any collusion in which Mr. Trump's campaign may or may not have been engaged. Where those investigations may lead in anybody's guess in their early stages. In any case, in the early days of his administration, President Trump has taken little advantage of the Republican majorities in Congress, the tax reform legislation notwithstanding.

Certainly, a president who faces opposition majorities in Congress has what has become an almost insurmountable barrier to policy making. Parties out of the White House that enjoy majorities in Congress may or may not be able to agree on alternatives, but they can unite in opposition to the president's program, and the president has less opportunity to appeal effectively to factions within the opposition party.

The separation of powers is built on prevent mechanisms, such as a bicameral legislature which may be composed of houses controlled (if at all) by differing coalitions, or the presidential veto. Beyond constitutional provisions, there are legislative rules, particularly the filibuster in the Senate, that serve as barriers to positive policy making. The filibuster has become particularly challenging since the mere threat of a filibuster, rather than the requirement of an actual filibuster, requires sixty votes even to get a controversial proposal to the floor of the Senate.

Thus, in the separation of powers system, party unity in Congress can serve just as much or more to frustrate policy as to facilitate it, and in recent years Congress has leaned more frequently toward frustration (Mann & Ornstein 2012).

The separation of powers and the polarized party system can combine not only to frustrate policy, but to positively produce a crisis or near crisis of governance. The most dramatic example are the occasions when the federal government has shut down because of policy disagreements over the budget, or policy disagreements in which the budget is the vehicle for proposed resolution. Recent federal government shutdowns have occurred over the budget conflicts between President Clinton and Republican majorities in Congress in 1995, and about a Republican proposal to defund the Affordable Care Act in 2013. These shutdowns are threatened or take place around a "fiscal cliff" when the federal government is encountering the limits of the debt ceiling, but the debate is as much or more about fundamental questions of the federal government's role in the economy and society (Paulson 2015). As President

Trump completes his first year in office, there has been another brief shutdown, this time over failure to negotiate legislation concerning illegal immigration. While previous shutdowns were mostly the work of Republican majorities in Congress while the Democrats occupied the presidency, the most recent shutdown was more the work of a Democratic minority in the face of a Republican president. With both parties in a polarized Congress using the tactic, we face the threat of more policy gridlock and government shutdowns.

Of course, in a parliamentary system, such a political crisis would lead to the government "falling," but does not necessarily "shut down" the executive branch. The crisis is resolved with the emergence of new leadership, by choice of a majority party or coalition, by a new general election, or by other means. In parliamentary systems, polarized parties or multiparty systems featuring relatively ideological parties are common. Gridlock can happen in a parliamentary system as well as in the American separation of powers, but parliamentary gridlock occurs when there is no clear governing majority. The separation of powers in the United States can frustrate even elected majorities, which was actually one of the intentions of the framers.

However, the separation of powers is not, by itself, the cause of gridlock. The separation of powers has often been productive in policy terms. Nor are the polarized parties, by themselves, the cause of inaction. But historically, the separation of powers has operated through umbrella parties, which seem to have passed from the scene. It is the uneasy relationship between the separation of powers and a polarized party system that promotes policy stasis and gridlock.

In short, we often have policy paralysis because we have developed a parliamentary party system without developing parliamentary government.

TOWARD A RESPONSIBLE PARTY SYSTEM?

Both major political parties have come in for criticism in recent years for their partisanship and ideological dogmatism, and for the venom of public discourse in politics. Yet, it remains paradigmatic to cite the famous statement of E. E. Schattschneider (1942) that "modern democracy is unthinkable save in terms of parties."

Chapter 2 presents a discussion of why the United States was likely to have a two-party system, and why the two parties were likely to be umbrella parties. To review, the reasons are cultural and constitutional. The United States is a diverse society with a variety of competing interests, creating a social setting in which umbrella parties are more functional than ideologically polarized parties. American society is a classic liberal society in which the belief in private property and individual liberty is so nearly unanimous that support for capitalism is almost unanimous, and there is historically not much space for a polarized party system. Finally, federalism and the separation of powers make competition between national programmatic parties and resulting party government unlikely.

The social and political constraints aside, there was often interest in developing "responsible" parties, both in academic circles that predated the emergence of today's polarized parties. In 1950, Schattschneider led a committee of the American Political Science Association to issue a report arguing that responsible, programmatic political parties would give the American public clearer policy choices than the umbrella parties did (APSA 1950). The report generated criticism (Key 1966, Kirkpatrick 1971, Ranney 1954) citing the social realities and usefulness of umbrella parties, and support (Manuel & Cammisa 1999; Paulson 2000, 2007; Sundquist 1992).

Elite Realignment

The same debate about the virtue of responsible programmatic parties versus umbrella parties has been conducted among party elites. As long ago as the New Deal era, President Franklin D. Roosevelt was pushing for a more programmatically liberal Democratic Party when he conducted an unprecedented campaign against incumbent conservative Democrats in the 1938 Congressional primaries. In 1944, as FDR was preparing to run for a fourth term, he and Wendell L. Willkie, the liberal Republican who had been his opponent in 1940, talked through intermediaries about the possibility of each of them leaving their own party to form a new progressive party in America. The plan was aborted after Willkie's death before the election, and FDR's death the following year, no meeting between them having taken place (Barnard 1966; Neal 1989, 316–17).

Thomas E. Dewey (1966), who opposed Willkie for the Republican presidential nomination in 1940 and 1944, favored the retention of umbrella parties. In a series of lectures at Princeton University in 1950, Dewey argued that umbrella parties were appropriate to the diversity of interests in American society, and that in an ideological party system, the Democrats would win elections and the Republicans lose, almost all the time.

It took Barry Goldwater to actually run a campaign that would move the country away from umbrella parties and toward polarized parties (Novak 1965, Perlstein 2009, White 1965), in the words of his supporter, Phyllis Schafly (1964), "a choice not an echo." In his vision, the Republican Party should become America's conservative party, as in fact, it has.

Chapters 2 and 3 discussed the decisive factional struggles in both major parties and the staggered electoral realignment that followed after the 1960s. Elite realignment has accompanied party and electoral realignment:

In 1952, Senator Wayne Morse of Oregon switched parties from Republican to Democratic to support Adlai E. Stevenson for president.

In 1964, Senator J. Strom Thurmond of South Carolina and Rep. John Bell Williams of Mississippi, conservative Democrats, switched to the Republican Party in support of Goldwater for president.

In 1971, Mayor John V. Lindsay of New York, a liberal Republican, switched to the Democratic Party. He was an unsuccessful candidate for the Democratic presidential nomination in 1972.

In 1972, Rep. Ogden Reid of New York, a liberal Republican, followed Lindsay into the Democratic Party. At about the same time, Rep. Donald Riegle of Michigan, also a liberal Republican, became a Democrat.

After chairing Democrats for Nixon in 1972, John B. Connally of Texas became a Republican. He was an unsuccessful candidate for the Republican presidential nomination in 1980.

In 1994, after the Republican victory in the midterm elections, Senator Richard Shelby of Alabama, a conservative Democrat, switched to the Republican Party. He still retains his Senate seat. Also in 1994, Senator Ben Nighthorse Campbell of Colorado also switched from the Democrats to the Republicans. A number of other conservative Democrats also switched parties after the 1994 election (Wilcox 1995).

In 2000, after the contested presidential election, Senator Jim Jeffords, a liberal Republican, reidentified himself as an independent. Thereafter, Senator Jeffords caucused with the Democrats.

Senator Arlen Specter of Pennsylvania, a moderate-to-liberal Republican who had experienced problems winning renomination in his previous primary, switched parties to run for reelection as a Democrat in 2010. Senator Spector lost the Democratic primary, and Pat Toomey, who had barely lost to Specter in the 2004 Republican primary, won the Senate seat.

Party realignment leading to polarized parties has occurred both from the bottom up, starting with the voters, and from the top down. Voter realignment and elite realignment have over the past five decades has promoted ideological polarization between our political parties. The constitutional separation of powers has combined with polarized parties to produce policy gridlock in government.

POLARIZATION LOOKING FORWARD

Ideological and party polarization reached its initial turning point based around cultural issues, particularly race (Carmines & Stimson 1989). Huckfeldt and Kohfield (1989) were not alone in arguing that race was displacing class as a determining factor in shaping issues and electoral coalitions. On the political agenda of early postindustrial society, issues were becoming more postmaterialist (Inglehart 1977, 1981), including debate and polarization over women's rights, abortion, the environment, and war and peace. At a time when economic growth was still taken almost for granted, Walter Dean Burnham (1970, 141) made the following comparison of cultural and economic issues:

> So long as these cultural struggles are intense "world view" conflicts, there is one thing that cannot be done with them. They cannot be treated in a "more-or-less" fashion . . . as if they were equivalent to conflicts over tariffs, or minimum wages. They inherently involve not questions of more-or-less, but either-or.

However, in recent years, Americans (and citizens of other advanced capitalist societies) are encountering issues related to increasing income inequality and structurally limited economic growth, creating a zero-sum politics about a zero-sum economy. Economic issues are now experienced as being just as polarizing and challenging to compromise as cultural issues were when Burnham made his comment. According to Poole and Rosenthal and their colleagues, race and class have collapsed into a single bundled issue. DW-Nominate scores today indicate that divisions between party coalitions in Congress are now almost entirely on the left-right economic dimension, and that increasing party polarization is related to increasing economic inequality (Bonica et. al. 2015, Hare and Poole 2014, McCarty et. al. 2016).

It appears as if party polarization has developed economic foundations in the soil of American society. We have polarized parties facing polarizing issues. Polarization and a new economy have become structural realities we must confront in considering the prospects for American democracy in the twenty-first century.

That discussion will be the subject of chapter 6.

NOTE

1. Congressional election data drawn from Jerrold G. Rusk, *A Statistical History of the American Electorate* (Washington, DC: CQ Press, 2001) and from the website of the Clerk of the U.S. House of Representatives, at http://history.house.gov/Institution/Election-Statistics/Election-Statistics.

Chapter Six

The Trump Era and Beyond
Postindustrial Democracy in America

The focus on the character of Donald Trump, investigations into his conduct as a candidate and as president, into the involvement of the Russians in the 2016 campaign, and any connections between the Trump campaign and the Russians are important for what they might tell us about our national security or the vulnerability of our democratic institutions to foreign interference. At this writing, it is premature to base any analysis of the Trump presidency on where those investigations will lead. By the time this commentary reaches public view, we may know more, and it would probably make any early guess as to the outcome look silly.

In a discussion about the health and future of American democracy, Donald Trump presents a problem but he is not *the* problem. He is a symptom. The challenges facing American democracy are fundamental and structural, and go beyond the character, behavior, or term of office any one individual. However, the controversies concerning the Trump campaign and the Trump administration are resolved, anywhere from complete exoneration of the president to his impeachment, resignation, or indictment, the structural challenges to the future of American democracy will remain.

This chapter examines the prospects for American democracy in the twenty-first century, extending well beyond the age of Trump. The following analysis will discuss American political culture, considering particularly the perspectives of Alexis de Tocqueville; the changing economy, considering particularly postindustrial modernization and globalization; and the institutions and political development of American democracy in the twenty-first century.

DEMOCRACY IN AMERICA:
THE VISION OF ALEXIS DE TOCQUEVILLE

Introducing their edition of *Democracy in America* by Alexis de Tocqueville (2000), Harvey C. Mansfield and Delba Winthrop state their belief that *"Democracy in America* is at once the best book ever written on democracy and the best book ever written on America." Whether it is that or not, they do not overstate the case by much. Simply put, de Tocqueville's observations on America remain compelling enough to be applied here to modern political economy and the prospects for American democracy almost two centuries later. Moreover, it is important to remind ourselves of observations like de Tocqueville's, and to refresh a historical perspective, because the future is only history that has not yet happened.

Four of de Tocqueville's observations are key to our evaluation of twenty-first century democracy in America: the equality of conditions, individualism, and the classless consciousness, omnipotence of the majority, and how inequality of conditions and aristocracy could result grow from industry. The first three address the cultural roots of America, and how Americans think about the issues we face, while the last presents the experience of growing inequality in America today.

Equality of Conditions

For Alexis de Tocqueville (2000: 46), the most fundamental characteristic about the "social state of the Anglo-Americans" was that it was "essentially democratic." Above all, nothing about America "struck my eye more vividly than the equality of conditions (3)."

In discussing democracy and the equality of conditions, de Tocqueville seems to equate the two without defining either. In the process, he is considering some of the classic questions posed by democratic theory: What is the relationship between equality and liberty? How much majority rule best preserves a democratic polity? How much social and economic equality is essential to democracy? In 1835, as de Tocqueville sees it, democracy is a virtually inevitable force of history, advancing on all fronts in both "Christian Europe" and America. What made America particularly interesting for de Tocqueville was the fact that America was not far beyond its social birth, but was nevertheless the country where the great "democratic revolution" was most advanced, and where democracy could be best observed for all the hope and fear it offered civilization.

De Tocqueville's "equality of conditions" is less than substantive material equality and more than an illusion. Its basis is in upward social mobility.

Americans are not economically equal, but they live in a dynamic society in which they are not tied to an ascriptive class status. Their economic relations are established not by birth, but by contract and the market. As citizens, Americans are free to participate in political life. Add popular sovereignty to the "equality of conditions" and you have democracy.

Individualism and Classless Consciousness

According to Tocqueville, the philosophy of Americans is shaped by the equality of conditions. They operate in a classless consciousness, and see themselves as free individuals, not as members of a social class. Americans do not understand alternatives to this philosophical approach, according to Tocqueville, because they have no examples of any in their history. They enjoy an equality of conditions without ever having had to become equal.

Individualism and the dynamic nature of society disguise the linkage between individual and mass opinion from Americans. According to Tocqueville (2000: 587):

> In democracies . . . all men are alike and do things that are nearly alike. They are subject to great continual vicissitudes; but as the same successes and same reverses come back continually, the name of the actors alone is different, the play is the same. This aspect of American society is agitated because men and things change continually; and it is monotonous because all the changes are similar.

What gives Tocqueville hope and admiration for American democracy is the American capacity for "self-interest well understood." While people in aristocratic societies are held together by tradition, inheritance, and noblesse oblige, citizens in America are linked by civil society. America has a constitution that at once protects popular sovereignty and limits majority rule, and civil associations through which Americans with interests in common participate in public life. But these associations must be distinguished from parties that represent a class. These associations are formed by individuals who perceive a common interest. The ability of Americans to form these associations, along with a constitutional structure that limits government, gives them the capacity to protect their liberty from majority tyranny.

Omnipotence of the Majority

Nevertheless, for Alexis de Tocqueville, Americans were at risk of majority tyranny. For Tocqueville, beliefs in mores, conceptualized in political science as national character or political culture, are the central ingredient to understanding a people and their society. What makes opinion so important in democracies, of course, is the doctrine of sovereignty of the people.

In the America of the 1830s, according to Tocqueville, sovereignty of the people is more than a doctrine, it is a dogma. The majority not only governs policy, it governs thought (Tocqueville 2000, 244–45):

> I do not know of any country where, in general, less independence of mind and genuine freedom of discussion reign than in America.
>
> ... In America, the majority draws a formidable circle around thought. Inside those limits the writer is free; but unhappiness awaits him if he dares to leave them. It is not that he has to fear an auto-da-fe, but he is the butt of mortifications of all kinds and of persecutions every day. A political career is closed to him; he has offended the only power that has the capacity to open it up. Everything is refused him, even glory ... Chains and executioners are the course instruments that tyranny formerly employed; but in our day tyranny has perfected even despotism itself ...
>
> Princes ... had made violence material; democratic republics in our day have rendered it just as intellectual as the human will it seeks to constrain. Under the absolute government of one alone, despotism struck the body crudely so as to reach the soul; the soul, escaping from those blows, rose gloriously above it; but in democratic republics, tyranny does not proceed in this way; it leaves the body alone and goes straight for the soul.

In America, the content of the dogma is found in the ideological hegemony of classic liberalism, the Lockean belief in a society based on individual liberty and private property. Tocqueville recognized this in the classless consciousness and the view Americans had of themselves as free individuals. More than a century after Tocqueville, Louis Hartz (1955, 58–59) agreed:

> This then is the mood of America's absolutism: the somber faith that its norms are self-evident. It is one of the most powerful absolutisms in the world ... American absolutism ... lacked even the passion that doubt might give.
>
> It was so sure of itself that it hardly needed to become articulate ... American pragmatism has always been deceptive because, glacierlike, it has rested on miles of submerged conviction, and the confirmation ethos which that conviction generates has always been infuriating because it has refused to pay its critics the compliment of an argument.

Inequality of Conditions Reborn

Despite his belief in the inevitability of the advancement of democracy and the equality of conditions, Alexis de Tocqueville saw the potential for the development an inequality of conditions in American society. America, Tocqueville thought, would inevitably industrialize. The very individualism that was central to American democracy would promote industrialization. Americans loved the pursuit of wealth and obtaining it; they also respected all callings that would enable individuals to pursue material well-being. According to Tocqueville (2000: 526), "the tastes and habits that are born of equality naturally lead men toward commerce and industry." Industrialization would produce both an urban working class and among the owners of industry, an industrial aristocracy.

Not so focused on individual income as we are today, Tocqueville (2000, 530–32) followed Adam Smith and predated Karl Marx in anticipating the relations of production in the industrial system:

> I have shown how democracy favors developments in industry and multiplies the number of industrialists without measure; we are going to see the path by which industry in its turn could well lead men back to aristocracy . . .
>
> When the artisan engages constantly and uniquely in the manufacture of a single object, in the end he performs his work with a singular dexterity. But at the same time, he loses the general faculty of applying his mind to the direction of his work. Each day he becomes more skillful and less industrious, and one can say that the man in him is degraded as the worker is perfected.
>
> The master and worker here have nothing alike and each day they differ more . . . Each occupies a place that is made for him that he cannot leave . . .
>
> What is this, if not aristocracy?
>
> The friends of democracy ought constantly to turn their regard with anxiety in this direction . . . for if ever permanent inequality of conditions and aristocracy are introduced anew into the world, one can predict they will enter by this door.

While Tocqueville was projecting this possibility of an industrial class system, he also saw the established inequality of conditions in the America of his day in relations among "the European . . . the Negro and the Indian." He comments on the injustices of slavery and the expropriation of land from Native Americans by the Anglo-American, and he foresees tragedy for the "unfortunate races." In the second volume of *Democracy in America*, when discussing why "great revolutions will become rare," Tocqueville (2000, 611) offers his famous caveat: "If America ever experiences great revolutions, they will be brought about by the presence of blacks on the soil of the United States: that is to say, it will not be the equality of conditions, but on the contrary, their inequality, that will give rise to them."

In raising these issues, Alexis de Tocqueville presents the current question of our inquiry: If the equality of conditions is an essential characteristic of American democracy, what are the prospects for American democracy in the twenty-first century if an inequality of conditions becomes more generalized?

ECONOMIC GROWTH AND DEMOCRACY IN POSTINDUSTRIAL SOCIETY

Democracy in America has always been founded on liberty, economic growth, social mobility, and the development of a capitalist economy. While capitalism does not produce substantive economic equality, American democracy and capitalism have developed together by at least an approximation of Tocqueville's equality of conditions, with enough economic opportunity to provide social mobility, and the improvement of material life from one generation to the next. While the experience of social mobility has not been equal either, equality of opportunity seems to have grown, at least until the last quarter of the twentieth century.

The Rise and Fall of the High Growth Economy

The generation after World War II marks the moment which serves for most Americans, expert or not, consciously or not, as the reference point for the American economy and political institutions working approximately as they should. Critics of President Trump refer to his policy agenda as threatening to dismantle the postwar global order. Certainly, Trump policies on international trade, the environment and immigration present a general threat to international economic and political cooperation. But there seems to be little understanding in the public discourse of the policy regime that was assembled in the postwar period, the economic growth that policy regime promoted, or for how much was done to dismantle it, with severe long-term economic consequences, almost a half century ago.

Certainly the postwar era, between 1944 and 1973, represents a peak for the marriage between economic growth and affluence on the one hand, and elite-mass consensus on political institutions and public policy on the other, both in the United States, and in other advanced democratic capitalist polities.

Massive government intervention in the international and national economies played a major role in creating postwar economic growth. It was achieved with a high level of elite consensus and bipartisan support, and was based on three cornerstones of policy: The Bretton Woods Agreement, the Veterans Administration, and the Employment Act of 1946.

The Bretton Woods Agreement, forged among allied diplomats and economists planning for the postwar world, created two international institutions: The World Bank and the International Monetary Fund (IMF). The World Bank was designed to provide credit for reconstruction and development, while the IMF was to provide for stability among national currencies for international trade. While officially adapting a global gold standard, the Bretton

Woods conference in practice adapted a dollar standard. The American dollar would be frozen in value at $35 to the ounce of gold. Countries engaging in international trade could mitigate inflation and maintain the value of their currencies by trading their currency in to the IMF and taking out dollars. Supplemented by the Marshall Plan for recovery in Europe and a series of international trade agreements, the arrangement encouraged global trade, investment, and development.

In 1946, Congress created the Veterans' Administration. The GI Bill effectively paid back veterans returning from war by providing four years of higher education and relatively easy access to loans for homes. In an atmosphere in which there was fear of a slump in the business cycle to prewar levels, the GI Bill had the added practical effect of encouraging veterans to stay out of the job market while earning their degrees. In the longer term, the GI Bill created a generation of income earners, consumers and tax payers for a growing economy.

Also in 1946, the Congress adapted the Employment Act, which for the first time made the federal government responsible to adopting policies to promote economic growth. The focus was on fiscal policy guided by the theory of John Meynard Keynes (1964). Keynes, the British economist who codrafted the Bretton Woods Agreement, argued during the depression that government intervention and fiscal policy would be necessary to recovery. In the longer term, the government should run budget deficits when the business cycle was turning down, acting as a consumer to stimulate demand and combat unemployment. During periods of growth, government should run a surplus to fight inflation. Monetary policy, not so strongly advocated by Keynes, would offer similar tools with interest rates, which would be reduced as the business cycle turned down to generate credit, and raised as it turned up to fight inflation.

Over the next two decades, the countercyclical policy worked reasonably well. By 1964, with the Kennedy tax cut, the United States officially adopted a budget that would balance at "full employment." Over the next few years, economists predicted confidently that the business cycle had been effectively neutralized (Heller 1967, Okun 1970). Their claims were supported by extended economic growth at about 5 percent in mid-to-late 1960s.

Fiscal policy, of course, is not content neutral. A structure for economic growth was developed in the United States on three fronts, all based on systems of public investment and private profit. Policies on all three fronts promoted not only economic growth, but political consensus as well.

The first ingredient was national defense. The Cold War meant that important elements of the war economy were never dismantled, and defense spending resulted in a policy of "military Keynesianism," promoting a military-industrial complex that became a central feature of the American economy, and the bipartisan foreign policy, which was a cornerstone of elite consensus. In the late 1950s and early 1960s, defense spending accounted for about half of the federal budget, about 10 percent of GDP (*Economic Report of the President* 2017, 585).

Second, the federal government engaged in extensive investment in social infrastructure, the centerpiece of which was the Federal Highway Act of 1956. The Federal Highway Act was at once a major source of employment and represented a public investment in private profit for automobiles, oil, steel, and real estate. It was nothing short of a national land-use program that facilitated urban sprawl, the growth of suburbs, the use of the automobile, and oil, and was presented also as a transport system for national defense. An indicator of elite consensus on the Federal Highway Act is that it passed by voice vote in the House and 89–1 in the Senate (CQ 1957, 406).

Finally, economic growth fueled the development of the welfare state. Originally designed to protect middle-class and working-class life, from Social Security to Medicare, the welfare state expanded to encompass the War on Poverty in the 1960s. In addition to humanitarian considerations, incremental redistribution enabled low-income Americans to become more active consumers, promoting business profits, economic growth, and consensus in the legitimacy of the American system. Between 1959 and 1973, the proportion of Americans living in poverty was cut in half, reduced from 22 percent to 11 percent (Stanley & Niemi 2000, 362).

To some degree, the success of the Bretton Woods/Keynesian policy regime made its collapse almost inevitable, through the changes it brought in the international economy. The system promoted general economic growth well beyond the United States, particularly in Western Europe and Japan. American dominance of international trade was erased by a number of factors. First, Americans were consuming more. Second, the role of the dollar as a world currency reduced its real value, making American products overseas more expensive, and foreign products in the United States less expensive. Third, the Vietnam War, in addition to breaking down elite consensus, was funded partly by printing money, and proved inflationary. Finally, and most visibly, American demand for oil exacerbated a growing international trade deficit.

In an effort to restore the balance of international trade, President Nixon floated the dollar in 1971, taking the dollar off the gold standard and the world off the dollar standard. He was hoping that the declining value of the dollar would restore the American balance of trade by making American products overseas less expensive and foreign products more expensive for Americans. But oil was central to the problem, and the oil embargo of

1973 ended the postwar economic expansion, and with it, what had become close to an elite consensus on Keynesian economics. A decade in the 1970s featuring two recessions, oil shocks and stagflation paralyzed Keynesian formulas as policy tools.

Economic growth has remained the general rule for the American economy, but growth since the early 1970s has not been as sustained at high rates, nor as well-distributed among the population at large. When the economy is going strong, growth rates are about half of what they were in the 1960s.

Since Nixon floated the dollar, fiscal and monetary policy has yielded uneven results at best. Ford and Carter faced oil shocks and recessions. The Reagan administration, despite free market rhetoric and the promise of a balanced budget, offered tax cuts and military Keynesianism, with the result that federal budget deficits played a role in recovery from a recession and subsequent economic growth. President George H. W. Bush, encountering the deficit, pushed a tax increase through Congress with bipartisan support, resulting in a recession, and was defeated for reelection. Democrat Bill Clinton was elected promising a middle-class tax cut, but facing an inherited budget deficit, instead balanced the budget by the end of his two terms. In exchange, the Federal Reserve Board, chaired by Alan Greenspan, kept interest rates low, and economic growth was steady.

Budget deficits reappeared after a tax cut, the terrorist attacks on the United States, and war in the Middle East. The Great Recession of 2008–2009 led the Obama administration to offer a massive budget stimulus, resulting in an unprecedented deficit (in current dollar terms) while the Federal Reserve Board reduced interest rates to almost a functional zero. Today, because of the budget deficit and continuing low interest rates, the federal government has little flexibility, in either its fiscal or monetary tools, to respond to the business cycle.

Low Growth Capitalism

Marc Levinson (2016) has offered an excellent summary of the economic policies of the growth period, and concluded that the outcomes of the postwar period were historically more unique than they were normal, and are unlikely to be replicated. Robert J. Gordon (2016) makes the same argument, applying it to a longer period of time and building it on inventions, more than government policy. Gordon considers the century from 1870 to 1970, the second industrial revolution, to be unique for the pace of innovation and new products that contributed to economic growth and lifestyle change. Gordon and Levinson thus both conclude that the rate of economic growth experienced in the twentieth century is not likely persist.

Today, economic growth is not simply a cyclical issue, it is a structural issue. Below, four structural limitations on economic growth in postindustrial societies will be discussed: the aggregate size of the economy, the changing structure of the workforce, the changing structure of the international economy, and the "fiscal crisis of the state."

Ironically, affluence and the aggregate size of the economy is one of the impediments to maintaining rates of economic growth, which is not all bad news. The economy today is almost four times as large in real-dollar GDP terms as it when growth rates peaked over 6 percent in 1966 (*Economic Report of the President* 2017, 568). Therefore, when the business cycle is high, at about 3 percent, it represents more real-dollar growth than there was in 1966. There is the bad news, however. The first problem is philosophical: today's growth may represent financial growth and not real wealth. The second problem is practical and material. The capacity to reinvest, whether in a business, or government representing society at large, is measured by rates of growth, not absolute growth. An economy four times as large needs to maintain its rate of growth so that real material growth is also at least four times as large. In today's economy, at the top of the business cycle, the capacity of society at large to reinvest is approximately half of what is was at the top of the business cycle fifty years ago, all other things being equal.

For Karl Marx (1867), this was the classic crisis of the "declining rate of profit," applied now to society. But the rate of profit problem is not narrow or ideological. For Adam Smith and free-market theorists, it would involve competition and saturated markets. For the business accountant, it would refer to the "law of diminishing returns."

The second factor in structural low growth in the changing structure of the work force. After World War II, "Fordism" signaled a social bargain, operating on the premise that a well-paid workforce could afford to buy what it produced, increasing business profits (Harrington 1986). However, while rising compensation increases profits, if profits do not rise much faster than compensation, the result is a declining rate of profit and capacity to reinvest. For a couple of decades after World War II, there remained a strong base of middle-income, industrial jobs to go with the growing number of white-collar and service jobs. Today, almost 80 percent of the workforce is in services, information, and management, split between low-paying service jobs, and higher-paying, high-skill, and technocratic jobs, with an abscess in the middle. The proportion of workers in industrial jobs has been more than cut in half, to less than 20 percent. While much of the blame in political discourse, particularly from Donald Trump, has been placed on international trade and illegal immigration, the change in the nature of work has much more to do with technological change and automation. Nevertheless, the structure of the job market is being altered by globalization, and the jobs that are exported are not random. Middle-income, goods-producing jobs disappear as businesses take advantage of cheap labor in less-developed countries. The decline of middle-income employment if it continues would leave us with the growth of two types of workers: Those with low pay whose limited capacity to consume threatens rates of profit, and high-pay workers, whose compensation threatens rates of profit.

While there may be lower aggregate economic growth, there will be pockets of rapid growth in small businesses or sectors with new technologies, rising and falling in waves of increasing frequency. Where there is low growth, unemployment will increase, while high growth will create new jobs along with labor displacement. The likelihood is that while the total number of jobs may increase, so will structural unemployment, and the income gap in a bipolar labor market will be exacerbated.

Third, the changing structure of the international economy limits growth in postindustrial societies. The United States was the leading trade power in the world after World War II, and played a major role in reconstructing its competitors, particularly in Western Europe and Japan. Now, the United States no longer dominates trade, and no longer controls the terms of trade, as it did when the dollar was the functional global standard. In particular, the United States does not unilaterally control the terms of trade for oil. Certainly, the days of rapidly increasing energy costs have been replaced by more price fluctuation. Energy supply has been supplemented by research and development in the private sector, including fracking and growth in renewable energy. But the energy economy is as international as the economy at large, and the maintenance of oil interests involves costs not well measured in market terms, such as environmental limits, and national security and military commitments. Americans and the citizens of other advanced democratic capitalist societies still cannot assume easy access to energy or other natural resources. The days of economic well-being for Americans that went with the postwar economy are gone, and will not be recreated.

Issues of war and peace, of course, have a direct impact on international economic relations. In the years after World War II, the United States and some of its allies, most particularly France, found themselves in wars to maintain colonialism or neocolonialism. The Vietnam War may yet be understood in history as the last war of the Cold War and the first war of the North-South world. More recently, Americans and the allies have been engaged in the war to combat extreme Islamist terrorism, with its costs in human life, as well as its material costs. The length and consequences of this war are not yet clear. Indeed, the limits of this war in time and geography remain unknown. It is a global war, and may persist as a relatively permanent reality, with measurable economic cost, in addition to human cost.

The global environment will deeply influence the international economy and the potential for growth. The negotiations over climate change not only present a compelling environmental issue, but an economic one. Developing countries yet to reach a point of industrialization passed by more advanced economies look for a way toward economic growth that can fit within a global environmental framework, while more advanced countries debate the balance between economic growth and environmental preservation. The fact that the United States and China agreed on anything was the real achievement of the Paris Accords, before President Trump announced the United States' withdrawal. But the question of limits to growth that we may face, first posed more than forty years ago, remains.

Immigration issues are placing stress on the American economy, as they are on national economies wherever the populations of developing and more advanced economies cross borders. So long as there is contact among the peoples and economies, and so long as there are great disparities of wealth in the global economy, immigration problems and their costs will remain.

Finally, the "fiscal crisis of the state" presents a severe limit on economic growth (O'Connor 1973). The potential of government budgets or interest rates to stimulate economic growth when it is low in the market is much more limited today than it was fifty years ago, for two reasons: the tax cut policy paradigm, and the changing structure of the federal budget in the United States.

In response to the oil shocks, stagflation, and recession, the Reagan administration offered its deep tax cuts, which passed Congress with some bipartisan support, leaving a deep structural deficit in the federal budget. Since then, it has been politically counterproductive to suggest tax increases, putting an effective limit on ambitious government spending. Even the Clinton administration had to rely on monetary policy as the instrument for raising economic growth, while achieving a balanced budget. The Great Recession of 2008, discussed above, weakened the capacity of the federal government to use fiscal or monetary policy even further. The Obama stimulus package, along with almost zero interest rates combined to stimulate economic growth. The deep deficits of the years right after 2008 have now returned to prerecession levels, but remain constraining on fiscal policy. Meanwhile, the Federal Reserve Board is moving toward raising its very low interest rate, despite continuing low rates of economic growth, hoping to create some future flexibility to once again use monetary policy to stimulate growth.

The decline in economic growth presents more than an economic threat to the American way of life. Recessions can actually facilitate business investment and the restoration of rates of profit while the business cycle is down. But they do not benefit most of the American population, who lose jobs and income. Since the financial panic of 2008, the gross domestic product increased by 25 percent through 2015, while corporate profit increased by 50 percent over the same period (*Economic Report of the President* 2017, 567–71). According to Thomas Picketty (2014), if the rate of return on capital, measured at least in part by corporate rates of profit, is greater than the rate of economic growth, the result is an increase in income inequality. Income inequality, in turn, strikes at the heart of Tocqueville's "equality of conditions."

Zero-Sum Democracy in America

If Alexis de Tocqueville was right that the "equality of conditions" is a central ingredient of democracy, the long, uneasy marriage between capitalism and democracy faces a dual threat, not only in the United States, but in other democratic capitalist polities, as well. First, capitalist economies in postindustrial societies have become structurally low-growth economies. Second, low growth in capitalist economies threatens political consensus and democracy.

During the postwar period of rapid economic growth, Americans were widely considered "exceptional" for the degree of consensus at both the elite and mass levels of the mainstream culture, for their classless consciousness compared with the populations of other advanced democratic capitalist polities, and for their strong public confidence in their political institutions.[1] In both the academic world, and in society at large, the pluralist model of democracy seemed to justify, as well as to explain, the operation of American government and the political economy. According to pluralist theory, public policy is decided in modern democracies through a process of conflict and compromise among competing interests.

Pluralist theory acknowledges that democratic capitalism does not function by majority rule, for three reasons. First, there are constitutional and legal limitations. In the United States, the separation of powers limits the power of the majority, just as the Bill of Rights provides protections for liberty against the majority. Second, while capitalism produces unprecedented wealth, it also produces at least a degree of economic inequality. Third, advanced democratic capitalist societies are complex, diverse, and specialized, with competing interests that make the emergence of majorities of the whole unlikely. Nevertheless, pluralist theorists conclude pluralism is as democratic as possible in the modern world, providing sufficient approximations of majority rule and equality. Robert Dahl (1956, 1961, 1971, 1989), perhaps the leading representative of pluralist theory, called his model "polyarchal democracy."

Acknowledging the absence of direct democracy, David Truman (1959) found power in a pluralist democracy in an "intervening structure of elites," concluding that "ordinary people cannot act except through organization and in response to the initiative of small numbers of leaders."

According to the pluralist model, this small number of leaders represent competing interests, but they also have a shared interest in system maintenance. During the postwar period of growth, there was strong elite consensus in American politics, but it has declined over the past half century, starting with civil rights and Vietnam, but spreading to economic issues since the 1970s. The familiar analogy of an economic pie would help explain this. If the pie is growing, elites can negotiate over who gets how many new pieces of the pie. When the pie is not growing, you have a zero-sum economy, and it is likely you also have zero-sum politics. Under those conditions, anybody's gain must be somebody's loss. No deal is forthcoming.

In either scenario, the people respond to "the intervening structure of elites." When elite consensus is strong, mass consensus is likely to follow. When there is a decline in elite consensus, there is likely to be a decline in mass consensus. Today's polarized politics is a reflection of a polarized electorate making choices offered by a polarized elite. As noted in chapter 5, Poole and Rosenthal and their colleagues lend empirical support for this generalization, with their finding that income inequality promotes political polarization (Bonica et. al. 2015, McCarty et. al. 2016, Poole & Rosenthal 1984, 1997).

THE TRUMP ERA AND BEYOND: PROSPECTS FOR AMERICAN DEMOCRACY

The public drama of the Trump presidency in its first year has focused on the personality of the president, his statements, and his actions. There is little doubt that the tasteless, immature, and divisive behavior of President Trump presents, at the very least, a short-term threat to American democracy and our political institutions. But the challenges we face go far beyond this president.

President Trump: Toward a Policy Agenda for Structural Change?

At this writing, public attention regarding the Trump administration is focused on the investigations into Russian interference in the 2016 election, and the possibility of collusion between the Trump campaign and/or transition team and the Russians. One investigation was based in the FBI until James Comey was fired, and is now more independent under the direction of Robert Mueller. There are two additional investigations in Congress, one each by the Senate Select Intelligence Committee, and the House Select Intelligence Committee. The Senate investigation, chaired by Senator Richard Burr, Republican of North Carolina, has appeared to be more successful at both making some progress and maintaining some bipartisanship. Where these investigations will lead, anywhere from exoneration of the president on one extreme to his impeachment on the other, is still a wide-open question. Any assumption that President Trump will adhere to constitutional norms in response to these investigations has already been placed in serious doubt. These investigations are an important constitutional matter, and a serious test of the separation of powers in a polarized era, but public impressions about them are premature at best, and will not be discussed in detail here. It should be noted, however, that in today's globalized economy, we can expect international efforts to influence election campaigns across national boundaries only to increase. Some of those efforts will be clandestine and aggressive, as in the Russian case, and some will actually be legally legitimate.

In addition, there are growing investigations into allegations of sexual misconduct in the workplace and society at large, starting in Hollywood, spreading through news media organizations, and into the U.S. House of Representatives and Senate. These allegations are similar to multiple allegations leveled at Donald Trump during the 2016 campaign, now threatening to come back and haunt him again in the White House. If anything, Trump's personal behavior in office, including his tweets and comments about his critics, has inflated public impressions that he does not respect the American constitutional system or institutions of government. While public condemnation of sexual misconduct is likely to stimulate a long-term cultural change in mores, the shorter-term impact on the Trump presidency remains unclear at this writing.

The investigations of Trump, his campaign, and administration have drawn comparisons with the Watergate scandal and the resignation of President Nixon. In that case, too, there were multiple investigations, by the FBI, by the Justice Department's special prosecutor, by the Senate Select Committee, and the House Judiciary Committee. Partisan politics certainly played a role in the Senate and House investigations. But as we saw in chapter 5, the ideological polarization of parties had not yet taken hold in Congress in 1973 and 1974. While Senator Sam Irvin, Democrat of North Carolina, the chair of the Senate Select Committee, seemed to be persuaded early on that there was a scandal to uncover, Nixon was counting on the support of conservative Democrats to remain in office. While there were partisans on both sides predisposed to find scandal or not, there seemed to be a common purpose among most members of both Congressional committees to get to the truth. In the end, a minority of Republicans joined the united Democrats on the House Judiciary Committee in voting to impeach Nixon. In today's polarized atmosphere, despite efforts to the contrary on the Senate Intelligence Committee, there seems to be a strong inclination to attack or defend President Trump based on partisan interests. At this writing, President Trump has a very low standing for a new president in public opinion evaluations of his performance in office. But so far, unlike Nixon's ultimate experience, Trump seems to be holding his base.

Donald Trump was elected president in 2016 at least partly due to a decline of the "equality of conditions." The votes he gained from declining industrial and mining areas came from voters who were once disproportionately Democrats, but who are now afraid of losing not only their jobs, but also their way of life. To the degree that working-class conservatism has been a factor in voting behavior for almost half a century, its expression of economic vulnerability seemed much more immediate in 2016.

Trump certainly presented issues related to postindustrial modernization more effectively than did Hillary Clinton and the Democrats. He made issues of deindustrialization part of his campaign to a degree that Clinton did not, and as a result carried Pennsylvania, Michigan, and Wisconsin, which delivered the election (see chapter 4). This does not mean he actually communicated an understanding of the nature of the issues; he did not. By blaming office holders for socioeconomic trends that long predate them and will continue for some time regardless of who holds office, he demonstrated that he does not understand the issues we face. But he talked about what was worrying voters living in once productive areas now in economic decline, and he posed some of the right questions about issues his opponent did not emphasize. As a result, in an election year of unrest and dissatisfaction, Trump ran as the change agent, while Clinton was stuck with the mantle of the status quo.

Nevertheless, those who voted for Donald Trump out of frustration at the impact of the economy on their lives were not expressing a class consciousness, nor were they voting for a clear policy agenda for change. They were voting against the status quo as they saw it. While Clinton and the Democrats were defending the policies of the Obama administration, Trump was promising to "make America great again." One candidate was locked in an unsatisfactory present, while the other was looking to go back to the "good old days." Both appealed to electoral coalitions that emerged in the 1960s. No one was talking seriously about the future.

Consider debate on the policy agenda offered in the early days of the Trump administration. On the economic issues, the Republicans generally stick to their support of policies of capital accumulation, while the Democrats support distributive policies, both taking little account of structural change.

On health insurance, for example, the Republicans in Congress propose to repeal and replace "Obamacare" with most of the changes designed to deregulate health insurance. Although some Democrats support a single-payer system of health insurance, most still concentrate on defending the Affordable Care Act. The Democrats prefer to leave a system supplementing

Medicare and Medicaid in place, while the Republicans prefer to rely on the market. Neither party presents a plan that takes into account both the realities of the health care market and the federal budget. A proposal for a genuinely comprehensive national health insurance, for example, could begin to pay for itself by rendering Medicare and Medicaid redundant, but even the Democrats have yet to produce such a proposal.

After nearly a year of frustration, the Trump administration and Republicans in Congress experienced significant legislative success with the passage of a package on tax reform and tax cuts. The focus of the legislation was on a permanent 40 percent cut in tax rates for corporations but the deal was enhanced for Republicans by the inclusion of the repeal of the mandate to buy health insurance that had been central to the Affordable Care Act. The midterm elections of 2018 will reveal any short-term partisan political consequences of the controversial legislation, but the real policy outcomes may not be clear for a decade, after the temporary individual tax cuts provided in the legislation are scheduled to expire. For now, President Trump and the Republicans are claiming the tax reform legislation as a victory.

The Democrats generally opposed the direction of the tax reform proposals and support plans to tax the rich to fund government programs. Neither party deals effectively with the fact that the federal government is mired in a structural budget deficit, laden with mandatory expenditures, including Medicare, Medicaid, and interest on the national debt. Furthermore, in the postindustrial economy, no one can reasonably expect aggregate economic growth by itself to provide a way out of the deficit.

On immigration, President Trump takes a relatively hard line toward undocumented immigrants, while most Democrats support a policy closer to a route to citizenship. Both Republicans and Democrats emphasize how immigration policy should be enforced or practiced, rather than discussing what outcomes immigration policy should seek to create. At this writing, negotiations on immigration reform are once again being initiated, with the focus on border security, the DACA (Deferred Action for Childhood Arrivals) program begun by the Obama administration, chain (family-unification) immigration, and the visa lottery. The degree of today's party polarization in Congress is indicated that as President Trump was celebrating his first year in office, an inability to negotiate an extension of DACA was the central issue of still another shutdown of the federal government, however brief.

In office, President Trump has followed his campaign rhetoric by pulling away from international agreements on trade and the environment. His administration is negotiating amendments to the North American Free Trade Agreement (NAFTA). He has announced withdrawal from the Trans-Pacific

Partnership (TPP), and from the Paris Accords on climate change. While both parties are divided internally on international trade policy, the climate change decision plays into the ideological polarization between the parties.

Neither party seems ready to address the fundamental interdependence of immigration, international trade, climate change, and other environmental issues, along with international terrorism. They are all global issues whose resolution will require international policy cooperation and structural change in the global economy, which will in turn feed back with fundamental change in the lives of Americans.

President Trump has also promoted his policy agenda, and further pushed ideological polarization, by his appointment and Senate confirmation of Neil Gorsuch to the Supreme Court. Less observed but perhaps even more important, Trump has been made numerous appointments to Courts of Appeals and the District Courts. Trump's impact on the federal judiciary will apparently be lasting, and the degree of his impact will be influenced by how long he remains in office, and whether the Republicans retain the Senate in 2018.

Donald Trump was elected president with an expectation among his supporters that he would change the system. He has taken steps toward change in the international institutional arrangements, but he has shown little historical understanding of those arrangements or respect for how institutions of American government operate. But his policy direction, aimed at restoring an old order that really never existed, does not address the issues of the future. So far, neither do alternatives offered by his opposition.

Polarized Parties and Polarizing Issues in the American System

Much of the foregoing analysis, in this and previous chapters, has concentrated on ideological polarization and party polarization in American politics. We have always had ideological polarization within classic Lockean liberal premises. But until a half century ago, that polarization occurred more within parties than between them. The umbrella parties both spanned the ideological spectrum usually with the result of mitigating polarization and ensuring that policy would not be paralyzed in the separation of powers system. Ironically, when policy was paralyzed to the point of Civil War over the issues of slavery and secession, it was because umbrella parties could not deliver national majorities to resolve the issue. This tragedy in the American experience leaves us with two lessons. First, the current moment does not represent the worst of polarization in American history. That is the good news. But the second lesson is the bad news. The Civil War was to a significant degree, the war of the industrial revolution in America. Is the end of the industrial age going to drive Americans to violence as a political tool? Or can we now manage our institutions into a new age better than we did in 1861, well enough to make the decisions we face by democratic and constitutional means?

Today, we live in a postindustrial society and global economy in which we cannot assume extended periods of economic growth. In the capitalist system, economic growth provides the new pieces of the pie that allows individuals who do not own capital to derive income from increasing increments of wealth. In the absence of growth, we have a zero-sum economy, and zero-sum politics. The foundations for Tocqueville's "equality of conditions," or for equal economic opportunity and upward social mobility, are undercut, and so are the foundations for a political consensus on the legitimacy of democratic capitalism.

Thus, we face polarizing issues about both economic growth and the distribution of wealth that go to the heart of American culture. Virtually all of the economic issues we face today can be understood as a showdown between proposals for capital accumulation for investment versus distributions of income or wealth to protect those who do not own capital. We face similar, more extreme challenges in a global economy to which we are tied. Historic colonialism and current neocolonialism are at the center of issues of war and peace, including the global war against international terrorists in which we are engaged. Global environmental issues, including climate change, demand resolution, as does the issue of immigration, which is global, not just a matter for American borders. Some Americans pretend we do not have to deal with these problems and crises, but the longer we wait to take action on these twenty-first century issues, the more extreme the policy measures required will be.

Writing about America for a Chinese readership, Alfred DeGrazia (1975) put it this way:

> If America were to confront the future frankly, it would have to make decisions for which it is psychologically unprepared. Its actual risks would not increase: It is important to realize this fact; no decision that America might take to realize a new peaceful world order would require more sacrifices than the future will demand of it in any case.

Facing polarizing issues, there is a potential upside to polarized political parties. As the members of the American Political Science Association committee, cited in chapter 5, noted, "responsible" parties offering distinct programs give the voters a clearer choice when they go to the polls. If there was a virtue to the umbrella parties that persisted into the middle of the twentieth century, those parties are nevertheless now gone. A polarized party system is what we have, and what we must learn to operate. But we are presented with the opportunity of political parties that might legitimately present extreme alternatives for the choices we face.

A polarized party system operates reasonably well with a parliamentary government, but as discussed in chapter 5, Americans do not have a parliamentary government, and it is not realistic to believe we could have one in the foreseeable future. But the advantage of parliamentary government in a polarized or multiparty system is that majority parties or coalitions can govern. In the American separation of powers system, mechanisms exist by constitutional design, or by design of the rules of a legislative body, that limit or even prevent majority rule. The separation of powers relies on conflict being tempered by compromise and consensus, a condition we cannot rely upon in today's polarized environment.

The constitutional mechanisms that limit the electoral power of the majority include the following:

The separation of powers itself limits the power of majorities to govern, even through the elective branches. In the Constitution, only the House of Representatives was originally designed to represent the electorate. Until 1913, the U.S. Senate was appointed by state legislatures to represent states.

The Electoral College was designed to limit popular majorities. The Constitution authorized state legislatures to choose the manner of electing electors, a provision that still survives. Not until 1836 did every state but one (South Carolina) choose electors by popular vote.[2] It remains possible, although not likely, for the winner of the national popular vote to lose the presidency in the Electoral College, which, of course, is what happened in 2016.

Finally, the American system includes a system of staggered elections. We elect the House and one-third of the Senate every two years, and the president every four years. We do not have the national elections that are found in many parliamentary systems.

The American republic was not designed to operate by majority rule, but polarized parties will only frustrate each other's capacity to govern by consent of the governed in the separation of powers system, unless we enhance majoritarian institutions in American government. Unfortunately, today's polarization has functioned to strengthen the limits of the power of the electorate in American government.

The filibuster has drawn the most public attention as the leading barrier to majority rule in the U.S. Senate. While the removal of the filibuster tradition may seem attractive, no Senate in the near future is likely to go for it. But the filibuster should at least be required to actually function when it is being used. Since 1975, on most bills, proposals, and nominations, 60 out of 100 votes is necessary to bring a bill to the floor, since 60 votes is required to overcome a filibuster. The Senate should return to the time before 1975, when Senators actually had to engage in a filibuster, after a bill came to the floor, to keep it from coming to a vote. When Senators have to actively filibuster a bill, at least they have something to lose, considering other legislation they might prefer to bring to the floor.

Distributions of seats in the House of Representatives in most states is a partisan process in the state legislature. The result is that majorities of state legislatures often design as many Congressional districts as possible to be safe for their party. In recent years, largely as a result of the gerrymander, only about fifty House seats across the country are genuinely contested from one election to the next. Nonpartisan checks on legislative redistricting would increase the number of contested seats in the U.S. House of Representatives, and in state legislatures. Today's polarized environment, and the interest incumbents have in protecting themselves may be why such checks, found in some states, are not more common across the country.

The current condition of campaign finance is a major factor not only in political polarization itself, but in the rancorous temper of discourse, and represents a threat to free and fair elections. The Supreme Court decision in *Citizens United v. Federal Election Commission* (2010) upheld the precedent that corporations (and by extension labor unions and other interest groups) are legal persons (*Santa Clara County v. Southern Pacific Railroad Company*, 1886) and that campaign finance was free speech protected by the 1st Amendment. Thus, while financial contributions to campaigns could be limited by campaign finance reform, direct expenditure to express political views could not (*Buckley v. Valeo*, 1976). The result is that corporations, labor unions and other groups can spend money without limit on their own advertising on issues or for or against candidates. While the candidates themselves endorse their own advertisements as being approved, advertising by outside groups can often increase the acrimony and bitterness of the campaign.

Often, those who oppose *Citizens United* cite the wrong problems in their criticism of the court's opinion, namely that it is nonsense to identify corporations as "people" (no one does), as if the court's recognition of corporations as "persons" is new law (it is not). Further, opponents criticize *Citizens United* for deciding that campaign finance is speech. But if campaign finance is not speech, what is it?

A more reasonable criticism of *Citizens United* would be based on a vigorous effort to reduce the scope of the decision with an application of the *rational basis* test. Speech is a fundamental right, and limiting it requires a demonstration of a narrowly tailored policy rationally related to a compelling governmental interest. The argument that may have a chance in court is not that corporations are not "persons" or that campaign finance is not speech, but that the government has a compelling interest to guarantee fair elections, and that regulation of campaign finance is narrowly tailored and rationally related to that purpose.

The internet and social media both aggravate ideological polarization in American politics. On the internet, Americans seem to consult websites that appeal only to views they already have. The same can be said for the more mainstream television, where conservatives tend to watch Fox News and liberals watch MSNBC. On social media, it seems that people will say things that they would not say face-to-face, or in more formal settings. The behavior of President Trump on Twitter is an example that certainly does not contribute to intelligent public discourse, appealing as he does to the lowest common denominator. It should be noted that there is really little difference between Trump using social media and Franklin D. Roosevelt giving "fireside chats" on the radio, going over the heads of communication elites directly to the people. The real issue is the *content* of what the president tweets: Is it tasteful and worthy of the fact that he is the president of the United States? Have his comments been vetted as policy within the executive branch? Is he legitimately contributing to public agenda? Is he enhancing the intelligence of public debate? Is he literally doing his job by presiding over the public agenda and facilitating public debate?

As discussed earlier in this chapter, Alexis de Tocqueville noted the "omnipotence of the majority" in American culture, and the tendency to draw a "formidable circle around thought." Or to use the language of Louis Hartz, American "absolutism" treats any thinking outside classic Lockean liberalism as un-American. That cultural habit seems of have morphed in the last half century so that Americans, at least at the ideological extremes, treat their fellow citizens with whom they disagree as if they are "un-American" and outside the circle within which thought should be enclosed. President Trump has contributed to that cultural tendency with often tasteless, personal attacks on his political opponents.

The potential saving grace from this polarization may be found in civil society, that virtue observed by Tocqueville of Americans to organize for a shared public interest. While threatened by polarization, this characteristic of American culture lingers visibly, particularly in local service organizations Americans join to promote a common "self-interest well understood." It is that spirit that has been muted among political elites and to a lesser but growing degree, among American citizens themselves in our national politics, as public discourse has become literally more uncivil.

Ironically, in our polarized era, our political parties, even polarized parties, are the institutions which should frame public issues to encourage debate and democratic decision making. The parties remain our institutions that can aggregate interests, structure support and opposition on issues, and perform linkage between public opinion as expressed in elections and public policy in government. It is up to party elites to perform this function, although in recent years they have collectively placed higher priority on appealing to the electoral base of their own parties and winning elections than on governing. At one time, political parties moderated the ideological extremes in society, but over the last half century they have come to reflect and exaggerate them.

Polarization itself is not the leading threat to American democracy today. Nor is President Trump the leading threat, although he certainly aggravates matters. The foremost threat to American democracy is the uneasy marriage of the separation of powers to a polarized party system, resulting in policy gridlock and the public distemper in political discourse.

Twenty-First Century Democracy in America

In addition to party polarization in a separation of powers system, two central challenges face American democracy in the twenty-first century. First, American democracy is not all that democratic. Second, the changing national and international economies threaten to make it less so, regardless of who is the president of the United States.

The discussion above in this chapter concentrated on mainstream pluralist theory because of the attention it pays to competing interests. If the economy is not growing substantially, those interests and the elites who represent them are playing a zero-sum game. But the vulnerability of American democracy is also revealed by well-developed bodies of theory that take issue with pluralism, finding more power in "democratic" capitalist societies, including the United States, in the hands of a select ruling class. Theories of elite power (Bachrach 1967, Domhoff 1967, Lowi 1982, Macpherson 1977, McConnell 1967, Mills 1956, Schattschneider 1960, Schumpeter 1942), locate power in a select few, identifying the elites by patterns of social relations and power in social institutions, including government in general and the administrative state in particular. Neo-Marxist theorists (Macpherson 1965, 1989, Mandel 1978, O'Connor 1973; Wolfe, 1977, 1981) are more specific, locating power in the capitalist class in society at large, even if government itself operates through relatively democratic political institutions.

It has not been the purpose of the foregoing study to examine these important critical theories of democracy. That has been and shall remain the subject of numerous studies on power and democratic theory. The mention of them here is to recognize that these theories pose questions about modern democracy in capitalist societies that are likely to receive more attention. These critical theories sidestep the issue of who is in office and how they got there to deal with the structure of power in society. They all address the contradiction posed by social inequality in democratic capitalist polities.

This is the same question we face in addressing a decline in the "equality of conditions" Alexis de Tocqueville foresaw almost two centuries ago. What will happen to the legitimacy of American democracy if Americans lose their faith in the opportunity to be upwardly mobile, to obtain the American dream that Tocqueville saw, and that generations of Americans have experienced? What will happen to the classless consciousness that Tocqueville and so many others have observed, if there is increasing substantive material inequality in American life? Tocqueville himself posed this question when he foresaw the rebirth of inequality in America as accompanying industrialization and commercialism. These questions move beyond the legitimate questions of racial, sexual, and other inequalities of personal identity that have been addressed with increasing intensity in recent decades, to the question of social class inequality which has seldom been addressed in American culture. Indeed, if economic inequality continues to grow, growing class consciousness may become an essential ingredient to strengthening democracy in America.

Finally, what will happen to American democracy if Americans' confidence in their political institutions continues to decline? The Constitution of the United States itself offered a design for a classic liberal republic, popular government without majority rule. The separation of powers was meant, above all, to protect liberty by limiting majority rule to operate against the concentration of power (Hamilton, Jay & Madison 1966).[3] Two centuries later, the democratization of American politics would serve to protect rather than threaten liberty. Today, we live in a political economy in which in the decline in the health of democratic institutions would yield a more functionally authoritarian American government, with or without Donald Trump, even without changing the Constitution originally designed to preserve liberty. Authoritarianism exercised through "democratic" institutions remains the danger Tocqueville warned about in *Democracy in America*.

The critiques of democratic theory and the operation of the American government under the Constitution reveal what has been a hybrid system of government by the people with legal and economic limits on the majority. When economic growth has been the general rule and Americans had faith in their future, it has worked generally well. But if we face long-term low economic growth and zero-sum politics with an associated decline of both elite and mass consensus, the contradictions in the hybrid system can no longer be finessed. We cannot yet tell whether a political crisis is immediately in the offing during the Trump administration, although events seem to have made a crisis in the near term more likely than not. But the challenges we face in the twenty-first century are fundamental and structural. They go well beyond the success or failure of one president.

Democracy in America in the twenty-first century will either become much more democratic or much less so. Either way, in the twenty-first century, how Americans experience their economic lives and their relationship with their government is changing fundamentally—for better or for worse.

NOTES

1. *American exceptionalism* is a term widely misused in current American political discourse, in that it is claimed to mean that America is somehow superior to other countries. The term actually applies to a body of theory about America, traced back to Alexis de Tocqueville, which finds Americans both interesting and different for the degree of democratization in their society, the "equality of conditions" and for the fact that Americans enjoy an "equality of conditions" without having to had endure a real social revolution to get there.

2. South Carolina did not elect electors by popular vote until after the Civil War.

3. See particularly The Federalist #10 and #51 by Madison.

Conclusion

At the new year 2018, Freedom House has released its annual report (Freedom House 2018) on the state of freedom and democracy in the world. It concludes that democracy and freedom are both in retreat, both globally and in the United States. It places responsibility for the global decline to a significant degree on the 45th president of the United States, Donald Trump, particularly on his policies aimed at reducing American involvement in the world. It attributes the weakening of American democracy at home to the conduct of President Trump in office, and to elites of both parties, for ideological polarization leading to policy gridlock and declining public confidence in our political institutions.

Certainly, Donald Trump has done little good and visible harm to both freedom and democracy. But as Freedom House acknowledges, the threats to democracy predate Trump, and even if we avoid the worst in his time, they will persist beyond him. Moreover, the focus of discussion on Trump tends to the distract from the longer-term structural challenges facing democracy in the United States and around the world.

The United States and other advanced democratic capitalist societies confront similar issues even if the specific applications differ from country to country. We face problems of low-growth economies, rapid economic change with growing and declining sectors and regions, and persistent economic inequality, along with cultural divisions and nationalisms, both at home and abroad. In domestic polities the experience is political disunity, while around the world the issue is war and peace. The age of polarization in the United States has aggravated cultural disunities that can be traced throughout our history, including a Civil War a century and a half ago.

Today we have a president who almost celebrates ignorance of the issues and only exaggerates disunity, political parties that articulate disunity, and a constitutional separation of powers gridlocked by disunity.

We are living through a moment of great danger, and it is reasonable to conclude that democracy is in crisis, facing threats from abroad, as well as at home, and from ourselves. But we have been here before. We somehow survived the Civil War, even if it left wounds that remain. The onset of World War II represented about as dark a moment as we are experiencing globally today.

We have also had times in our history that we might like to replicate today. As imperfect as the Constitution is, it represents a spirit of compromise among its authors, and a sense that the common good outweighs narrow individual interests that we would do well to revive. We ended slavery, which required a war and fundamental structural change for our society. We recognized civil rights, at least as a foundation of law, and the struggle for equality continues into our troubled present moment.

Perhaps the model we can best understand is the period during and after World War II, when American elites and masses united on a sense of the common good, not only to win the war, but to win the peace that followed. An international economic system was negotiated and built, and an economy that was both profitable to businesses and beneficial to most of the population at large was constructed. A bipartisan policy scheme led to a period of progress and relative general wealth lasting about a generation.

That system was far from perfect, and it began to come unglued fifty years ago. Today, President Trump is at work on dismantling what remains of it.

Public policy cannot now reconstruct an arrangement that was more appropriate for another time. But it is that spirit that must be replicated, the idea that self-interest is best served when tied to the common good. In that spirit, the social consensus among elites and masses does not have to agree on issue outcomes, but in debating polarizing issues, there must be an understanding that our fellow citizens with whom we disagree are only motivated by the same sense of the common good. Among political elites, that means placing the legitimacy of the debate ahead of the narrow self-interest of staying in office. That may seem to be a dream in today's politics, but it is a reality that has been periodically achieved before.

American democracy today rests on the same foundation that Alexis DeTocqueville observed almost two centuries ago: A civil society based on "self-interest well understood."

Bibliography

ADA. 2017. www.adaction.org/pages/publications/voting-records.php.
Aldrich, John H. 1995. *Why Parties? The Origin and Transformation of Party Politics in America*. Chicago: University of Chicago Press.
Ambrose, Stephen E. 1984. *Eisenhower as President*. New York: Simon & Schuster.
Andersen, Kristi. 1976. "Generation, Partisan Shift, and Realignment: A Glance Back at the New Deal." In *The Changing American Voter*, by Norman H. Nie, Sidney Verba, and John R. Petrocik. Cambridge, MA: Harvard University Press.
———. 1979. *The Creation of the Democratic Majority: 1928–1936*. Chicago: University of Chicago Press.
APSA. 1950. *Toward a More Responsible Two Party System*. New York: Rinehart.
Apter, David. 1964. "Ideology and Discontent." In *Ideology and Discontent*, by David Apter. New York: The Free Press.
Arbour, Brian. 2016. "Racial Attitudes in the Highland South in 2008 and 2012." *paper presented at the Northeastern Political Science Association conference*, 1. November 11, 2016, Boston.
Archer, J. Clark, Fred M. Shelly, Peter J. Taylor, and Ellen R. White. 1988. "The Geography of U.S. Presidential Elections." *Scientific American*, 44–51.
Archer, J. Clark, Fred M. Shelly, Fiona M. Davidson, and Stanley D. Brunn. 1996. *The Political Geography of the United States*. New York: Guilford.
Aronowitz, Stanley. 1992. *False Promises: The Shaping of American Working Class Consciousness*. Durham, NC: Duke University Press.
Bachrach, Peter. 1967. *The Theory of Democratic Elitism*. Boston: Little, Brown.
Baker, Peter. 2017. "Nixon Tried to Spoil Johnson's Vietnam Peace Talks, Notes Show." *New York Times*. January 2. https://www.nytimes.com/2017/01/02/us/politics/nixon-tried-to-spoil-johnsons-vietnam-peace-talks-in-68-notes-show.html (accessed July 8, 2017).
Barber, James David. 1972. *The Presidential Character: Predicting Performance in the White House*. Englewood Cliffs, NJ: Prentice-Hall.

Barnard, Ellsworth. 1966. *Wendell Willkie: Fighter for Freedom.* Marquette: Northern Michigan University Press.

Bartels, Larry. 1988. *Presidential Primaries and the Dynamics of Public Choice.* Princeton, NJ: Princeton University Press.

———. 1998. "Electoral Continuity and Change, 1868–1996." *Electoral Studies,* 301–26.

———. 2000. "Partisanship and Voting Behavior, 1952–1996." *American Journal of Political Science,* 35–50.

Bartlett, Donald L., and James B. Steele. 1992. *America: What Went Wrong?* Kansas City, MO: Andrews and McNeel.

Bean, Louis H. 1948. *How to Predict Elections.* New York: Knopf.

Bell, Daniel. 1973. *The Coming of Postindustrial Society: A Venture in Social Forecasting.* New York: Basic Books.

Birch, Anthony H. 1993. *Concepts the Theories of Democracy.* London: Routledge.

Black, Earl, and Merle Black. 1992. *The Vital South: How Presidents are Elected.* Cambridge, MA: Harvard University Press.

Bluestone, Barry, and Bennett Harrison. 1982. *The Deindustrialization of America.* New York: Basic Books.

Bonica, Adam, Nolan McCarty, Keith T. Poole, and Howard Rosenthal. 2015. "Congressional Polarization and its Connection to Income Inequality." In *The Sources, Character and Impact of Congressional Polarization,* by James A. Thurber and Antoine Yoshinaka, 357–77. New York: Cambridge University Press.

Broder, David. 1978. "Introduction." In *Emerging Coalitions in American Politics,* Seymour Martin Lipset, ed. San Francisco: Institute for Contemporary Studies.

———. 1980. "Democrats." In *The Pursuit of the Presidency 1980,* Lou Cannon, Haynes Johnson, Martin Schram, Richard Harwood, and David Broder, eds. New York: G. P. Putnam's Sons.

Brown v. Board of Education. 1954. 347 U.S. 483.

Brown v. Board of Education II. 1955. 349 U.S. 294.

Buckley v. Valeo. 1976. 424 U.S. 1.

Buell, Emmett. 1996. "The Invisible Primary." In *In Pursuit of the White House: How We Choose Our Presidential Nominees,* by William G. Mayer. Chatham, NJ: Chatham House.

Burnham, Walter Dean. 1970. *Critical Elections and the Mainsprings of American Politics.* New York: Norton.

———. 1975. "Insulation and Responsiveness in Congressional Elections." *Political Science Quarterly* 90: 411–35.

———. 1978. "American Politics in the 1970s: Beyond Party?" In *Parties and Elections in an Anti-Party Age,* Jeff Fishel, ed. Bloomington: Indiana University Press.

———. 1991. "Critical Realignment: Dead or Alive?" In *The End of Realignment? Interpreting American Electoral Eras,* Byron E. Shafer, ed. Madison: University of Wisconsin Press.

———. 1996. "Realignment Lives: The 1994 Earthquake and its Implications.." In *The Clinton Presidency: First Appraisals,* Colin Campbell and Bert A. Rockman, eds. Chatham, NJ: Chatham House.

Busch, Andrew E. 2012. *Truman's Triumphs: The 1948 Election and the Making of Postwar America.* Lawrence: University Press of Kansas.

Bush v. Gore. 2000. 531 U.S. 98.

Campbell, Angus. 1960. "Surge and Decline: A Study of Electoral Change." *Public Opinion Quarterly* 24: 397–418.

Campbell, James E. 1985. "Explaining Presidential Losses in Midterm Congressional Elections." *Journal of Politics* 47: 1140–57.

———. 1986. "Predicting Seat Gains from Presidential Coattails." *American Journal of Political Science* 30: 165–83.

———. 1987. "A Revised Theory of Surge and Decline." *American Journal of Political Science* 31: 965–79.

———. 1993. *The Presidential Pulse of Congressional Elections.* Lexington: University Press of Kentucky.

———. 2006. "Party Systems and Realignments in the United States." *Social Science History*, 359–86.

Carmines, Edward G., and James A. Stimson. 1989. *Issue Evolution: Race and the Transformation of American Politics.* Princeton, NJ: Princeton University Press.

Carney, Eliza Newlin. 2015. "Party Unity: Standing Together Against Any Action." *CQ Weekly*, March 16: 37–45.

Ceaser, James W., and Andrew E. Busch. 2001. *The Perfect Tie: The True Story of the 2000 Presidential Election.* Lanham, MD: Rowman & Littlefield.

Centers, Richard. 1949. *The Psychology of Social Classes.* Princeton, NJ: Princeton University Press.

Cherry, Robert W. 1985. *A Righteous Cause: The Life of William Jennings Bryan.* Boston: Little, Brown.

Chester, Lewis, Godfrey Hodgson, and Bruce Page. 1969. *An American Melodrama: The Presidential Campaign of 1968.* New York: Viking Press.

Citizens United v. Federal Election Commission. 2010. 558 U.S. 310.

Clerk, U.S. House of Representatives. 2017. http://history.house.gov/Institution/Election-Statistics/Election-Statistics.

Clubb, Jerome M., William H. Flanigan, and Nancy H. Zingale. 1990. *Partisan Realignment: Voters, Parties and Government in American History.* Boulder, CO: Westview Press.

CNN. 2016. www.cnn.com.

Cohen, Marty, David Karol, Hans Noel, and John Zaller. 2008a. "The Invisible Primary in Presidential Nominations, 1980–2004." In *The Making of the Presidential Candidates 2008*, by William G. Mayer. Lanham, MD: Rowman & Littlefield.

———. 2008b. *The Party Decides: Presidential Nominations Before and After Reform.* Chicago: University of Chicago Press.

Collatt, Donald S., Stanley Kelley, and Ronald Rogowski. 1981. "The End Game in Presidential Nominations." *American Political Science Review*, 81–99.

Cooper v. Aaron. 1958. 357 U.S. 566.

Corrado, Anthony. 2012. "Financing Presidential Nominations in the Post-Public Funding Era." In *The Making of the Presidential Candidates 2012*, William G. Mayer and Jonathan Bernstein, eds. Lanham, MD: Rowman & Littlefield.

Cowan, Geoffrey. 2016. *Let the People Rule: Theodore Roosevelt and the Birth of the Presidential Primary.* New York: Norton.

CQ. 1999. "Influential Since the 1940s, the Conservative Coalition Limps into History in 1998." In *CQ Almanac 1998*, B9–B11. Washington, DC: CQ Press.

———. 1957. *Congressional Quarterly Almanac 1956.* Washington, DC: Congressional Quarterly.

Crotty, William. 1983. *Party Reform.* New York: Longman.

Dahl, Robert A. 1956. "Polyarchal Democracy." In *A Preface to Democratic Theory*, by Robert A. Dahl. New Haven, CT: Yale University Press.

———. 1961. *Who Governs? Democracy and Power in an American City.* New Haven, CT: Yale University Press.

———. 1971. *Polyarchy.* New Haven, CT: Yale University Press.

———. 1989. *Democracy and Its Critics.* New Haven, CT: Yale University Press.

Davis, Kenneth S. 1994. *FDR: The New York Years, 1928–1933.* New York: Random House.

DeGrazia, Alfred. 1975. *Eight Bads, Eight Goods: The American Contradictions.* New York: Doubleday.

DeVries, Walter, and V. Lance Terrance. 1972. *The Ticket Splitter: A New Force in American Politics.* Grand Rapids, MI: W. B. Eerdmans.

Dewey, Thomas E. 1966. *Thomas E. Dewey on the Two Party System.* New York: Doubleday.

Domhoff, G. William. 1967. *Who Rules America?* Upper Saddle River, NJ: Prentice Hall.

Downs, Anthony. 1957. *An Economic Theory of Democracy.* New York: Harper & Row.

Duverger, Maurice. 1972. *Party Politics and Pressure Groups.* New York: Thomas Y. Crowell.

Economic Report of the President. 2017. Washington, DC: U.S. Government Printing Office.

Eisenhower, Dwight D. 1965. *Waging Peace.* New York: Doubleday.

FEC. 2016. *Federal Election Commission.* Washington, DC: http://www.fec.gov/press/campaign_finance_statistics.shtml (accessed July 16, 2016).

Fiorina, Morris. 1981. *Retrospective Voting in American National Elections.* New Haven, CT: Yale University Press.

Ford, Gerald R. 1979. *A Time to Heal: The Autobiography of Gerald R. Ford.* New York: Harper & Row.

Freedom House. 2018. https://freedomhouse.org/report/freedom-world/freedom-world-2018. Retrieved January 17, 2018.

Gallup Poll. 2016. www.gallup.com/poll/10120/history-shows-january-frontrunner-often-does-win-democratic-nomination.aspx (accessed July 16, 2016).

Gamson, William. 1962. "Coalition Formation at Presidential Nominating Conventions." *American Journal of Sociology*, 157–71.

Goodwin, Doris Kearns. 2013. *The Bully Pulpit: Theodore Roosevelt, William Howard Taft, and the Golden Age of Journalism.* New York: Simon & Schuster.

Gordon, Robert J. 2016. *The Rise and Fall of Economic Growth: The U.S. Standard of Living Since the Civil War.* Princeton, NJ: Princeton University Press.

Greenstein, Fred I. 1982. *The Hidden Hand Presidency: Eisenhower as Leader.* New York: Simon & Schuster.

Habermas, Jurgen. 1973. *Legitimation Crisis.* London: Heinemann.

Hadley, Arthur T. 1976. *The Invisible Primary.* Englewood Cliffs, NJ: Prentice-Hall.

Hamilton, Alexander, John Jay, and James Madison. 1966. *The Federalist Papers.* Edited by Roy P. Fairfield. New York: Doubleday.

Hare, Christopher, and Keith T. Poole. 2014. "The Polarization of Contemporary American Politics." *Polity* 46: 411–29.

Harrington, Michael. 1986. *The Next Left.* New York: Holt.

Hartz, Louis. 1955. *The Liberal Tradition in America.* New York: Harcourt, Brace & World.

Heller, Walter W. 1967. *New Dimensions of Political Economy.* Cambridge, MA: Harvard University Press.

Hofstadter, Richard. 1963. *Anti-Intellectualism in American Life.* New York: Vitage Books.

Huckfeldt, Robert, and Carol Weitzel Kohfield. 1989. *Race and the Decline of Class in American Politics.* Chicago: University of Illnois Press.

Inglehart, Ronald. 1977. *The Silent Revolution: Changing Values and Political Styles Among Western Publics.* Princeton, NJ: Princeton University Press.

———. 1981. "Postmaterialism in an Environment of Insecurity." *The American Political Science Review* 75: 880–900.

Jacobson, Gary C. 1990. *The Electoral Origins of Divided Government: Competition in U.S. House Elections, 1946–1988.* Boulder, CO: Westview Press.

Jensen, Richard. 1978. "Party Coalitions and the Search for Modern Values" in Seymour Martin Lipset, ed. *Emerging Coalitions in American Politics.* San Francisco: Institute for Contemporary Studies.

Kahn, Herman, and Anthony J. Wiener. 1967. *The Year 2000: Speculation on the Next Thirty-Three Years.* New York: Macmillan.

Kazin, Michael. 2007. *A Godly Hero: The Life of William Jennings Bryan.* New York: Anchor.

Keech, William R., and Donald R. Matthews. 1977. *The Party's Choice.* Washington, DC: Brookings Institution.

Key, V. O., Jr. 1949. *Southern Politics in State and Nation.* New York: Knopf.

———. 1955. "A Theory of Critical Elections." *Journal of Politics*, 3–18.

———. 1959. "Secular Realignment and the Party System." *Journal of Politics*, 198–210.

———. 1966. *The Responsible Electorate.* Cambridge, MA: Harvard University Press.

Keynes, John Meynard. 1964. *The General Theory of Employment, Interest and Money.* New York: Harcourt, Brace & Jovanovich.

Kirkpatrick, Evron M. 1971. "Toward a Responsible Two-Party System: Political Science, Policy Science, or Pseudo Science?" *The American Political Science Review* 65: 965–90.

Koenig, Louis W. 1971. *Bryan.* New York: G. P. Putnam's Sons.
Ladd, Everett Carll. 1977. *Where Have All the Voters Gone?* New York: Norton.
———. 1978. "Shifting Party Coalitions–1932–1976." In *Emerging Coalitions in American Politics*, by Seymour Martin Lipset. San Francisco: Institute for Contemporary Studies.
———. 1980. "Liberalism Upside Down: The Inversion of the New Deal Order." In *The Party Symbol: Readings on Political Parties*, William Crotty, ed. San Francisco: W. H. Freeman and Company.
———. 1981. "The Brittle Mandate: Electoral Dealignment and the Presidential Election of 1980." *Political Science Quarterly*, 1–25.
———. 1991. "Like Waiting for Godot: The Uselessness of 'Realignment' for Understanding Change in Contemporary American Politics." In *The End of Realignment? Interpreting American Electoral Eras*, Byron E. Shafer, ed. Madison: University of Wisconsin Press.
Ladd, Everett Carll, with Charles Hadley. 1978. *Transformations in the American Party System: Political Coalitions from the New Deal to the 1970s.* New York: Norton.
Lane, Robert E. 1962. *Political Ideology: Why the American Common Man Believes What He Does.* New York: The Free Press.
Lawrence, David G. 1997. *The Collapse of the Democratic Presidential Majority: Realignment, Dealignment and Electoral Change from Franklin Roosevelt to Bill Clinton.* Boulder, CO: Westview Press.
Leip, Dave. 2016. www.uselectionatlas.org.
———. 2017. www.uselectionatlas.org.
Levine, Lawrence W. 1965. *William Jennings Bryan, Defender of the Faith: The Last Decade, 1915–1925.* New York: Oxford University Press.
Levinson, Marc. 2016. *An Extraordinary Time: The End of the Postwar Boom and the Return of the Ordinary Economy.* New York: Basic Books.
Lowi, Theodore J. 1982. *The End of Liberalism.* New York: Norton.
Macpherson, C.B. 1965. *The Real World of Democracy.* Toronto: Anansi.
———. 1977. *The Life and Times of Liberal Democracy.* New York: Oxford University Press.
———. 1989. "Do We Need a Theory of the State?" In *Democracy and the Capitalist State*, by Graeme Duncan. Cambridge: Cambridge University Press.
Mandel, Ernest. 1978. *Late Capitalism.* New York: Verso.
Mann, Thomas, and Norman J. Ornstein. 2012. *It's Even Worse Than it Looks: How the American Constitutional System Collided With the New Politics of Extremism.* New York: Basic Books.
Manuel, Paul Christopher, and Anne Marie Cammisa. 1999. *Checks and Balances? How and Parliamentary System Could Change American Politics.* Boulder, CO: Westview Press.
Marx, Karl. 1867. *Capital: The Process of Capitalist Production as a Whole.* Edited by Frederick Engels. Vol. 3. New York: International Publishers.
Mayer, William G. 1996. "Forecasting Presidential Nominations." In *In Pursuit of the White House: How We Choose Our Presidential Nominees*, by William G. Mayer. Chatham, NJ: Chatham House.

———. 2003. "Forecasting Presidential Nominations, or My Model Worked Just Fine, Thank You." *PS: Political Science and Politics*, 153–57.

———. 2008a. "Voting in Presidential Primaries." In *The Making of the Presidential Candidates 2008*, by William G. Mayer. Lanham, MD: Rowman & Littlefield.

———. 2008b. "What the Founders Intended: Another Look at the Origins of the American Presidential Selection Process,." In *The Making of the Presidential Candidates 2008*, by ed. William G. Mayer, 203–34. Lanham, MD: Rowman & Littlefield.

Mayer, William G., and Andrew E. Busch. 2004. *The Front-Loading Problem in Presidential Nominations*. Washington, DC: Brookings Institution.

Mayhew, David. 2002. *Electoral Realignments: A Critique of an American Genre*. New Haven, CT: Yale University Press.

McCarty, Nolan M., Keith T. Poole, and Howard Rosenthal. 2016. *Polarized America: The Dance of Ideology and Unequal Riches*. Cambridge, MA: MIT Press.

McConnell, Grant. 1967. *Private Power and American Democracy*. New York: Knopf.

Mills, C. Wright. 1956. *The Power Elite*. Oxford: Oxford University Press.

Miroff, Bruce. 2007. *The Liberals' Moment: The McGovern Insurgency and the Identity Crisis of the Democratic Party*. Lawrence: University Press of Kansas.

MSNBC. 2016. www.msnbc.com.

Murray, Robert K. 1976. *The 103rd Ballot: Democrats and the Disaster at Madison Square Garden*. New York: Harper & Row.

National Party Conventions 1831–1984. 1987. Washington, DC: Congressional Quarterly.

Neal, Steve. 1989. *Dark Horse: A Biography of Wendell Willkie*. Lawrence: University Press of Kansas.

New York Times. 2016a. https://www.nytimes.com/elections/results/president.

———. 2016b. https://www.nytimes.com/interactive/2016/11/08/us/politics/election-exit-polls.html (accessed April 6, 2017).

Nichols, David A. 2017. *Ike and McCarthy*. New York: Simon & Schuster.

NLRB v. Jones and Laughlin Steel Corporation. 1937. 301 U.S. 1.

Nordloh, David J. 1981. *William Jennings Bryan*. Bloomington: Indiana University Press.

Norrander, Barbara. 2000. "The End Game in Post-Reform Presidential Nominations." *Journal of Politics*, 999–1013.

———. 2010. *The Imperfect Primary: Oddities, Biases, and Strengths of U.S. Presidential Nomination Politics*. New York: Routledge.

Novak, Robert. 1965. *The Agony of the G.O.P. 1964*. New York: Macmillan.

O'Connor, James. 1973. *The Fiscal Crisis of the State*. New York: St. Martin's Press.

Okun, Arthur. 1970. *The New Economy of Prosperity*. New York: Norton.

Parmet, Herbert S., and Marie B. Hecht. 1968. *Never Again: A President Runs for a Third Term*. New York: Macmillan.

Paulson, Arthur. 1985. *Political Attitudes of the Unemployed: Interviews With Fifteen Men*. Boulder: PhD dissertation, University of Colorado.

———. 1998. "The Political Economy of Postindustrial America." In *America in the 21st Century: Challenges and Opportunities in Domestic Politics*, by Kul B. Rai, David F. Walsh, and Paul J. Best, 21–48. Upper Saddle River, NJ: Prentice Hall.

———. 2000. *Realignment and Party Revival: Understanding American Electoral Politics at the Turn of the Twenty-First Century.* Westport, CT: Praeger.

———. 2007. *Electoral Realignment and the Outlook for American Democracy.* Boston: Northeastern University Press.

———. 2015. "From Umbrella Parties to Polarized Parties." In *Polarized Politics: The Impact of Divisiveness on the U.S. Political System*, William Crotty, ed. Boulder, CO: Lynne Reiner.

Perlstein, Rick. 2009. *Before the Storm: Barry Goldwater and the Unmaking of the American Consensus.* New York: Nation Books.

Peters, Charles. 2005. *Five Days in Philadelphia: 1940, Wendell Willkie, and the Political Convention that Freed FDR to Win World War II.* New York: PublicAffairs.

Phillips, Kevin. 1969. *The Emerging Republican Majority.* New Rochelle, NY: Arlington House.

Picketty, Thomas. 2014. *Capital in the Twenty-first Century.* Cambridge, MA: Harvard University Press.

Plessy v. Ferguson. 1896. 163 U.S. 537.

Polsby, Nelson W. 1978. "Coalition and Faction in American Politics: An Institutional View." In *Emerging Coalitions in American Politics*, Seymour Martin Lipset, ed. San Francisco: Institute for Contemporary Studies.

———. 1983. *The Consequences of Party Reform.* Oxford: Oxford University Press.

Poole, Keith T., and Howard Rosenthal. 1984. "The Polarization of American Politics." *Journal of Politics* 46: 1061–79.

———. 1985. "A Spatial Model of Legislative Roll Call Analysis." *American Journal of Political Science* 29: 357–84.

———. 1991. "Patterns of Congressional Voting." *American Journal of Political Science* 35: 228–78.

———. 1997. *Congress: A Political-Economic History of Roll Call Voting.* New York: Oxford University Press.

Rabinowitz, George and Stuart Elaine MacDonald. 1986. "The Power of the States in U.S. Presidential Elections." *American Political Science Review*, 65–87.

Rae, Nicol. 1989. *The Decline and Fall of the Liberal Republicans: From 1952 to the Present.* New York: Oxford University Press.

———. 1994. *Southern Democrats.* New York: Oxford University Press.

———. 1998. "Party Factionalism, 1946–1996." In *Partisan Approaches to Postwar American Politics*, Byron E. Shafer, ed. New York: Chatham House.

Ranney, Austin. 1954. *The Doctrine of Responsible Party Government: Its Origins and Present State.* Urbana: University of Illinois Press.

———. 1975. *Curing the Mischiefs of Faction: Party Reform in America.* Los Angeles: University of California Press.

Reiter, Howard L., and Jeffrey M. Stonecash. 2010. *Counter-Realignment: Political Change in the Northeast.* Cambridge: Cambridge University Press.

Riker, William H. 1982. "The Two Party System and Duverger's Law." *The American Political Science Review* 76: 753–66.
Ritchie, Donald A. 2007. *Electing FDR: The New Deal Campaign of 1932*. Lawrence: University Press of Kansas.
Rusk, Jerrold G. 2001. *A Statistical History of the American Electorate*. Washington, DC: CQ Press.
Santa Clara County v. Southern Pacific Railroad. 1886. 118 U.S. 394.
Scammon, Richard, and Ben Wattenburg. 1970. *The Real Majority*. New York: Howard-McCann.
Schafly, Phyllis. 1964. *A Choice, Not an Echo*. Alton, IL: Pere Marquette Press.
Schantz, Harvey L. 1996. "Sectionalism in Presidential Elections." In *American Presidential Elections: Process, Policy and Political Change*, Harvey L. Schantz, ed. Albany: State University Press of New York.
Schattschneider, E. E. 1942. *Party Government*. New York: Rinehart.
———. 1960. *The Semisovereign People: A Realist's View of Democracy*. New York: Holt, Rinehart & Winston.
Schechter Poultry Co. v. U.S. 1935. 295 U.S. 495.
Schlozman, Kay Lehman, and Sidney Verba. 1979. *Injury to Insult: Unemployment, Class and Political Response*. Cambridge, MA: Harvard University Press.
Schumpeter, Joseph. 1942. *Capitalism, Socialism and Democracy*. New York: Harper.
Schwartz, Bernard. 1993. *A History of the Supreme Court*. New York: Oxford University Press.
Silbey, Joel H. 1991. "Beyond Realignment and Realignment Theory." In *The End of Realignment? Interpreting American Electoral Eras*, Byron E. Shafer, ed. Madison: University of Wisconsin Press.
Smith v. Allwright. 1944. 321 U.S. 649.
Smith, Margaret Chase. 1972. *Declaration of Conscience*. Edited by William C. Lewis. New York: Doubleday.
Speel, Robert W. 1998. *Changing Patterns of Voting in the Northern United States: Electoral Realignment, 1952–1996*. University Park: Pennsylvania State University Press.
Springen, Donald W. 1991. *William Jennings Bryan: Orator of Small Town America*. Westport, CT: Greenwood Press.
Stanley, Harold W., and Richard G. Niemi. 2000. *Vital Statistics in American Politics*. Washington, DC: CQ Press.
Stanwood, Edward. 1888. *History of Presidential Elections*. Cambridge, MA: Riverside Press.
Steger, Wayne. 2015. *A Citizen's Guide to Presidential Nominations*. New York: Routledge.
Stonecash, Jeffrey. 2006. *Political Parties Matter: Realignment and the Return of Partisan Voting*. Boulder, CO: Lynne Reiner.
Sundquist, James L. 1983. *The Dynamics of the American Party System: Alignment and Realignment of Political Parties in the United States*. Washington, DC: Brookings.

———. 1992. *Constitutional Reform and Effective Government.* Washington, DC: Brookings Institution.
Tanenhaus, Sam. 2016. "How Trump Can Save the GOP." *New York Times Sunday Review*, July 10: 1, 4–5.
Tocqueville, Alexis de. 2000. *Democracy in America.* Harvey C. Mansfield and Delba Winthrop, eds. Chicago: University of Chicago Press.
Touraine, Alain. 1971. *The Post-Industrial Society.* New York: Random House.
Truman, David B. 1959. "The American System in Crisis." *Political Science Quarterly* 74: 488–89.
U.S. v. Darby. 312 U.S. 100. 1941.
Wattenberg, Martin P. 1990. *The Decline of American Political Parties: 1952–1988.* Cambridge, MA: Harvard University Press.
Weigel, David. 2016. "'Racialists' are Cheered by Trump's Latest Strategy." *The Washington Post*, August 20: 1.
West Coast Hotel Co. v. Parrish. 1937. 300 U.S. 379.
White, Theodore H. 1965. *The Making of the President 1964.* New York: Atheneum.
———. 1973. *The Making of the President 1972.* New York: Atheneum.
Wilcox, Clyde. 1995. *The Latest American Revolution? The 1994 Elections and Their Implications for Governance.* New York: St. Martin's Press.
Willkie, Wendell L. 1943. *One World.* New York: Simon & Schuster.
Wilson, James Q. 1985. "Realignment at the Top, Dealignment at the Bottom." In *The American Elections of 1984*, by Austin Ranney. Durham, NC: American Enterprise Institute/Duke University Press.
Witcover, Jules. 1977. *Marathon: The Pursuit of the Presidency 1972–1976.* New York: Viking Press.
Wolfe, Alan. 1977. *The Limits of Legitimacy.* New York: The Free Press.
———. 1981. *America's Impasse: The Rise and Fall of the Politics of Growth.* New York: Pantheon Books.

Index

12th Amendment, 6
24th Amendment, 23, 29, 80, 105

Active-Positive Presidents, 10–11
Active-Negative Presidents, 11
Affordable Care Act, 117–118, 138–139
Agnew, Spiro T., 47
Alien and Sedition Acts, 8
Alt-right, 8
American Conservative Union, 112–113
Americans for Constitutional Action, 112–113
Americans for Democratic Action, 112
Anderson, John B., 48
Anti-Federalists, 18
Anti-war movement, 26
Apter, David, 9
Arthur, Chester A., 30

Barber, James David, 10–11
Bartels, Larry, 53–54
Bean, Louis H., 77–78
Biden, Joseph, 64
Bill of Rights, 135
Blaine, James G., 30
Bloomberg, Michael, 70
Boehner, John, 72
Borah, William E., 31
Bradley, Bill, 52

Bretton Woods Agreement, 128–130
Brown, Jerry, 48
Brown v. Board of Education, 36
Bryan, William Jennings, 8, 19–21
Buckley v. Valeo, 45, 143
Burnham, Walter Dean, 9, 105, 122
Burr, Aaron, 6, 18–19
Burr, Richard, 136–137
Bush, George H.W., 40, 48, 54, 85, 104, 131
Bush, George W., 7, 40, 45–46, 52, 54, 96
Bush, Jeb, 57–58
Byrd, Harry F., 20
Bush v. Gore, 7

Campaign finance, 45–46, 50–51, 58, 143–144
Campaign Finance Reform Act of 1971, 45
Campaign Finance Reform Act of 1974, 45, 51
Campbell, Ben Nighthorse, 121
Campbell, James, 112
Carson, Ben, 57–58
Carter, Jimmy, 29, 46–49, 52, 55–56, 79–80, 85, 131
Chafee, Lincoln, 64
Charlottesville, Virginia, 8

Christie, Chris, 57
Church, Frank, 48
Citizens United v. FEC, 45, 50, 143
Civil rights, 4, 23–26, 29, 36–39, 72, 112–114, 136, 150
Civil Rights Act of 1957, 36
Civil Rights Act of 1960, 23, 36
Civil Rights Act of 1964, 23, 26, 29, 38, 112–114
Civil War, 17, 19, 140, 149–150
Class consciousness, 17–18, 125, 146
Cleveland, Grover, 4, 7, 21, 30, 32
Clinton, Bill, 5, 29, 54, 100, 105, 117–118, 131
Clinton, Hillary, 1–2, 5, 9, 12, 29, 50–51, 54, 64–71, 75–76, 91–100, 138
Comey, James, 5, 10, 100, 136
Congressional Quarterly, 112, 115
Conkling, Roscoe, 30
Connally, John B., 45, 121
Constitution of the United States, 6, 12, 16–18, 23, 29, 76, 101, 103, 105, 115, 118–119, 121, 125 135, 137, 141–142, 146, 150
Coolidge, Calvin, 31
Cooper v. Aaron, 36
Corker, Bob, 9
Cruz, Ted, 58–64, 71

Dahl, Robert A., 135
Davenport, Russell, 3, 34
Davis, John W., 21–22
Dean, Howard, 46, 50
Declaration of Independence, 16–17
Deferred Action for Childhood Arrivals (DACA), 139
DeGrazia, Alfred, 141
Democracy in America, 124–127, 146
Democratic National Convention, of 1896, 20; of 1912, 20; of 1924, 19, 21; of 1928, 21–22; of 1932, 22; of 1936, 22; of 1940, 23; of 1944, 23; of 1948, 23–25; of 1952, 24; of 1960, 26; of 1968, 27–28, 43; of 1972, 28–29; of 1980, 49; of 2016, 64, 66, 69–70, 99
Democratic Presidential Primaries, of 1932, 22; of 1968, 26–28; of 1972, 26–29; of 1976, 29, 48; of 1980, 49; of 2000, 52; of 2004, 46, 50; of 2008, 50; of 2016, 1, 50, 56, 65–68;71–72
Democrats for Nixon, 121
Dewey, Thomas E., 33–35, 37, 42, 120
Dole, Robert, 45, 54
Dukakis, Michael, 55
DW-Nominate scores, 113, 122

Eisenhower, Dwight D., 11, 35–38, 47, 56
Elections, legitimacy of, 5–7.
Elections, of 1800, 6; of 1824, 6–7, 18; of 1860, 78; of 1876, 7; of 1880, 19, 79, 81; of 1888, 7; of 1896, 19, 31, 77–79, 81, 108; of 1916, 19, 32, 79; of 1928, 19; of 1932, 33, 78–79, 81, 108; of 1936, 22, 33–34, 81; of 1940, 3, 23, 34, 120; of 1944, 19, 34, 79, 81, 85; of 1946, 105; of 1948, 19, 24, 35, 79, 108; of 1952, 79; of 1956, 79; of 1960, 79; of 1964, 78–79, 81, 85, 99, 103–112;81, 85, 104; of 1968, 11, 79, 85–89, 104, 107, 110; of 1972, 78–79, 85, 99, 104–105, 107–108; of 1976, 79–80, 85; of 1980, 79–81; of 1988, 85, 104, 110; of 1992, 11, 85, 94, 110–111; of 1994, 104–105, 121; of 2000, 7, 85, 121; of 2004, 96–97; of 2008, 97, 99; of 2012, 81,91–97; of 2014, 105
Election of 2016, 1–2, 5, 7–9, 11, 75–76, 79, 89–100, 118, 123, 136–138;142; States in 2016 election, 89–94; Florida 91–92; Iowa, 93–94; Michigan, 92, 138; Ohio, 92; Pennsylvania, 92–93, 138; Wisconsin, 92, 138
Electoral College, 142

Elitist theory of democratic capitalism, 145
Equality of conditions, 13, 124–127, 135, 138, 141, 146
Exit polls, 2016 election, 94–101; Demographics, 94–97; Issues, 97–101

"Fair Play" Amendment, 36
Federal Highway Act of 1956, 36, 130
Federalism, 17, 120
Federalists, 18, 77
Filibuster, 118, 142–143
"Fiscal crisis of the state," 132, 134
Flake, Jeff, 9
Floating the dollar, 130–131
Flowers, Gennifer, 5
Folsom, Jim, 8
Forbes, Malcolm S., 45
Fortune, 33
Ford, Gerald, 46–49, 56, 85, 131
Fordism, 132
Fox News, 144
Fraser, Donald M., 27–28, 43
Freedom House, 149
Freedom Riders, 26
Front-loading, 44–45, 50–56
Full employment, 129

Gallup Poll, 34
Gamson, William, 55, 62, 66
Garfield, James A. 30
Garner, John Nance, 22
Gingrich, Newt, 50, 104–105
Goldwater, Barry, 29, 32–33, 37–40, 48, 56, 79, 104, 120–121
Gordon, Robert J., 131
Gore, Albert, 7, 29, 52, 54
Gorsuch, Neil, 140
Government shutdowns, 118–119
Grant, Ulysses S., 30
Great Recession of 2008–2009, 15, 99, 131, 134–135
Great Society, 117
Greenspan, Alan, 131

Hamilton, Alexander, 18
Harriman, W. Averill, 24
Hart, Gary, 4, 52
Hartz, Louis, 126
Hofstadter, Richard, 9
Hoover, Herbert C., 31
House Intelligence Committee, 5
House Judiciary Committee, 137
Huckabee, Mike, 57
Humphrey, Hubert H., 24, 26–28, 56, 79

Inequality of conditions, 124, 126–127
"Inversion of the New Deal Order," 9, 98–99
International Monetary Fund, 128–129
Invisible Primary, 50–58, 64–65, 71
Irvin, Sam, 137

Jackson, Andrew, 6, 8, 18–19, 86
Jefferson, Thomas, 6, 18–19
Jeffords, Jim, 121
Johnson, Andrew, 30
Johnson, Hiram, 31
Johnson, Lyndon B., 10–11, 26–27, 104, 117
Justice Department, 118, 137

Kaine, Tim, 70, 91
Kasich, John, 58–64, 71
Keech, William R., 52
Kefauver, Estes, 24
Kennedy, Edward M., 49, 52, 54, 56
Kennedy, John F., 10, 18, 24, 26, 37, 85
Kennedy, Robert F., 26–27
Kennedy tax cut, 129
Kerry, John, 46, 55, 96
Keynes, John Meynard, 129
Keynesian Economics, 129–131
Know-Nothings, 8
Krock, Arthur, 34
Ku Klux Klan, 21

Ladd, Everett Carll, 9, 99
LaFollette, Robert M., 31

League of Nations, 8, 31
Lend-Lease, 34
Levinson, Marc, 131
Lewinski, Monica, 5
Lewis, John, 5
Liberal Republican Party, 30
Lincoln, Abraham, 19, 30
Lindsay, John V., 121
Locke, John, 16–17
Lodge, Henry Cabot, 35, 37
Long, Huey, 8, 20
Low growth capitalism, 131–135
Luce, Henry, 3, 34

MacArthur, Douglas, 36
Mackinac Conference, 34
Madison, James, 18
Main Street Republicans, 30–32
Mansfield, Harvey C., 124
Marshall Plan, 129
Marx, Karl, 127, 132
Matthews, Donald R., 52
Mayer, William G., 50–51
McAdoo, William Gibbs, 21
McCain, John, 9, 52, 55
McCarthy, Eugene, 26–27
McCarthy, Joseph R., 36
McConnell, Mitch, 9
McGovern, George, 27–29, 43, 46, 52, 56
McGovern-Fraser Commission, 27–28, 43–44
McKinley, William, 31
Medicaid, 138–139
Medicare, 130, 138–139
Military Keynesianism, 129–130
"Modern Republicanism," 36
Mondale, Walter, 44, 52, 54
Morse, Wayne, 121
MSNBC, 144
Mueller, Robert, 5, 136
Multi-party system, 16, 119

Neo-Marxist theory of democratic capitalism, 145

"Never Trump" Republicans, 63–64, 71
New Deal, 19, 22–23
New York Herald Tribune, 4, 34
New York Times, 34
Nixon, Richard M., 9–11, 36–38, 40, 46–48, 79, 85, 104, 114, 130–131, 137–138
Norrander, Barbara, 55, 62, 66, 68
Norris, George W., 31
North American Free Trade Agreement (NAFTA), 117, 139–141
North Atlantic Treaty Organization (NATO), 117

Obama, Barack, 8, 49, 51, 54, 70, 75, 85, 91–94, 96, 98–99, 107, 117, 131, 134, 138–139
Oil shocks, 49, 131, 134
O'Malley, Martin, 64
"Omnipotence of the majority," 124–126, 144
One World, 4
One-party system (south), 19–20

Paris Climate Accords, 117, 134, 140
Parker, Alton B., 21
Passive-Positive Presidents, 11
Paul, Rand, 57
Pendleton Act, 30
Phillips, Kevin, 8–9, 99
Picketty, Thomas, 135
Plessy v. Ferguson, 19
Pluralist theory, 135–136, 145
Political geography in Presidential elections, 78–85
Polarization, evaluated, 121–122, 140–145
Polarizing issues, 86, 89
Polsby, Nelson, 30
Poole, Keith T., 113, 122, 136
Postindustrial democracy, 13, 100, 128–136
Presidential Character, 10–11
Princeton University, 120
Progressive era, 31–32

Rae, Nicol, 31–33, 60–61, 72
Rational Basis test, 143–144
"Reagan Democrats," 79–80, 99
Reagan, Ronald, 11, 38, 40, 45, 47–48, 52–54, 56, 79, 85, 104, 117, 131, 134
Realignment, 12, 78–85, 105–112
Realignment, interactive, 78, 85
Realignment, surge, 78, 85
Reid, Ogden, 121
Republican National Committee, 35, 62
Republican National Convention, of 1876, 30; of 1880, 30; of 1912, 32, 47; of 1940, 33–34; of 1944, 34; of 1948, 35; of 1952, 35–36; of 1960, 37; of 1964, 38–40; of 1976, 47–48; of 2016, 62–64
Republican Presidential primaries, of 1912, 31–32, 47; of 1940, 33; of 1944, 34; of 1948, 35; of 1952, 35; of 1964, 37–38; of 1976, 47; of 1980, 45, 48; of 1996, 45; of 2012, 50, 57; of 2016, 1, 3, 56–64, 71–72
Responsible party government, 13, 119–122
Riegle, Donald, 121
Rockefeller, Nelson, 4–5, 36–38, 47, 56
Romney, George, 47
Romney, Mitt, 50, 54, 57, 61, 92–93
Roosevelt, Franklin D., 3, 19, 22–23, 32–33, 81, 117, 120, 144
Roosevelt, Theodore, 10, 18, 31–32, 47
Root, Oren, 3
Rosenthal, Howard, 113, 122, 136
Rubio, Marco, 57–58, 60–61, 63
Russians, 2016 election, 2, 5, 11, 69, 100, 118, 123, 136–137
Russell, Richard B., 24
Ryan, Paul, 9, 62, 72

Sanders, Bernie, 1, 54, 64–72, 99
Santa Clara County v. Southern Pacific Railroad Company, 143
Schafly, Phillis, 120
Schattschneider, E.E., 119–120
Schultz, Debbie Wasserman, 69
Schweiker, Richard, 47
Scopes Monkey Trial, 21
Scott, Hugh, 35
Scranton, William W., 38
"Self-interest well understood," 126, 150
Senate Intelligence Committee, 5
Senate Select Committee, Watergate, 137
Seniority system, 20
Separation of Powers, 12–13, 18, 100, 103, 115, 118–121, 135, 137, 140, 142, 145–146, 150
Shelby, Richard, 121
Smith, Adam, 127, 132
Smith, Alfred E., 19, 21–22, 36
Smith, Margaret Chase, 36; "Declaration of Conscience" and, 36
Social Security, 130
Solid South (Democratic), 19–20, 81, 104, 108–110
Specter, Arlen, 121
Stagflation, 131, 134
Stassen, Harold E., 35–36
States in Presidential elections, 76–85
Stein, Jill, 70
Stevenson, Adlai E., 24, 121
Superdelegates (Democratic), 44, 65, 68–69
Super Tuesday, 44, 52, 58–61, 65
Supreme Court of the United States, 7, 10, 19, 22, 36, 140, 143

Taft, Robert A., 33–36, 56
Taft, William Howard, 31–32, 47
Talmadge, Herman, 20
Thurmond, J. Strom, 24, 121
Time-Life, 3, 33
Tocqueville, Alexis de, 13, 40, 123–128, 135, 141, 144, 146, 150
Toomey, Pat, 121
Trans-Pacific Partnership, 69, 117, 139–140
Treaty of Versailles, 8
Truman, David, 135

Truman, Harry S., 23–24, 77
Trump, Donald, 1–5, 7–13, 15, 33, 40, 57–64, 70–72, 75–76, 91–100, 117–119, 123, 128, 132–134, 136–140, 144–146, 149–150
Two-party system, 12, 15–18, 40, 119–120
Two-thirds rule, 20–21, 29; repealed, 22
Typologies of Presidential nomination contests, 52–55

Udall, Morris K., 48
Unhyphenated Americans, 8.

Van Buren, Martin, 18–19
Vandenburg, Arthur, 33–34, 47
Van Doren, Erita, 4
Veterans' Administration, 128–129
Vietnam War, 11, 23, 26–27, 42, 47, 130, 133, 136
Voting Rights Act of 1965, 23, 29, 80, 105
Voting Records in Congress, 112–116

Walker, James J., 22
Walker, Scott, 57

Wall Street Republicans, 3, 30–32, 35, 42
Wallace, George, 8, 28–29, 48, 56, 79, 85
Wallace, Henry A., 23–24
Warren, Earl, 36
Warren, Elizabeth, 64
Watergate, 11, 46, 48, 85, 114, 137
Webb, Jim, 64
Welfare state, 86, 130
White, F. Clifton, 37
Wilcox, Clyde, 105
Wilk, Edith, 4
Williams, John Bell, 121
Willkie Clubs, 3
Willkie, Wendell, 3–4;33–35;38, 47, 120
Wilson, James Q., 104
Wilson, Woodrow, 8
Winthrop, Delba, 124
World Bank, 128
World War I, 8
World War II, 2, 8, 31, 128, 132–133, 150

Yates, Sally, 10

Zero-sum democracy, 135–136

About the Author

Arthur Paulson is professor emeritus of political science at Southern Connecticut State University. Before his retirement, he served as the university's pre-law advisor, president of the Faculty Senate, and chair of the Department of Political Science.

His research focuses on political parties and electoral realignment in American politics. He is the author of *Electoral Realignment and the Outlook for American Democracy* (Northeastern University Press/University Press of New England, 2007), and *Realignment and Party Revival: Understanding American Electoral Politics at the Turn of the Twenty-first Century* (Praeger, 2000) and several book chapters, articles, and papers on electoral politics.